The Shape of the Round Table:
Structures of Middle High German Arthurian Romance

This book begins by dissociating itself from two biases that have constrained much of the scholarship on the structure of Middle High German Arthurian romance: the traditional prejudice in favour of the three great romances (*Erec, Iwein,* and *Parzival*) and the notion that structural analysis is merely the handmaiden of interpretation. By expanding the corpus under consideration to include all twelve romances, Professor Schultz is able to develop a structural model that attempts to do justice to the entire genre, not merely to its most famous representatives. By pursuing structural analysis for its own sake, he is able to investigate structures of many different kinds, not merely those that advance a single interpretation.

The book falls into three principal parts. The first treats the semantic building blocks of Arthurian romance: the World, Society, the Other, the Hero, the Mediator, and the Recipient. Each of these represents a body of traditional meaning; in combination they generate the characteristic roles, themes, and spatial structures of romance. The second major part treats the individual episode: first its *skeleton*, the linear structure of the archetypical episode and its principal variants; then *substance*, the realization of this skeleton by the addition of actors and their attributes, perspectives, and ostensible causes; finally, *surface*, the consequences of the narrator's activity in generating the actual text. The third part of the book works through these same categories from the perspective of the entire romance: the varieties of skeletal structure that determine its overall shape; the ways in which the addition of substantial elements fosters coherence; the importance of the narrator in determining our understanding of an entire romance and our conception of romance as a literary genre.

The book concludes with a brief coda devoted to contradiction. Schultz shows that the numerous internal inconsistencies of Arthurian romance – a feature of the genre for which it has often been taken to task – can be explained in a number of ways: as the result of a peculiarly medieval devotion to local detail; as the consequence of intrinsic tensions in the structure of the genre; and as the reflection of certain general properties of literary texts.

JAMES A. SCHULTZ is a member of the Department of Germanic Languages and Literatures at Yale University.

JAMES A. SCHULTZ

THE SHAPE OF THE
ROUND TABLE

Structures of
Middle High German
Arthurian Romance

UNIVERSITY OF TORONTO PRESS

Toronto Buffalo London

© University of Toronto Press 1983
Toronto Buffalo London
Printed in Canada

ISBN 0-8020-2466-1

Canadian Cataloguing in Publication Data

Schultz, James A. (James Alfred), 1947-
   The shape of the Round Table : structures of
   Middle High German Arthurian romance
   Bibliography: p.
   ISBN 0-8020-2466-1
   1. Arthurian romances – History and criticism.
   2. German poetry – Middle High German, 1050–1500 –
   History and criticism. 3. Epic poetry, German –
   History and criticism. I. Title.
   PT203.S38   831'.03'09351   C82-095195-1

FOR EFRAÍN

ist unser minne ane kraft,
sone wart nie guot geselleschaft.

Iwein, vv 5109–10

Contents

Contents

A Word of Thanks

I would never have turned to the study of medieval narrative nor, most likely, to medieval studies at all, but for the example of Michael Curschmann. His teaching first tempted me to investigate the literature of the German Middle Ages; he advised me as I wrote the doctoral dissertation that subsequently provided the blueprint for this book; and his own scholarship has inspired me at every turn. Where I have succeeded, it is because I have tried to match his example; where I have failed, it is because I am unable to do so.

My education in the narrower, academic sense would have been impossible had it not been for my parents and their devotion to education in its broadest possible sense. Their generous support of all kinds, even as I pursued a field as unlikely as medieval German, has been unstinting and invaluable. Without that support this project would have been impossible.

Nor could I have completed this project without the support and encouragement of Efraín Barradas. His own prolific scholarship has been both an inspiration and a goad. His unshakable comradeship has enabled me to maintain the sense of purpose without which my initial curiosity about Middle High German would never have developed into a book on Arthurian romance.

My study has profited greatly from the suggestions of Joan Ferrante, Ingeborg Glier, Arthur Groos, and Robert Hanning, who read the manuscript and offered their advice on how to improve it. As a novice medievalist, I am especially grateful for the help that they, with their much greater experience, have so generously given. The book as it stands before you has profited as well from the interest and care of Prudence Tracy of the University of Toronto Press, who has guided the publication from the start, and from the sympathetic rigour and practised eye of Judy Williams, also of the University of Toronto Press, and Elizabeth Stouffer, who read the work at several stages.

For two years the Columbia University Council for Research in the Humanities awarded me summer grants that enabled me to work on this project. The Frederick W. Hilles Publication Fund of Yale University and the National Endowment for the Humanities have helped underwrite the costs of publication. I am grateful for their support.

A Word on Citations, Notes, and Unfamiliar Literature

Citations from modern scholars that appear in the text have been translated into English. Where translations already exist, I have used them; where they do not, I have supplied my own. I have not translated the citations in the notes, although I have quoted from translations wherever they are available. In every case, regardless of the language cited, the short title and the first page reference in the notes refer to the original; the second page reference refers to the translation, if one has been used.

References to the critical literature in the notes have been kept as brief as possible. For full bibliographical information, consult the bibliography.

To facilitate access to a body of literature that may be unfamiliar to many English-speaking readers, I have listed in the second part of the bibliography recent English translations of the medieval works discussed, where such translations exist. For the less familiar Middle High German romances I have included English summaries in the appendix.

References in the text and in the notes to the Middle High German Arthurian romances as well as to a number of other frequently cited works are given in parentheses. The name of the work, and occasionally its author as well, is indicated according to the abbreviations listed in the following table; the number following the indication of the work refers to the verses or strophes cited. For complete bibliographical information, consult the bibliography.

C   Heinrich von dem Türlin, *Diu Crone*
CCh Chrétien de Troyes, *Le Chevalier de la charrete*
CCl Chrétien de Troyes, *Cligés*
CE   Chrétien de Troyes, *Erec et Enide*
CP   Chrétien de Troyes, *Le Conte du graal (Perceval)*

CY   Chrétien de Troyes, *Le Chevalier au lion (Yvain)*
D   der Stricker, *Daniel von dem Blühenden Tal*
E   Hartmann von Aue, *Erec*
ETr   Eilhart von Oberge, *Tristrant*
G   der Pleier, *Garel von dem Blüenden Tal*
GM   [Konrad von Stoffeln], *Gauriel von Muntabel*
GTr   Gottfried von Strassburg, *Tristan und Isold*
I   Hartmann von Aue, *Iwein*
L   Ulrich von Zatzikhoven, *Lanzelet*
M   der Pleier, *Meleranz*
Nbl   *Das Nibelungenlied*
P   Wolfram von Eschenbach, *Parzival*
T   der Pleier, *Tandareis und Flordibel*
W   Wirnt von Gravenberc, *Wigalois*
Wm   *Wigamur*

THE SHAPE OF THE ROUND TABLE

INTRODUCTION

Prescriptive Interpretation and Descriptive Poetics

Just eight hundred years ago, according to the accepted chronology, Hartmann von Aue composed his *Erec* and thereby introduced Arthurian romance into Germany. In doing so he established a tradition that flourished brilliantly for about thirty years and with diminishing lustre for perhaps another seventy. Yet even after 1280, when the composition of new works in the direct line of Hartmann seems to have ceased, the Arthurian tradition remained alive in Germany. *Parzival* was still considered popular enough in 1477 to make its way into print. Sixteen years later *Wigalois* appeared in a prose adaptation which had seen ten editions by 1664. Then it was less than a century before Bodmer published his reworking of *Parzival*; the original followed in 1784; and, one after the other, the rest of the medieval romances were edited and published throughout the nineteenth century. The works were of interest not only to scholars but also to authors and, as is well known, to composers as well. Through their mediation the Arthurian tradition once again became part of the general culture.

It is not surprising that a tradition of such vitality should have attracted the interest of literary critics. Some have been drawn to the greatest of the romances, *Erec*, *Iwein*, and *Parzival*, for these exercise the kind of fascination on scholars that any masterpiece does. Others have studied Middle High German Arthurian romance in the broader context of medieval European vernacular literature; they have investigated the incorporation of classical traditions, the impact of Christian thought, the authority of French models, and the relation to other genres. Still others have sought to place the German romances in the larger Arthurian tradition by tracing their roots back to Celtic folklore and their influence down to the present day.

Over the last several decades scholars have become increasingly fascinated by the structure of the Middle High German Arthurian romance and have attempted to analyse it from every conceivable point of view. They have divided up the romances according to the position of initials in the manuscripts and according to the places where the narrator interrupts the story with his comments. They have detected the patterns of Christian historical and exegetical thought, the structures of folklore and myth, and the stages of psychological development. They have compared the structures of Middle High German Arthurian romance with those of their French sources and with those of other genres. They have not always agreed.

And yet, among many German scholars at least, a general consensus has been achieved with regard to the linear organization of Arthurian romance. A romance, according to this consensus, will fall into two main parts, separated by a crisis, each of which will portray the Arthurian themes – love and adventure, society and the individual – in a characteristic way. Two scholars contributed more than any others to the development of the bipartite model: Hugo Kuhn in his interpretation of Hartmann's *Erec*, which appeared in 1948, and Erich Köhler, whose discussion of the romances of Chrétien was published eight years later.[1] Since then the model has become a critical commonplace, and one can find it repeated at every turn: Kurt Ruh incorporates it in his general study of courtly romance; Christoph Cormeau prefixes it to his study of two later romances; Walter Haug repeats it en route to his analysis of Wolfram's *Parzival*.[2]

Yet the concord of scholarly voices, seductive as it is, has lulled us into granting the bipartite model an authority that its architects never intended. The model, which was developed in the analysis of the works of Chrétien, Hartmann, and Wolfram, has been taken as the single and universal standard for *all* Arthurian romances. Thus Kurt Ruh divides *Lanzelet* into two parts, even though there is no crisis to separate them, and holds that the theme of the first part is Lanzelet's search for his name, even though his lack of one does not once occur to the hero in the fifteen hundred lines before it is revealed.[3] Thus Wolfgang Mitgau, in his generally convincing study of *Wigalois*, feels obliged to disengage a 'Haupthandlung' divisible by two – even though he himself divides the entire work into four parts.[4] Thus Wolfgang Moelleken tries to show that the relation of love and marriage plays a central role in Stricker's *Daniel*[5] – even though *Daniel* is notorious, and rightly so, for ignoring the theme of love almost completely.[6] In every case a model that was developed for the most celebrated romances has been transferred to the less famous ones on the assumption that the masterpieces define the genre; yet in every case the lesser works have been made to fit the model only through the concerted determination of the scholars. One might paraphrase the narrator of *Wigalois*, who says of certain listeners: 'si bietent lihte d'oren dar: ir muot stet aber anders war' (W:98–9); the critics seem to attend to the work at hand, but really their minds are elsewhere, on the works of Hartmann and Wolfram.

We see then that, although there is widespread agreement on the structure of German Arthurian romance, this general agreement has not been without its dangers. The bipartite model describes the canonical romances – in German, that is, *Erec*, *Iwein*, and *Parzival* – in a way that we, in the second half of the twentieth century, find convincing. There is, however, no reason to assume that this model necessarily defines the structure of the entire genre. Ruh, Mitgau, and Moelleken believe that, by talking of the lesser romances in the accepted vocabulary, they will be able to rescue them for the canon; but it is not at all clear that they have not distorted the works in doing so. Their devotion to critical tradition has turned what was originally a perfectly defensible set of descriptive observations on a few works into a prescriptive poetics for an entire genre. If a work can be made to fit the prescription, it is considered a legitimate Arthurian romance; if no one can be found to champion its orthodoxy, it is forced into literary-historical exile, like *Gauriel*, *Wigamur*, or the works of der Pleier. The critical literature, it seems, recognizes only one province in the kingdom of Arthurian romance; if you want to live there you have to look like Erec.

It must be obvious, however, that a structural definition that accommodates less than half the corpus remains just that: a structural definition of less than half the corpus. If we want to understand the structure of all the Middle High German Arthurian romances, then we will have to remove the works of Hartmann and Wolfram from their privileged position. No one will deny that *Erec*, *Iwein*, and *Parzival* are the masterpieces of our genre, yet this is irrelevant to an investigation of genre structure. As Northrop Frye notes: 'Such words as "classic" or "masterpiece" tell us nothing about the structure of literary works: they refer to social acceptance, and there are no inherent formal qualities that classics or masterpieces have that other works do not have.'[7] Indeed, our appreciation of the 'masterpieces' can only increase once we know which of their characteristics are unique and which true of Arthurian romance as a whole.[8] The celebrated bipartite structure, for instance, is not in fact a feature of the entire genre but only of the canonical works. If we want to study the structure of Middle High German Arthurian romance as a genre, then we must consider all the German Arthurian romances, from *Erec* to *Tandareis*, as equally legitimate witnesses to the structural principles that underlie the genre.

We must consider all the *German* Arthurian romances. While it is true that German romance authors repeatedly pillaged the French Arthurian corpus, the German tradition is not the same as the French. The pillage was selective: *Erec* and *Yvain* were adapted into German and exercised considerable influence; *Cligés* seems to have been adapted but to have had very little impact;[9] the *Charrete* is present only in more or less accurate allusions (I:4290–302, 4530–726, 5678–81; P:357,20–4, 387,1–8, 583, 8–11; C:2097–126, 24505–22). The German *Parzival* was clearly inspired by Chrétien, and *Wigalois* must have been influenced by *Le Bel Inconnu*.[10] Without any doubt, the German poets drew on the French tradition for material and inspiration, but they drew on their sources to fit the requirements of what was, after Hartmann at least, a German genre. One is tempted to advance reasons why some elements appealed to them and others did not, but any such explanations will remain unconvincing unless they are based on an understanding of what German writers considered the essential features of the genre. Only by limiting the investigation to the German romances will we be able to isolate those features.

Of course, much of what is true of the German romances is true of the French as well, just as most of Kuhn's observations about *Erec* apply both to Chrétien's work and to Hartmann's adaptation. Observations about romance structure are most likely to attain general validity when they reflect the basic categories and structures of the genre. And yet there are many features that distinguish the German romances from their French ancestors: they reveal different attitudes to conventional topoi, to the relation of narrator and audience, to the place of cities in the social order. One could, of course, attempt an investigation of Arthurian romance that would do justice to the works of Chrétien and his descendants, both French and German. I have chosen a less ambitious but, in view of national differences, no less compelling project: the study of all the German Arthurian romances. What we lose in breadth we will gain, I hope, in precision.

I have chosen to study all the German *Arthurian* romances. While there can be no doubt that Arthurian romance shares important traits with other departments of Middle High German literature, it is distinguished from them in important ways as well. One might, for instance, very well have included the Tristan romances and attempted a description of Middle High German courtly romance. Yet the Tristan romances are in many ways quite different from the Arthurian romances: their linear structure is less paratactic; their ending is necessarily tragic; society fills an altogether different function.[11] Again I have chosen the narrower corpus; in defence of this choice, I will try, whenever possible, to point out those particular features that distinguish Arthurian romance from other Middle High German traditions. In this way we will gain some sense of the system of genres of which Arthurian romance is a part.[12] We will want to pay particular attention to the systematic distinctions between Arthurian romance and its nearest relatives, the Tristan romances, but also, from time to time, to those between Arthurian romance, on the one hand, and heroic epic or the so-called *Spielmannsepik* on the other.[13]

By basing the study of German Arthurian romance on a corpus that includes all the extant works, we free the structural analysis of the genre from the hegemony of the canonical works. But that hegemony is only one of the constraints by which it has traditionally been shaped. It has been shaped as well by the widespread critical conviction that structural analysis is merely the handmaiden of interpretation. Hugo Kuhn considered the bipartite composition of *Erec* as part of his effort to fix the meaning of the work; naturally, only those structural features interested him that would further his interpretation.[14] And Erich Köhler pursued structural analysis as part of a larger project to relate twelfth-century French romance to the organization of the society in which it was composed: he too limited his consideration of structure to those features that would be useful in that larger project.[15] It must be obvious, however, that the attempt to provide a complete analysis of the structure of German Arthurian romance will be undermined just as much by limiting the kind of evidence that is allowed as by restricting the corpus from which evidence is sought. If the study of romance structure aspires to be complete, then it must be freed from its ancillary role and allowed to pursue the investigation of structure even where structure does not yield clear meaning.

In separating the study of structure from the determination of meaning, I follow Todorov's distinction between poetics and interpretation: 'Two different objects, *structure* and *meaning*, are implied here by two distinct activities: *poetics* and *interpretation*. Every work possesses a structure, which is the articulation of elements derived from the different categories of literary discourse; and this structure is at the same time the locus of the meaning. In poetics, one rests content with establishing the presence of certain elements within a literary work. But it is possible to achieve a high degree of certainty, for such knowledge may be verified by a series of procedures. The interpretive critic undertakes a more ambitious task: that of specifying – or it might be said of *naming* – the work's meaning. But the result of this activity cannot claim to be either scientific or "objective."' Todorov admits that the opposition is, in practice, never pure, but that one will choose in a given investigation to stress one term or the other. He continues: 'It is anything but an accident if, in studying a genre, we have taken the perspective of poetics. Genre represents, precisely, a structure, a configuration of literary properties, an inventory of options.'[16]

The study of romance structure must be freed not only from the service of interpretation but also from questions of history, at least initially. To be sure, an Arthurian romance was written at a specific historical moment for a given audience. Although these facts doubtless left their mark on the texts, the nature of the relationship between literature and the real world – especially in the Middle Ages – is not easily fixed. What did Landgraf Hermann have to do with *Parzival*? We can only guess. Was the *Lanzelet* audience familiar with the French Lancelot tradition? We can't really tell. Who wrote *Iwein*? Hartmann von Aue you answer. But what if you had said Bligger von Steinach, would that have made any difference? We might have had to repair once more the flimsy biography we have constructed of Hartmann's life, but our understanding of *Iwein* would hardly be affected at all. Since I am concerned here only with the internal structure of Arthurian romance, it is possible to ignore speculation about Hartmann's life and consider only the more concrete evidence of *Iwein*. I will limit myself, that is, to that which can be found in the texts themselves. Thus, for my strictly Arthurian purposes, there are two Hartmans: one is the narrator of *Erec*, the other of *Iwein*. We know a great deal more about them than about that third Hartmann to whom the first two owe their existence.[17]

Questions connected with the relation of an individual author, Hartmann, to a single work, *Iwein*, are not, however, the kind of literary-historical questions that are most likely to arise in the course of an investigation such as this. Studying the structure of a single genre, we are more likely to question the relations between the literary structures we discover in the analysis of that genre, Arthurian romance, and the social, political, and ideological structures of the world in which that genre flourished, Germany around the year 1200. Yet we will not pursue these questions either, for, if we approach the literature with the categories of extra-literary structure already firmly in hand, there is every reason to suppose that our literary analysis will be prejudiced by these predetermined, extra-literary categories: literature becomes evidence. We will pursue here what from the literary-historical point of view must be a preliminary undertaking: the independent investigation of genre structure. Only when these literary structures have been established on their own can they be incorporated with confidence in larger literary-historical investigations.

By freeing structural analysis from the service of interpretation and history we will be able to pursue the analysis of romance structure for its own sake. Where previous studies have focused on thematic structure or on the linear structure of episodes – always with regard to meaning – we will be able to investigate many varieties of structure. Where the usual approach yields a few thematic oppositions (*minne* and *aventiure*; society and the individual) and an articulated series of episodes (bipartition), we will develop a model that comprises patterns of organization at many levels and reveals as well the systematic relations these patterns sustain among themselves. I have oriented my model on the familiar division of literary discourse into semantic, syntactic, and verbal aspects, a division that provides the blueprint for the model and offers therefore the most convenient headings for its description.

First, then, we will establish the essential semantic categories of Arthurian romance and explore the systems they form. We will discover six such categories – I will call them *functions* – that, in static combination, determine the thematic axes of Arthurian romance, the structures of romance space, and the roles on which Arthurian characters are based. The six functions also enter into dynamic combinations and thus determine the structure of romance episodes. We will investigate first the basic episode syntax – the structure of the episodic *skeleton*. We will go on to discuss the techniques by which this bare skeleton acquires distinctive features – which I will call *substance*. Finally, we will consider the verbal systems of Arthurian romance – the *surface* by which we have access to the work – and try to establish the ways in which our perception of the episodic structure is affected by the manner in which it is conveyed.

An Arthurian romance, however, is composed not of a single episode but of a series of episodes. Therefore, having considered single episodes, we will want to move back one step to the point where the systems we have just isolated, episodes, become the terms of a new larger system, romance. From this new perspective the different types of episodes themselves represent the essential categories. We will first want to investigate the different types of relationships into which groups of episodes can enter, that is, the syntax of entire romances. We will explore both the romance skeleton and the connections that are generated when that skeleton is realized, when it acquires substance. Finally, we will consider the verbal surface of the entire romance, the effect of transmission on the whole.

By the time we conclude our progress from level to level, the 'essential semantic categories' with which we began will no longer seem so clear. We will recognize that they are of interest only to the extent that they are part of other systems; we will see that all the various structures we isolate are of interest, indeed can only be recognized, on account of the relationships they sustain with each other.[18] This perception of structure as a many-layered system of structures brings to mind Roland Barthes's fruit and vegetable simile, which may provide as good a way as any to compare the traditional image of Arthurian structure with my own. '... If up until now we have looked at the text as a species of fruit with a kernel (an apricot, for example), the flesh being the form and the pit being the content, it would be better to see it as an onion, a construction of layers (or levels, or systems) whose body contains, finally, no heart, no kernel, no secret, no irreducible principle, nothing except the infinity of its own envelopes – which envelop nothing other than the unity of its own surfaces.'[19]

CHAPTER ONE

Six Functions:
The Essential Semantic Categories
of Arthurian Romance

THE SYSTEM OF FUNCTIONS

You are standing in the rear doorway of a darkened theatre. All at once
the back section of the stage is illuminated and a landscape comes to life:
you hear the familiar sounds of birds and streams but would not be
surprised by the appearance of dwarfs, dragons, or other supernatural
creatures. Now another group of lights comes up and draws your attention away from the landscape. You observe instead a richly dressed and
courteous company: knights joust as their ladies watch; newcomers
arrive and are welcomed by those already present; all sit down to a
lavish feast. A group of individual figures appears on stage: perhaps you
notice the damsel who seems to entreat the aid of the courtly company;
or else you might distinguish a giant off in the woods or possibly a
maiden weeping by the body of her fallen champion. Now a moving
spotlight draws your attention to the figure of a single knight. Guided by
this spotlight you follow him as he departs with the damsel in need of
aid, as he overcomes the giant in the woods, as he avenges the fallen
knight, and as he returns to join the festive company.
 A voice begins to speak. You soon realize that it belongs not to one of
the figures on the lighted stage but to a barely visible soul standing in the
semi-darkness just this side of the proscenium. He reports the words in
which the damsel seeks the court's assistance and the conversation she
has with the single knight as they set out. He portrays in gory detail how
the knight subdues the giant and recounts the life history of the weeping
maiden. Generally the speaker follows the actions of the knight in the
spotlight, but from time to time he will have the action stand still while
he dwells on the description of a dress or develops an extended simile.

But now other voices object: the description is too long, the simile far-fetched. You realize now that the theatre is full, that there is a public for this elaborate spectacle, and that this public feels free to interrupt the presentation from time to time with its own observations and objections.

What is happening in this theatre is Arthurian romance. When we read an Arthurian text, we stand in the back door and watch not just the action on stage, but the whole complex event. We might at this point continue to develop our theatrical model – by describing the sequence of actions that constitute a proper welcome, by investigating the order in which the single knight approaches the other individuals on stage, by analysing the strategy of the narrator's rhetoric – but I prefer to pause. Let us ignore for the moment these questions of sequence and consider instead the nature of the categories that our model implies.

Remember that the theatre was introduced in six stages. At one extreme was (1) the natural-magical landscape; in front of it, (2) courtly society. Next were (3) a collection of opponents and women who enter into individual relationships with (4) the hero. The narrator (5) stands between the action on stage and (6) the audience. These six stages correspond to the six essential semantic categories that constitute Arthurian romance: (1) the world, (2) the society, (3) the other, (4) the individual, (5) the mediator, (6) the recipient.

In considering these six categories we will want to keep in mind a distinction of Todorov. He maintains that 'a notion can be defined in two ways: either in terms of its internal organization or in terms of its functions. In the first case, one deals with a system of which this notion is the external limit; in the second, it is a constitutive element in another system. ... Let us call the first type of definition structural and the second functional.'[1] Since we are concerned primarily with the structure of whole romances, that is with a system in which the six categories are merely components, we will want to define these categories in terms of their function. True, we will take note of their structure from time to time, but only to the extent that it affects their function. To help keep this perspective in mind I will call the six essential semantic categories simply: functions.[2]

The World (W)

This function comprises everything above or beyond courtly society: the divine order and the natural order, the grail and exotic jewels, magic springs and the forests of adventure, fate and chance. In most romances these are perceived piecemeal: Laudine respects the Christian injunction against suicide (I:1895–8); Enite's horse was stolen from 'einem wilden getwerge' (E:7396); because of the rock on which he grew up Lanzelet will never be sad (L:234–40); Oringles von Limors comes upon Enite 'von geschihte' (E:6133); God sends Gasozein to rescue Ginover from her murderous brother (C:11285). Yet W is not just a grab bag contrived to contain all those disparate elements that will not fit in the other functional categories; it is rather a group in which the component elements, in spite of their disparity, all participate in one crucial opposition: the courtly world has no control over them, cannot explain them, and can be threatened by them.

This threat, to be sure, is not realized in all cases: the dwarf from whom Enite's horse was stolen is quickly forgotten, while Enite continues to enjoy the use of the wondrous animal. In other instances, however, the initial, seeming beneficence of W soon turns threatening: the rock on which Lanzelet grows up assures his happiness, yet it belongs to his foster mother, a water fay, whose own interests later lead Lanzelet into the prison of 'Mabuz der bloede'; and the same fate through whose timely interest Oringles is led to save Enite's life has, in fact, delivered her into the hands of her most dangerous enemy. We recognize then that W, although it may at times seem merely strange and may at other times reveal a friendly aspect, represents at least a potential threat to the courtly order. Keeping this in mind, we can agree with Erich Köhler when he writes: 'The world surrounding Arthur's court is an enchanted, demonized reality that reveals itself as a constant threat to the order represented by that court.'[3]

The various manifestations of W fall into two groups. The first includes the natural world in its 'normal' shape (forests and meadows), in exaggerated forms (giants and dwarfs), and in exotic forms (jewels from India and musical toys); the second group includes causal explanations, whether these be attributed to fate or chance, magic or providence. Let us now investigate these two groups more closely.

When Gasozein and Gawein marry Sgoidamur and Amurfina, King Arthur organizes a *hochzit* to celebrate the occasion. After fifteen days of partying the court receives news of a tournament at Orcanie, Arthur and his knights set off at once, ride 'gein dem walde Aventuros' (C:13932), and presumably reach their destination. Gawein, however, gets lost in the woods. While there he pursues a maiden on horseback who is carrying a dead knight and berating Parzival; he sees an army of six hundred knights burst into flame shortly after they have been killed by a sword and a spear that fight without human direction; he watches birds attack a bound giant while a naked maiden tries to ward them off; he comes upon a richly dressed old woman riding a unicorn and beating a Moor whom she leads by a rope. After a dozen such sinister encounters Gawein finally awakens in the middle of a field.

Although few Arthurian woods contain such surrealistic terrors as the Walt Aventuros, these terrors are in fact merely the emblematic exaggeration of the dangers that threaten any knight in any woods. Later in his narrative Heinrich speaks of 'ein grozer walt, der was nach vreise gestalt' (C:26205–6), and the same can be said of Arthurian forests in general: by nature they are dangerous. Often this danger finds its incarnation in strange creatures: giants (I:4915; D:1049); dwarfs (L:426; T:9972); serpents (I:3841; W:4956). Just as often an errant knight is likely to encounter the more familiar figure of another knight: Erec comes upon Guivreiz; Parzival fights Feirefiz; Tandareis is attacked by robber knights. In any case, whether it takes the shape of a dragon or a knight, an Arthurian hero can be sure, on entering the woods, of finding *aventiure*; every Arthurian woods is the Walt Aventuros.

While the forest is the primary geographical realization of W, and the giants and dragons who dwell in it are the most familiar incarnations of this same function, the tangible realization of W is not limited to the forest and its inhabitants. In *Daniel* and *Garel*, for example, monsters appear from out of the sea (D:1913; G:7224). In other cases the creatures of W leave their natural habitat to aid courtly society: the giant Esealt rescues Erec and Walwein from captivity (L:7530–63, 7602–23); the giant Malseron and his three comrades are won for Garel's cause (G:11863–956, 12130–297). Even when enlisted in the courtly cause, however, giants clearly belong to a world beyond courtly society, and this distinguishes them from figures like Guivreiz or the robbers who attack Tandareis; for knights, even when they contribute to the dangers of the woods, always retain their essential allegiance to the courtly realm. The concrete realizations of W include not only helpful giants but also inanimate objects: the stones that give happiness to Lanzelet (L:234–40) and Florie (W:792–800), for example, as well as those that give strength to Feirefiz (P:743,5–8) and Gawein (C:23430–4). If we recall how this last stone was won almost by accident from Gawein's opponent, Fimbeus (C:14937–75), and how it is later stolen by the 'Ritter mit dem boc' (C:24720–25012), then we will recognize as well how the beneficence of W always remains contingent. Finally, the tangible realization of W includes that which is strange because it is foreign: the mechanical eagle on Lanzelet's magical tent (L:4780–804) and the exotic merchandise displayed outside Schastel Marveile (P:562,22–563,18). These too are originally part of a world that lies beyond the limits of courtly society.

When Gwigalois enters the kingdom of Korntin, which has already been ten years under the dominion of Roaz von Glois, a heathen magician in league with the devil (W:3652–8), he encounters an elaborate system of demonic magic. Yet Gwigalois repeatedly places his fate in the hands of God (W:4344–7, 5811–2, 6005, 6974), God himself intervenes directly several times (W:6504–7, 6865, 6904, 7020–1), and Gwigalois finally liberates Korntin. The demonic magic of Korntin and the direct intercession of God represent, respectively, the hostile and friendly aspects of our second group of W, the group that includes causal explanations. Roaz's magic provides the single explanation for the vicious dwarf Karrioz and the protective smog into which he flees (W:6545–762), for the sword wheel (W:6773–84), and for the fire-throwing creature, Marrien (W:6931–70). The reason that Gwigalois is able to overcome this demonic magic is, as King Lar recognizes at the outset, that Gwigalois has been chosen by providence to liberate Korntin (W:4701, 4862).[4]

Even though the lengthy and explicit contest between demonic magic and divine providence can be found in Arthurian romance only in *Wigalois*, the existence of both a malignant and a beneficent causality plays an important role in almost every romance. A good deal of *Diu Crone*, for example, is dominated by the enmity of Fimbeus and Giramphiel and the assistance of Gansguoter. On the one hand, Giramphiel sends Gawein off to fight a dragon she thinks invincible (C:15035–48, 15270–87); she sends the maiden who organizes the 'Handschuhprobe' and the 'Ritter mit dem boc,' who steals a collection of valuable magical props (C:22990–25570); Gawein must fight Fimbeus to recover them (C:27936–28233); and then Giramphiel plans to tell King Arthur that Gawein is dead (C:28518–39). Even Gasozein's fight with Arthur is related to Fimbeus by means of the belt Gasozein claims to have from Ginover (C:4857–88). On the other hand, Gansguoter tries to dissuade Gawein from undertaking an adventure that is, in fact, an attack on himself (C:13060–73); he gives Gawein armour that dispels magic (C:27343–68); he repels a company of burning knights (C:27413–68); he lifts a portcullis and stills a magic river that protected the land of Fimbeus and Giramphiel (C:27503–658); and he gives Gawein a magic box that puts their court to sleep

(C:27692–700, 27846–900). Finally, Gansguoter's sister gives Gawein detailed advice on how to proceed to the grail (C:28466–590). Thus a great deal of Gawein's course is determined by the malignant magic of Giramphiel and Fimbeus or the beneficent magical powers of Gansguoter.

Erec, on the other hand, contains very little magic; instead, events are attributed to God. He is held responsible for details of staging such as the timely reappearance of Erec's horse (E:6726), for individual victories such as those over Iders and Mabonagrin (E:973, 9454), and for the outcome of the whole (E:10098). Although Erec, unlike Gwigalois, has not been specially chosen of God, still we sense that our hero's course is guided by a friendly providence. Frequently in Arthurian romance, however, events will be attributed neither to magic nor to God but simply to chance; that is, neither to a hostile nor a friendly causality but merely to an unknown one. Lanzelet comes to the Wahsendiu Warte 'von geschihten' (L:5125); Oringles comes upon Enite 'von geschihte' (E:6133).

So far we have not distinguished between the natural and the supernatural components of W. I assume that Landgraf Hermann in the course of his life witnessed no more miracles than I; yet I am sure that he believed in miracles. I suspect as well that Landgraf Hermann never saw a water fay, and I wonder whether he believed in water fays too. Augustine held that miracles differ from 'real' events only in their relative frequency;[5] perhaps the Landgraf believed that water fays differ from ordinary women only in the relative likelihood of meeting one. Perhaps, then, the romance authors populate their lakes with water fays for the same reason they dress their heroines in clothes from Scotland (W:811): to delight their listeners with a high concentration of unusual but not impossible properties.

Whatever the attitude of Landgraf Hermann or the romance authors, there is nothing unusual about water fays within the world of Arthurian romance. They are just as much at home there as miracles in Augustine's theology, and they fill a similar role. Miracles, as tangible signs of the omnipotence of God, or in the New Testament of the divinity of Christ, strengthen the Christian's faith in the divine order when he or she might be inclined to doubt it.[6] The magic of the water fay in *Lanzelet* has a similar function. It provides a single explanation for a series of otherwise unrelated adventures and makes us believe in an order where we would not have suspected one. As Todorov says: 'supernatural beings compensate for a deficient causality ... Thus the fairy who assures a character's fortunate destiny is merely the incarnation of an *imaginary causality* for what might just as well be called chance, fortune, accident.[7]

Within the work there is nothing at all 'imaginary' about supernatural causes; they are just as real as natural causes or divine ones. That Iwein challenges Ascalon by means of a magic well in no way renders the ensuing fight less legitimate than the fight with Aliers, whom Iwein challenges face to face. Functionally, then, there is no supernatural in Arthurian romance. It has been incorporated, along with natural laws and the will of God, into the repertory of causal explanations that stands at the service of the romance author. The water fay may not have been as real for Landgraf Hermann as an authorized miracle, but in the literary world of romance she is the functional equivalent of God.[8]

What we have just noticed of supernatural causality is true of providence and chance as well. At one moment Hartman says that God sent Oringles to keep Enite from killing herself (E:6117), and sixteen lines later he says that Oringles arrived 'von geschihte' (E:6133). Apparently the will of God and the workings of chance cannot be distinguished.[9] Within the work this is true, for they both belong to the same repertory of causal explanations and are thus functionally equivalent. The distinction between God, the water fay, and chance may affect our interpretation of Arthurian romances; it does not affect their structure.[10]

Wolfram understood the functional coherence of W better than anyone else. He took note of the forests of adventure, the strange foreign lands, the monsters and freaks, the magical properties, the chance and providence that occur in most romances isolated and without apparent relation to each other. He took these elements and transformed them into the woods of Sigune and Trevrizent, the exotic kingdoms of Feirefiz, strange creatures like Cundrie, the magic of the grail ritual, Parzival's chance encounters with Sigune, and the providence that leads him to Trevrizent. In each case the transformation that Wolfram effects integrates a traditional element of W into a new, clearly organized system, the world of the grail. The old realm of W continues to exist – for Gawan in the magic of Schastel Marveile, for Parzival in the forests of books fourteen and fifteen. It has been supplemented, however, by a new realm, one whose components have been chiefly borrowed from W but whose coherent organization has been patterned on that of our next function, S. Thus, out of an assortment of items that lay beyond the control of courtly society, Wolfram has fashioned a new system that functions independently of courtly society.[11]

The Society (S)

Where are we to place Arthurian romance in relation to the forces that were transforming European society in the twelfth and thirteenth centuries? Erich Köhler aligns Chrétien with those who oppose the centralization of power under the French king. Gert Kaiser believes that the romances of Hartmann reflect the aspirations of the *ministeriales* while *Wigalois* portrays the society from the perspective of the great princes. Helmut Brall finds that *Daniel* represents the opposite point of view, that of those lesser lords threatened by the growth of territorial powers.[12] These scholars have shown that the relations between the social order as portrayed in a romance and the society in which that romance was written and received are often complex and tendentious. And yet to the unaided eye the structure of the social order within Arthurian romance appears remarkably uncomplicated and, over the course of time, strikingly stable. After all, Erec and Iwein appear in *Gauriel* and seem to feel perfectly at home there.

This simplicity and stability are achieved by exclusion, both vertical and lateral. Our romances do not recognize any social organization lower than the class of knights. To be sure, lesser souls appear from time to time, scattered throughout the Arthurian landscape – a fisherman (P:142,11–144,16), a hermit (I:3283–344), poor peasants (W:5288–305) – while others, like the *spilman* (E:2158–62), are occasionally required to appear at court. Yet all these exist only as individuals and only by virtue of their momentary connection with the loftier world of knights and ladies. That real peasants and real fishermen sustain necessary relationships with each other as well as with a much larger social fabric is irrelevant to the authors of romance. Arthurian society is bounded not only vertically but also laterally: it includes forests, meadows, and castles but stops short of cities. Gert Kaiser remarks that, 'as a genre, Arthurian romance is, by definition, hostile to the city.'[13] We recognize this in our romances not only by the almost complete absence of cities but also by the contempt shown those things associated with them: Tristan thinks nothing of masquerading as a merchant, but when Gawein is called the same he takes it as an insult (P:360,6–29; C:17690–712).[14]

Because of these various exclusions the structure of the Arthurian social order is radically simpler than that of the real world in which our authors lived; and we, concerned with the internal organization of romance, are interested only in this simplified model. It allows for meaningful social relations only within the world of knights and ladies or, less often, dependent on that world. Court society, that is, is the only form of coherent social organization that our authors recognize. Although we can observe behaviour typical of this society throughout the romance world – in the welcome Garel receives at Merkanie (G:766–930); in the form of Lanzelet's fight with Iwaret (L:4463–555); in the standards against which Wirnt finds fault with his audience (W:2317–95) – courtly society clearly has its focus at the court of King Arthur. Arthur, Ginover, and the knights and ladies who surround them provide the models of behaviour for all estimable figures in the romances.

But what of the world of the grail or the kingdom of Gwigalois? Don't these represent alternative models, independent of Arthur's court and, in significant ways, opposed to it? Only to a certain extent. To the extent that they offer coherent social models, they depend for this coherence on their parody of the Arthurian pattern; to this extent they are merely *contrafacta* of Arthur's court. To the extent that these alternatives differ from their original, the differences depend for their meaning on their contrast with the familiar social relations at Arthur's; here also the court of King Arthur provides the standard. If we wish to understand the organization of romance society, then, we must investigate the social relations of Arthur's court.

The composition of Arthur's court, firmly established in the traditions of the genre, is familiar to anyone who has read more than a single romance.[15] Arthur stands at the centre, accompanied by his queen, Ginover; flanking him are his nephew, the model knight Gawein, and his seneschal, the problematical Keie. These can be augmented by a few traditional hangers-on (Segramors, 'Dodines der wilde') and the heroes of previous romances, sometimes including Tristan. But we are not concerned so much with the composition of Arthur's court as we are with its function. What profit do romance authors derive from the traditional triad – Arthur, Gawein, Keie – and the court that surrounds them? First, well-known figures like Gawein and Keie aid in the composition of effective scenes. Second, the court serves as a model of exemplary behaviour. Third, the ideology of Arthur and his court motivates most of the romance population. Fourth, the appearance of Arthur early in a work indicates genre.

Gawein is the greatest of Arthur's knights; of this there is never any doubt. When Hartman first introduces him to Germany he claims 'daz nie man so vollekomen ans künec Artuses hof bekam' (E:2743–4); Wolfram calls him 'der tavelrunder hoester pris' (P:301,7); and Heinrich, writing after the Arthurian literary tradition has established itself quite securely, can assert: 'alle aventiure von Gaweines tiure sagent' (C:29913–15). Gawein is Arthur's 'naehster vriunt' (E:4874) and most important counsellor (C:25828–68; D:358–80, 6220–43); he is celebrated as an expert in courtly protocol (W:343–83), as a model of discretion (D:373–80), and as the devoted servant of women (T:598–606). He possesses a special sensitivity in matters of the heart that enables him to recognize the reason for Parzival's anguish in the snow near the Plimizoel (P:301,7–25) and to know that love is the source of the young Meleranz's sorrow (M:2598–624). Gawein's special sympathy for lovers makes him the most frequent and most eloquent advocate for Tandareis and Flordibel when they have fallen into disfavour with Arthur (T:3595–744, 8085–9, 8217–28, 16049–123).

But Gawein is best known for his great prowess, and it is for this reason that he is the knight most often sought by those in need of a champion. Lunete (I:4165–78), the knight ravaged by Harpin (I:4520–7, 4727–33), the wicked daughter of the Grave von dem Swarzen Dorne (I:5663–77), Nereja (W:1899–1910), Amurfina (C:7796–817), and Sgoidamur (C:12879–86) all seek the aid of Arthur's most valiant knight. By virtue of this same celebrated prowess Gawein is the standard against which all romance heroes are measured. He fights Lanzelet outside of Limors, Iwein in judicial combat before Arthur, Parzival by the Sabins, Daniel and Gauriel outside Arthur's court, and in every case the hero's success demonstrates that he is equal to or better than the recognized standard of Arthurian valour. In most cases the fight ends in a draw (*Iwein, Daniel*) or is stopped just short of defeat for Gawein (*Lanzelet, Parzival*). In those cases where Gawein is actually defeated, however, the narrator (W:562–77) or the characters (GM:1640–4) remark on the enormity of such an event.[16] When for a single day Erec outshines Gawein at a tournament, Hartman pretends this is only possible through the special intervention of the narrator (E:2756–63)! But why do our authors try to spare Gawein the shame of outright defeat? And why do their narrators take such pains to preserve the reputation of Gawein when the glory of their heroes depends on his defeat? Because a defeated Gawein is useless to them. Only when Gawein is universally acknowledged as the best fighter in the Arthurian world can a contest between Gawein and the hero fill its function: the demonstration of the hero's own (nearly) matchless prowess.

Yet these contests do not serve merely to establish the hero at the top of a static hierarchy: they serve as well the dynamic function of incorporating the hero into Arthur's court. In *Daniel* and *Gauriel* the contest with

Gawein is connected with the initial introduction of the hero into the court; in *Lanzelet* the contest is meant to fill this purpose (Walwein is dispatched by Arthur expressly to fetch the renowned but as yet unseen Lanzelet) but does so only indirectly (at the tournament at Djofle, which follows immediately). In *Iwein* and *Parzival* the fight with Gawein serves to reintroduce the hero, after a long absence, to Arthur's court. Gawein functions as an agent of reintegration also in a number of episodes in which he does not actually fight the hero: he tricks Erec into visiting King Arthur against his will (the 'Zwischeneinkehr'); he participates in the rescue of Lanzelet from his captivity at Pluris; he is able to lead Parzival out of his trance in the snow and into the court in book six; and his advocacy of Tandareis and Flordibel eventually accomplishes their rehabilitation. In *Wigalois*, too, the figure of Gawein serves to tie the hero to Arthur's court – he is Gwigalois's father and, long before they learn of their relationship, his knightly mentor; but here Gawein's integrating function depends on static relationships, not on dynamic encounters.

While Gawein is celebrated as Arthur's most perfect knight, Keie is best known for his flaws. Of these the most notorious is his shameless tongue: he pretends to a heroism he does not possess (L:2889–901; I:2468–507, 4634–63; D:3239–64) and likes to berate the virtuous without any justification (I:810–36; P:298,8–299,12; G:600–24). Not only does Keie speak shamelessly, he acts in disgraceful ways as well: he attacks the wounded Erec and the defenceless Cunneware (E:4629[22]–32; P:151,21–152,22); and he tries to sneak off the field of combat rather than acknowledge defeat (C:3042–58). Keie has become so inured to shame that he does not notice when he himself is humiliated (I:2628–42; G:18816–17). As a result, primarily of Keie's attacks on them, Arthur's courtiers hate him (L:2902–6; D:3303–16; C:26089–90; G:18540–6). At the same time, most narrators take pains to point out that Keie, in spite of his many ugly qualities, is one of the bravest of the knights of the Round Table (I:2565–74; D:148–50; G:17857–8).

The traditional figure of Keie can be treated in one of two ways: seriously or comically. The author of *Erec*, for example, who tends towards the first approach, has his narrator offer an analysis of Keie's contradictory, four-part heart; half of it, at least, is filled with virtue (E:4636–64). In *Iwein*, Hartman claims that Keie must be a *tiurer helt*; otherwise Arthur would not allow him at court (I:2565–74). Wolfram goes farther, defending Keie against all detractors and assigning him the valuable social function of *merkaere* (P:296,13–297,29; cf. G:600). Hartmann and Wolfram – and also the author of *Garel* – agree not only in taking Keie seriously; they agree on his function as well. When the hero leaves Arthur's court Keie's antagonism must accompany him; and before the hero can return he must first overcome Keie in armed combat. Thus Keie chides Iwein when Iwein resolves to avenge Kalogrenant, but Iwein defeats Keie just before his reunion with Arthur. Keie affronts Parzival when Parzival first appears at court, but Parzival defeats Keie just before he next sees Arthur in book six. Keie mocks Garel as Garel sets off in Arthur's behalf, but Garel avenges himself, seventeen thousand lines later, just before he sees Arthur for the second time. In *Erec* Keie realizes only the second part of this pattern: he is not present when the hero leaves court but succumbs to the hero's prowess just before Gawein tricks Erec into stopping at Arthur's highly mobile camp.

Based on this evidence we might suppose that Keie is the precise opposite of Gawein: where Gawein's actions serve to integrate the hero into Arthur's court, Keie's resist that integration. But resistance to integration is not the precise opposite of integration. Keie's malice, in all the above cases, merely accompanies the hero's prior decision to leave court; his antagonism only complicates the hero's certain return. Where Gawein is the agent of integration, Keie merely aggravates the separation. This is not to disparage Keie's role. Gawein has a long-range function and Keie a local one; but our authors, as we shall see over and over again, are often much more interested in the local than in the overall effectiveness of their works.

Our authors' concern for local effect is especially clear in the case of those who treat Keie comically. On the one hand are those works in which we, along with Arthur's court, delight in Keie's humiliation. In *Lanzelet* everybody laughs as Keie is unhorsed into a ditch (L:2924–5), and in *Daniel*, where Keie is hurled from the hand of a giant and saved in his fall by a tree, we laugh as Arthur's knights curse the giant for his loose grip and the tree for breaking the fall (D:3303–16). On the other hand are works in which we are more likely to laugh with Keie than at him. In *Tandareis*, for instance, Keie criticizes Arthur for granting a rash boon, a criticism we have all wanted to make (T:367–77, 3272–319). He jokes with Tandareis after being captured and accepts in good humour a wonderful speech of Kalogriant, who reminds him of his celebrated victories against Erec, Iwein, Meleranz, Parzival, Joram, and Garel (T:2466–584). In *Diu Crone* Keie plays an especially attractive role: he dominates the 'Becherprobe' and the 'Handschuhprobe,' amusing the court as he mocks (C:1815–19, 25964). Although Gasozein discovers him asleep in a ditch, Keie vindicates himself in fighting giants – to the special satisfac-

tion of his advocate, the narrator (C:27023–6). Keie speaks long and elo-
quently on the virtues of the supposedly dead Gawein (C:16933–17091)
and on how the court will miss him, Keie, while he seeks the grail
(C:25965–26073). Yet even in *Diu Crone*, where Keie dominates so much
of the narrative, his role seldom has more than local importance: his combats duplicate those of others; his speeches are merely decorative; and the
lengthy 'Becherprobe' has not the slightest bearing on the rest of the tale.

Jürgen Haupt says that in *Lanzelet* Keie is without function but that
the scene in which he appears is quite effective.[17] Haupt means that Keie
does not fill the function that he, Haupt, has determined that Keie fills in
the works of Chrétien, Hartmann, and Wolfram. Yet the stock figure of
Keie enables Ulrich to fashion an effective scene. Is this not a function?
Romance authors are so fond of Gawein and Keie not for ideological
reasons (as Haupt and Emmel seem to believe)[18] but for pragmatic ones:
they require, for the effectiveness of their scenes, figures whose character
and function are already well known.

If we consider the fate of the great Arthurian heroes in romances other
than their own, then we will recognize the functional significance of
Gawein and Keie even more clearly. In *Erec* some of the later heroes are
listed (Lanzelot, E:1631; Iwein, E:1641; Tristram and Garel, E:1650), but
of course they are merely names. In *Iwein* and *Parzival* earlier works
provide literary examples, but their heroes do not actually appear as
actors (Erec, I:2792–8; Enite, P:143,29, 187,14; Lunete, P:253,10). In the
non-canonical romances, however, the heroes of the earlier works appear
as active members of Arthur's court. Erec – along with Tristant – plays an
important role in *Lanzelet*, in rescuing both Lanzelet from his captivity at
Pluris (L:6229–389) and Ginover from her abduction by Valerin (L:7259–
351). Der Strickaere includes Iwein in the same praise he accords Gawein:
'ich waene, diu sunne nie beschein zwene bezzer ritter danne sie' (D:256–
7); and he grants Parzival a somewhat less than glorious engagement of
his own (D:7176–215). Erec, Iwein, and Lanzelet join Gawein at Gwigalois's *hochzit* (W:9570–1) and in the campaign against Lion (W:10070–3).
The same three are active both in *Garel* and *Tandareis*, although they are by
no means so important as Gawein. In *Diu Crone*, Lanzelet, Iwein, Erec,
and Parzival take part in the 'Becherprobe' and the 'Handschuhprobe'
(C:2070–290, 24596–628), and their lack of success in these tests is attributed to various shortcomings we know from the works that bear their
names.[19]

Unlike his colleagues, who always grant Gawein greater honour than
the later heroes, the author of *Gauriel* seems to prefer the newcomers.

He devotes considerably more attention to Gauriel's fight with Iwein (GM:1658–903) than to his fight with Gawein (GM:1525–657), and he abandons his hero for several hundred lines to follow Erec on an adventure of his own (GM:1288–431, 2130–277). Clearly the author of *Gauriel* is quite taken by the distinguishing traits of these knights. Iwein's lion gets to fight Gauriel's ram, and Erec holds forth on the dangers of *verligen* (GM:2884–905).[20] We see then that, while the earlier authors had to make do with Gawein and Keie, the founding members of Arthur's court, the later authors were, after the composition of a few romances, able to draw on a larger company of well-known knights. And the authors used these later heroes just as they had always used Gawein: as figures whose recognized excellence and famous past histories could be exploited for the purposes of their own romances.[21]

Arthur's court, however, provides the romance with more than a cast of stock characters; it also establishes models of estimable behaviour. Many authors preface their narrative with a summary presentation of the virtues of Arthur's court (I:1–58; C:161–205; W:145–246; D:33–142), thus enabling us to judge the behaviour of others according to these standards. Wirnt, for instance, notes that Arthur's knights 'muosen dicke wagen durch lop den lip' (W:156–7). When, a hundred lines later, Joram challenges Arthur's knights outside his castle, or when, much later, Gwigalois insists on taking up the adventure announced by Nereja, we recognize at once that they are behaving according to the Arthurian pattern. Similarly, we witness Arthur organizing a *hochzit* on the occasion of Gwigalois's knighting. Princes come from all over; there is jousting and feasting and entertainment; all are caught up in the festive *vreude*; Arthur dispenses lavish gifts as his guests depart (W:1622–1716). When Gwigalois himself organizes a *hochzit* to celebrate his liberation of Korntin and his marriage to Larie (W:9054–798), the festivities, even though they are described at much greater length, follow exactly the same pattern as those we witnessed at Arthur's. We recognize thereby that our hero is living up to the Arthurian model.

Our knowledge of courtly behaviour is useful not only in evaluating knights but also in keeping our bearings in the forests of adventure. When Iwein arrives at the castle that has been ravaged by Harpin he is greeted by six well-dressed pages, then received by the lord, taken in to meet the ladies, disarmed, fed, and entertained (I:4359–405). Having watched Arthur welcome Lanzelet or Gawein back to court (L:7724–90; C:13690–737), we realize at once that Iwein has arrived at a castle where the conventions of courtly behaviour are respected; and we deduce therefore that his host is an admirable man. How differently we react when Iwein arrives at the castle of the 'pesme aventure,' where the porter receives him 'mit manegem droworte' (I:6174)! Arthur's court functions in the romance world rather as Versailles did in Europe of the seventeenth and eighteenth centuries. Where the conventions are observed we know at once that we are among the right sort of people; where they are flouted we take it as a bad omen and expect all sorts of other unpleasant surprises.

Arthur's court is the standard not only for characters within the Arthurian stories. It is also the standard against which romance narrators like to judge their own public. Hartman recommends the ways of Arthur's court to his listeners (I:18–20) and laments that nowadays the *vreude* of an Arthurian *hochzit* is no longer possible (I:48–52). Wirnt never tires of reminding his audience how badly their world compares with the virtuous age of which he is telling (W:2146–58, 2319–48, 2358–95, and many others). And, near the end of our tradition, der Pleiaere begins *Meleranz* with a panegyric on the virtue of an earlier age, only to follow it at once by a much longer attack on the wretchedness of his own age (M:1–100). As in so many other cases, here too Wolfram carries things farther than anybody else. He looks beyond the romance world and his audience, which is after all an integral part of that world, and holds up Arthur's court as a model to those who live beyond the realm of literary fiction. The court of Hermann of Thuringia, says Wolfram, would benefit from a figure like Arthur's Keie (P:297,16–29). Many have remarked that Arthurian romance society is an idealized version of the society for which the romances were written. This ideal is not merely celebrated in its own right within the romances themselves; it is also repeatedly invoked to show how far the society out of whose real life these ideals were generated falls short of them.

The court at Versailles did more than establish a code of etiquette; it provided as well a coherent ideology that inspired active emulation in other capitals throughout Europe. Reference to France helps us explain not only the table manners at Potsdam but also the development of the absolutist Prussian state. The same is true of Arthur's court. It not only supplies romance authors with stock characters and models of courtly behaviour, the tangible realizations of the function S that we have considered so far; it also offers a coherent ideology that inspires action. Let us turn now to those ways in which the conventions of Arthur's court motivate the action of romance, to those aspects of the function S, that is, that contribute to romance causality.

Among the most venerable customs at Arthur's court is the hunt of the white stag. We find it in *Erec* (E:1099–111) and in *Lanzelet* (L:6725–37); in *Diu Crone* Heinrich refuses to explain the convention since we have heard of it so many times already (C:16714–37). The popularity of this custom with romance authors, however, certainly derives less from its inherent interest than from its capacity to get things moving. As Kurt Ruh states, 'The hunt of the white stag is, in other words, *stimulans actionis*. ... it sets ... active chivalry in motion.'[22]

A similar function is filled by Arthur's troublesome habit of granting all requests in advance. The most disastrous instance, the details of which we know from the *Charrete*, causes him to lose his queen. This episode plays an auxiliary role in *Iwein* (I:4288–302, 4528–726) and *Garel* (G:31–90). Other examples of Arthur's addiction to the rash boon are not hard to find (L:5774–82 [which is recalled by Keie, T:367–77]; C:1008–66, 24937–55; T:579–82). Arthur is often criticized for his habit. The knight ravaged by Harpin says of the abduction of Ginover, 'der künec treit ouch die schande' (I:4526); Garel says to the king himself, 'ir wart guoter witze ein kint daz ir min frowen gabet hin' (G:142–3); and Keie blames all the troubles in *Tandareis* on the thoughtless speed with which Arthur granted Flordibel's request (T:2504–14). Yet in evaluating this criticism and in understanding why the rash boon is so popular with romance authors, we should keep in mind what Walter Haug says on the subject: 'the motif is occasionally used to criticize the thoughtlessness of the king ... Basically, however, it is a neutral introductory motif, a mechanism whose function is to set the plot in motion.'[23] Since Gawein is off trying to rescue the queen, Iwein must defend Lunete and fight Harpin; since all the court is off in the same pursuit, Garel alone can answer the challenge of Ekunaver.

Arthur's reluctance to eat until he has had news of some adventure is yet another convention of his court that serves to motivate the essential activity of our romances (L:5708–17; P:309,3–9, 648,18–22; C:12627–38; W:247–51; D:400–7; M:3175–97; T:335–41). Der Strickaere tells us clearly what Arthur has in mind:

daz tet er niht wan umbe daz,
daz sie sich regeten dester baz
und ritterschefte pflaegen
und sich da niht verlaegen.
er fuogte ir ere in alle wis,
davon bejagete er den pris.   (D:83–8)

The requirement that one fight before breakfast is, it turns out, merely a trick of Arthur's to get his knights under way.[24]

The remarks of der Strickaere can help us understand a great deal more than Arthur's reluctance to eat. They explain as well the function of the hunt of the white stag, the rash boon, and the great value attached to *ere*. All these customs and values are attributed to Arthur's court, and yet that is only a way of masking their true purpose. Arthurian romance depends on the series of contests undertaken by the hero; the customs and ideology of Arthur's court provide credible explanations for these contests. A knight must do what is asked in the name of his lady; he must fight another knight with upraised spear; he must seek *pris* and *ere*; Arthur hunts the white stag; he grants a rash boon. In every case the result is adventure. The result, that is, is an episode or perhaps a series of episodes. In order to generate the episodes of romance the knights must, in the terms of der Strickaere, *sich regen und ritterschefte pflegen*. The customs and ideology of Arthur's court provide ostensible causes for all this activity.[25]

The counterpart to the Arthurian conventions that require a knight to seek adventure is the *hochzit* that inevitably awaits him on his return. The forms of the *hochzit*, as we have seen, are clearly established: the knights will joust; there will be talk of love; the court will feast and be entertained; Arthur will dispense generous gifts; often there will be a wedding or knighting ceremony. All of this will induce that most precious state, courtly *vreude*.[26] A detail from *Lanzelet* reveals just how precious this collective emotion is considered. When Arthur rescues Ginover from the castle of Valerin, the pillaging of his army is said to avenge not the abduction of the queen but rather the fact 'daz Artus truric was gewesen' (L:7371); life without *vreude*, it seems, is as intolerable as life without Ginover.

In general the *vreude* of the court is entirely dependent on the success or failure of the hero. When in *Diu Crone*, for instance, a false report of Gawein's death reaches the court, all are plunged at once into the most eloquent grief (C:16745–17311). But when news arrives that Gawein is in fact still alive, the court is instantly able to mount a most elaborate festival – even though, as we have just been told, it is 'der geste bar (daz vil selten ie geschach)' (C:21826–7)! Suddenly there are storytellers, chess players, jousting, every kind of musical instrument known to the author, and, of course, *vreude* (C:22042–110). The *hochzit*, it turns out, depends not on the logistical possibility of mounting one, but on the fate of the hero. It is the inevitable reaction to his successful completion of an adventure or series of adventures.

All the activity of the Arthurian knight takes place between two poles. On the one hand are the tenets of courtly ideology that enjoin him to increase his *ere*; these dynamic injunctions require him to leave court and seek adventure. On the other hand is the *hochzit* that awaits him on his return, the static repose of courtly *vreude* that is his reward. We see then that the Arthurian court both requires and rewards precisely that undertaking – the search for adventure – that forms the backbone of Arthurian romance.

The presence of King Arthur, usually at or near the beginning of a work, identifies the work as an Arthurian romance and guarantees the validity of the conventions of that genre.[27] This is the principal function of Arthur and explains why he need undertake so little else. Ruh calls him 'semper movens immobilis.'[28] To be fair, we should acknowledge that Arthur is not quite so passive as the exegetes of the canonical works would have us believe. In *Parzival* he captures Ritschart de Navers in the skirmishes at Logrois (P:665,5–12); he wages an immense heroic battle in *Daniel* (D:2959–5807) and participates, rather unimpressively, in a battle in *Wigamur* (Wm:3256–67); he tourneys with distinction in *Tandareis* (T:13057–8, 13124–46, 16827–33) and also in *Wigamur* (Wm:2056–63); in *Diu Crone* Arthur fights a major contest with Gasozein (C:3273–5083), and in *Gauriel* he is prepared to accept the hero's challenge (GM:1904–67).[29] And yet this activity, even where it is considerable, never overshadows Arthur's principal function as guarantor of familiar conventions – conventions of behaviour among the romance population, literary conventions throughout the romance as a whole.

Arthur's presence, then, certifies a work as an Arthurian romance, and the conventions whose validity he guarantees are the conventions peculiar to that genre. As the distinctive conventions of Arthurian romance are more closely connected to the function S than to any other function, we might profitably pause for a moment to compare the characteristics of society we have just isolated in Arthurian works with the analogous features of their closest relatives, the Tristan romances. Clearly the Arthurian and Tristan traditions have more in common with each other than with any other Middle High German narratives. From the first German Arthurian romances to the last, our authors do not hesitate to include Tristan among the members of Arthur's court (E:1650; GM:3860; cf. G:2456–75). Eilhart devotes an entire episode to Tristrant's stay with Arthur (ETr:5016–487), and even Gotfrit alludes to Arthur, although not without a certain disdain (GTr:16861, 16900). Furthermore, some of the same scribes are responsible for the transmission of Gottfried's work and those of the Arthurian authors (the codex that contains *Tristan* ms F also includes *Iwein* ms D; the same scribe who copied *Tristan* ms M wrote *Parzival* ms G). And yet, in spite of the close relation of the two traditions, they imply entirely different attitudes towards the social order.

The members of Arthur's court form a cohesive, harmonious group; they only fight against each other by mistake. Gawein is the hero's closest friend and, in the long run, his function is always to reintegrate the hero into Arthur's court. The barons at Marke's court, on the other hand, are distinguished primarily by their envy; their greatest efforts are directed to separating Tristan from the court. To be sure, Keie seems sometimes to play a similar role at Arthur's, and yet his divisive behaviour is sporadic, inconsistent, and, in the end, neutralized by the essential harmony of the court.

We saw that Arthur's court provides patterns of courtly behaviour recognized as models throughout the romance world. His knights seek adventure; he presides at festivals. These customs are completely foreign to the court at Tintajel. Marke's cowardly barons would rather surrender their children than fight Morolt, and the Tristan authors, with a minor exception (GTr:524–736),[30] resolutely refuse to grant Marke a respectable *hochzit*. Gotfrit, as is well known, disdains to describe the festivities attendant on Tristan's knighting (GTr:5054–68) and collects a large assembly at Marke's wedding for the sole purpose of having them praise Isolt's beauty (GTr:12544–68). All Eilhart has to say on the same occasion is, 'die brutlouf wart riche' (ETr:2807).[31] This is not to say that the Tristan authors are unfamiliar with Arthurian conventions. When Eilhart's hero arrives at Arthur's, the narrator pauses to explain that it is the custom of Arthur's knights to ride off in search of adventure and honour (ETr:5046–58). Gotfrit twice mentions Arthur's name, both times in connection with the well-known Arthurian *hochzit*, in order to have a recognized standard of *vreude* against which he can measure the much greater *vreude* of Tristan and Isolt (GTr:16861–5, 16896–901).[32] The Tristan authors are clearly familiar with the significance of Arthurian behaviour, but they recognize it as something foreign. Eilhart pauses to explain these strange customs, Gotfrit regards them as inferior. Yet it is not simply a matter of taste. The Tristan authors clearly do not regard Marke's court as a model of courtly behaviour; it is a society of envious, cowardly men who have pitted themselves against the hero. Therefore they suppress even the most conventional forms of societal affirmation (*hochzit*) and deny the barons even the most ordinary expression of social usefulness (fighting). And the treatment achieves its result. We are not likely to regard Marke's court as worthy of emulation.

Nowhere is the difference between the social order at Karidol and that at Tintajel more obvious than in the ideological systems that they represent. Arthur's court requires its members to go out in search of *aventiure* and rewards them with a *hochzit* on their return; its knights live between the poles *arbeit* and *vreude*. Yet *arbeit* and *vreude* can hardly be separated, for they depend on and require each other. There will be no *vreude* if there has been no *arbeit*; there will be no *aventiure* without the promise of *hochzit*, the celebration of reintegration. Thus the individual is never pitted against the society in Arthurian romance, since the activities of the one depend on those of the other, and the conventions of their relationship are accepted by all.

In place of the Arthurian *arbeit* and *vreude* the Tristan tradition offers the famous pair *liep* and *leit*; these, too, cannot be separated. Yet they are not social values like their Arthurian counterparts. They are important values for Gotfrit and Tristan but not for Marke and his court. Society in the Tristan romances is concerned with *ere*, yet this value is of even greater concern to the hero and cannot by itself be said to motivate the romance. Marke's court, it turns out, does not possess a coherent ideology which can explain the behaviour of Tristan. This can only be explained by an individual emotion, love, and the conflicts that arise between the obligations of love and those of society. Just as social ideology does not explain the contests in which Tristan engages, so too it has no way of resolving them. Thus, while the Arthurian hero returns from his adventures to a great celebration organized in his honour, Tristan remains pitted against society to the end: *Erec* ends in *vreude*, *Tristan* in death.[33]

No matter what point of view we adopt, we find in the Tristan romances an entirely different social order from the one we find in Arthurian romance. The nature of the members that constitute the court, their behaviour, the presence or absence of a coherent ideology – at Tintajel all these work to drive the hero into exile and break the court asunder while at Arthur's they foster the hero's career and guarantee his return to a coherent society. Marke's court seeks disintegration, Arthur's, in the end, integration. This tendency to integration, manifest ultimately in the universal happy end, is, like so much else in our romances, rooted in the structure of the society of which Arthur is the head. It is not for nothing that we call our works *Arthurian* romances.

The Other (O)

Since W and S serve parallel functions in Arthurian romance, we were obliged, in order to distinguish them, to dwell on their difference in quality: W differs from S not because it includes characters and causes – S does the same – but because the characters of W are giants while those of S are Arthur and Gawein. O, on the other hand, can be given a purely functional definition. It comprises everything with which the function I – let us for the moment equate I with the hero – enters an individual relation. O has a negative and a positive aspect: on the one hand are all those who oppose the hero (O^-); on the other, all those with whom he enjoys a harmonious relationship (O^+). In the archetypical Arthurian episode, the two aspects of O appear in complementary distribution: Erec defeats Iders and wins Enite; Lanzelet kills Iwaret and gains Iblis; Garel defeats Vulganus and wins Laudamie. In every case the hero overcomes an opponent in armed combat and wins a woman as a result. By his own intervention the hero transforms O^- to O^+.

One suspects that deep in the pre-literary Arthurian subconscious O^- is a male in league with the threatening world of W, and that O^+ is a woman who is, or is destined to become, a member of courtly society. By wresting O^+ from O^- the hero wins his bride and introduces, or reintroduces, her to the world of S. But in the actual romances these clear allegiances no longer obtain. There are, of course, cases where an opponent is a creature of W (*Iwein*: Harpin; *Wigalois*: Roaz; *Garel*: Vulganus) and cases where the woman becomes the hero's bride (*Lanzelet*: Iblis; *Parzival*: Condwiramurs; *Garel*: Laudamie); but in other instances the opponent is indisputably courtly (Gawein; *Wigalois*: Schaffilun; *Garel*: Gilan) and the woman for one reason or another does not marry the hero (*Lanzelet*: Ginover; *Daniel*: Frouwe von dem Trüeben Berge; *Gauriel*: Asterian's daughter). In general that opponent from whom the hero wins his bride does behave according to courtly conventions (*Erec*: Iders; *Parzival*: Kingrun; *Daniel*: Matur) even when he has a special connection to W (*Iwein*: Ascalon; *Lanzelet*: Iwaret; *Meleranz*: Libers). Let us say, then, that O^- is an opponent whom the hero defeats in battle and O^+ a woman whom he liberates.

But even this formulation is too specific. Lunete denouces Iwein before Arthur's court; Sigune castigates Parzival after he leaves Munsalvaesche; Elaete banishes Gauriel at the outset of the romance: yet in each case the hero eventually regains the favour of the woman who rejects him. Parzival fights Feirefiz; Gauriel defeats Gawein and Iwein; Garel defeats Gilan: yet in each case the hero gains the friendship of his opponent. From these examples we see that O⁻ can be female and O⁺ male, and that the two aspects of O may represent no more than two attitudes of a single character towards the hero. We are left then with an abstract, functional definition: O⁻ is a resistance against which the hero struggles; O⁺ replaces O⁻ and enters into a harmonious relation with the hero. O⁻ is opponent; O⁺, companion.

Both opponent and companion are 'other,' but they are so to different degrees. In many episodes, this difference is expressed by the contrast between the anonymous knight with whom the hero fights and the named knight from whom he exacts surety. When Erec defeats Guivreiz, for instance, the hero demands nothing from his vanquished opponent 'wan daz ir mir ane schamen rehte nennet iuwern namen' (E:4470–1). Thus in the same moment that Guivreiz, by his defeat, ceases to be an opponent he also, by giving his name, becomes less strange; Guivreiz is transformed from a more intense form of the other to a less intense form. This process of incorporation continues when Erec reveals his name and it turns out that Erec's father, Lac, is well known to Guivreiz; Guivreiz then spontaneously offers himself as Erec's vassal and invites him home (E:4513–69). In *Iwein* and *Parzival*, when the hero fights Gawein, the change in degrees of 'otherness' is effected not at all as the result of the exhausting combats that are fought but entirely as the result of giving names. When the hero and Gawein become known to each other they are at once transformed from opponents into friends, a transformation that is visualized in both romances when the contestants throw away their swords (I:7495–7; P:688,21). Thus the more intense form of the other, O⁻, is changed into the less intense form, O⁺, through the very clear decrease in the degree of strangeness: learning names.[34]

The functions of O in Arthurian romance fall into the same two categories into which we divided W and S: tangible and causal. The tangible effects of O result from the specific characteristics of each opponent or companion. The hero, about whom we know nothing at the beginning of a romance, increases in definition as he reacts to one O after the other. Laudine is a courtly lady with a magic well; Harpin, a giant; Gawein, the model knight. Iwein becomes tangible for us not because he is 'biderbe hövesch und wis' (I:3752) but because of the way he reacts to Laudine, Harpin, and Gawein. In fact, Iwein can hardly be said to exist at all except as he is defined by what he encounters. He is defined both in relation to O⁻ (Laudine condemns him; Gawein fights him) and in relation to O⁺ (Laudine is his wife, Gawein his friend). Later authors refer to

Iwein as either 'der ritter mit dem lewen' (G:36; cf. GM:858–9, 1723) or 'von dem brunnen her Iwein' (W:10073; G:17682; T:12951, 16851). In each case he is distinguished by one of his combats.

Yet if the hero exists only as he achieves definition in relation to O, then the romance, which follows the progress of the hero, also depends for its existence on O. We have already mentioned that in the archetypical Arthurian episode the hero transforms O^- to O^+. The series of episodes, which is nothing but the succession of the repeated transformations of O, determines the linear organization of romance. This is the chief tangible function of O.

The causal effects of O parallel those of S. Just as the ideology of Arthur's court forces a knight to seek adventure, so the existence of O^- causes him to engage in combat. In this sense, O^- is the specific agent that enables the hero to realize the courtly injunction. Iwein has certainly always accepted the obligation to seek adventure, as Gawein states quite clearly (I:2899–901), but he depends on the appearance of Ascalon in Kalogrenant's story in order to be able to fulfil his desire. Just as O^- parallels the general cause, so O^+ is a specific form of the general courtly reward. Laudine fills for the single episode the role that the *hochzit* fills for the whole romance: each is a reward for success. By defeating Ascalon (O^-) Iwein gains Laudine (O^+); because Iwein has fulfilled the injunction to seek *aventiure*, courtly society organizes a *hochzit* that engenders *vreude* (I:2439–45).

If we consider the dynamics of Arthurian romance on a more abstract level, we see that W and S provide the genre with its causal and ideological framework. They form a static system, valid within literary history from *Erec* to *Tandareis* and within the romance world from Karidol to Korntin. O, on the other hand, can be located only within an individual work, where it fills a dynamic function. O^- provides a challenge, whether to society in general or to a particular knight, that engenders action. O^+ provides a goal for that action. O^- and O^+ function within the narrative as poles of action and repose. W and S provide Arthurian romance with its static causal and ideological framework; O, by its repeated transformation from O^- to O^+, marks narrative divisions of a single work.

The Individual (I)

The hero of *Erec* appears for the first time in line two and immediately establishes himself at the centre of the romance stage; ten thousand lines later Hartman is still talking about him. In romances whose prologues have survived, the hero may not appear until a bit later, but once he arrives he will behave just like Erec: he will demand our attention almost continuously. Hartman may interrupt the 'pesme aventure' to describe the appearance of the captive women (I:6192–220) or to let them tell their history (I:6319–406); he may pause to say a few words of his own about those who mean to do ill but accidentally do good (I:6663–75); we may even be distracted from Iwein's progress by the story of Ginover's abduction (I:4530–726), which is only tangentially related to the main narrative. And yet, no matter how eagerly we follow the digression, we never forget that Iwein is standing there, waiting to get on with his own adventures. Even in the extreme case of *Parzival*, where we follow the progress of a secondary hero for over five thousand lines, we do not forget that at the same time the real hero is fighting battles we do not witness. Indeed, the coherence of the whole depends on our ability to keep Parzival in mind, even when he is out of sight. Our constant awareness of an Arthurian hero provides a single, unifying focus for the work, and this single focus holds together even the most loosely constructed romances.[35]

In assuring the linear coherence of the work the hero's domination of the romance fills a structural, literary need. The tireless activity by which he accomplishes this domination satisfies at the same time an ideological demand, the requirement that an Arthurian knight devote himself ceaselessly to the acquisition of worldly renown. Young Gwigalois tells his mother that he must set out to seek adventure 'daz man mich von rehte baz erkenne danne ein andern man' (W:1296–7). Gwigalois, of course, is thinking only of the courtly injunction to seek *ere*, yet this corresponds precisely with the literary requirement that the hero be constantly before our eyes. He must dominate the work so that we, the audience, recognize him better than any other man. On this depends the coherence of the whole. Gwigalois's *ere* is contingent not only on the number of his combats but also on his success, and this ideological requirement also fills a structural need. To accomplish the transformation of O^- to O^+ – in other words, to generate an episode – the hero must be victorious over his opponent. We find then that Arthurian ideology provides causal justifications for behaviour of the hero that serves an essential structural function: the hero must be present throughout to guarantee the coherence of the whole; he must be victorious over his opponents to generate episodes.

The hero's domination of romance has a very simple cause: he is stronger than anybody else. That is, the significance of the hero's domination for romance structure and for the romance population derives from its significance for the hero's opponents. He defeats them all. He dominates them. Of the two kinds of subject that Greimas distinguishes, 'les sujets "savants" ... et les sujets "puissants,"'[36] Arthurian heroes clearly belong to the second category. Indeed, their inability to act other than puissantly is quite staggering. Trevrizent tells Parzival that the grail cannot be won by force. No matter; Parzival can't think of anything else to do, so he goes on fighting. Luckily for him Trevrizent was wrong. Iwein loses the favour of Laudine because he fights too long. Faced with a crisis that fighting has caused but that fighting cannot help, he goes mad; if he can't solve the problem by force of arms he falls to pieces. When Gwigalois wants to gain the favour of Nereja he provides a string of victories, and Tandareis is reconciled with King Arthur only by the help of three tourneys.

Imagine what Tristan would do in similar circumstances. Sometimes, to be sure, he would fight, for he too is stronger than anybody else. But he is just as likely to pick up his harp, to dress up as a pilgrim or a fool, or to outsmart his enemies in some other way. In addition to the *pouvoir-faire* of the Arthurian heroes, Tristan has an equally matchless *savoir-faire*; he is 'der sinnesame Tristan' (GTr:3091), 'der wise Tristan' (GTr: 6260; cf. ETr:1238). Of course Arthurian heroes do know some things, but what they know is merely the bare minimum needed to keep them fighting: they must rescue damsels in distress, they must accept every challenge. We are told occasionally that they know how to govern well, although – except in the case of Lanzelet – their kingship is never more than an afterthought.[37] The only important exception to the Arthurian rule is Daniel, who often pauses to reflect before undertaking a contest (D:1056–110, 1159–74, 1843–73), and who wins a number of these contests – Juran, the monster with the Gorgon head, the monster who bathes in blood, the abduction of King Arthur – as much through the exercise of his mind as by the strength of his arm.[38] But whereas the Frouwe von dem Liehten Brunnen can say of Daniel, 'siner wisheit der ist vil' (D:2350), all one can say of the rest of the romance heroes is that they are 'küene' and, at best, 'traecliche wis' (P:4,18). Even near the end of his course, Parzival, who can match Feirefiz in combat, is still 'leider niht so wis' (P:749,5) that he can equal him in words.

Fortunately Arthurian heroes have no great need of cleverness. The adventures they so assiduously seek are all adventures that have been preordained for them, and part of their preordination is that they can be accomplished by brute force. The economy with which the requirements of each adventure correspond to the capacities of the Arthurian hero is part of the magic of romance; it is also a sign of the hero's own pre-destination.[39] The hero has merely to be on stage – at Arthur's, in the woods, it hardly matters. Adventures will present themselves, and he will achieve them by virtue of his strength. There is always struggle, but there is never danger.

Although nearly all Arthurian adventures are achieved by brute force, they are not all the same. Lanzelet's attack on Galagandreiz is quite different from his defence of Ginover, and this defence differs completely from Parzival's defence of Jeschute. The differences among Arthurian adventures are crucial because they enable us to differentiate among Arthurian heroes: Parzival does not differ from Lanzelet because of what he *is* but because of what he *does*. Like the other characters in romance, our heroes are 'a-psychological,'[40] a point to which we will return later. Because they so completely lack an interior life, we can know them only as a result of their actions. They differ from their fellow characters not in insight or psychological interest, only in the success and quality of their adventures. Galagandreiz appears in one episode, Lanzelet in all episodes; Galagandreiz is defeated, Lanzelet always wins. Galagandreiz is no more than one particular kind of defeat; Lanzelet is the sum of a great variety of victories.

Because the episodes in which we see the hero differ from one another, we perceive him, in the course of a romance, from a variety of different aspects. This sequence of aspects has often been read as a course of development, a search for identity. Kurt Ruh believes that the program of the first part of *Lanzelet* can be 'formulated psychologically' as the hero's 'coming-to-himself, self-realization.'[41] Gustav Ehrismann regards *Parzival* as 'a novel of development in which the inner life of the hero unfolds with uniform psychological coherence.'[42] Erich Köhler, writing of adventure, speaks of the 'development of the hero to complete self-understanding.'[43] And recently Rainer Warning has written that the real 'queste' of the courtly hero is 'the search for oneself ... the search for identity.'[44]

I would oppose to these remarks an observation of Michel Huby: 'The Middle Ages do not recognize gradual development ... they know only the absolute of revelation, whether it comes from God or from some other who "teaches" you who you are.'[45] After seven lines of instruction (L:570–6) Lanzelet has mastered riding (L:592–5) and is able to distinguish himself at jousting (L:662–6). Gurnemanz needs only give a few words of advice before Parzival wins his first jousts (P:173,27–175,6).

Why does Parzival succeed so quickly? Because, as we are told, 'den twanc diu Gahmuretes art und angeborniu manheit' (P:174,24–5); Parzival is a hero by nature. Johfrit and Gurnemanz are not teachers; they are catalysts, agents in whose presence Lanzelet and Parzival can change at once from children to heroes.

Later developments in the life of an Arthurian hero occur just as suddenly and with just as little regard for psychological plausibility. After Iwein and Gawein return from their overlong circuit of tourneys, our hero suddenly remembers his wife (I:3082–7) and falls at once into a stupor 'als er ein tore waere' (I:3095); then Lunete arrives, delivers her message, and Iwein goes mad. There is no 'psychological coherence' to a character who completely forgets his wife for over a year and then goes mad when suddenly it occurs to him that he has wronged her. Nor is there any reason to suppose that Erec's adventures lead him 'to complete self-understanding.' He sets out with Enite for no reason that we know of, he remains unmoved by the repeated proof of her devotion, then, after his stubbornness has nearly killed them both, he is suddenly reconciled – again for reasons that are not at all clear (E:6775, 6781–2). The behaviour of Iwein and Erec clearly does not reveal the state of any plausible psyche so much as it reveals the needs of the narrative. Their behaviour reflects not psychological development but plot development.

By saying that the behaviour of Erec reflects the needs of the narrative we say that the behaviour of the hero, to the extent that it makes sense at all, does so not in a psychological context but in a literary one. The romance, after all, continues for several episodes after the reconciliation without the slightest hint that Erec is (still) searching for his identity. It is not Erec but the romance that must attain its identity. Ingrid Hahn is surely right when she says of *Parzival* that its hero as well as other characters are all incorporated in a 'process in which the truth emerges.'[46] Whatever the 'truth' of an individual romance, whatever its 'identity,' it is attained not because its hero develops but because the romance itself, which uses the hero like a puppet, has achieved its proper form. 'That which changes,' says Max Wehrli, 'is only the interpretation by the poet, formulated expressly or in symbols. The course of the action is not so much experienced by a hero as it is accomplished by the poet, who watches over and comprehends the whole.'[47]

Of the hero's identity, then, one can say at most that in the course of the romance it is realized: realized – that is, comprehended – by the romance population; realized – that is, actualized – by the romance author. Whereas the hero's domination of the romance depends on his unequalled strength, the realization of his identity depends on his general supereminence. He is not only the strongest but also the bravest, the best-looking, the most courteous, and so forth.[48] In the course of the romance the hero's excellence becomes gradually clearer to us – and to the characters within the romance – because we witness this excellence as it is realized in action – the only kind of proof that really counts – in one episode after the other. In the course of a work the boundaries of the romance world are rearranged and our understanding of the hero grows so that he can attain his true position – both in the romance world and in our estimation. Erec's reconciliation with Enite is only one stage in this process; it is evidently not the goal. The process of the romance must be completed by Erec's public success at the 'joie de la curt,' his acclamation at King Arthur's, and his triumphant return to Karnant. The happy ending of romance is attained not when the hero finds his true identity but when the perfect hero, the romance world, and the romance audience have achieved identity.

The single term that enables this identity is the supereminence of the hero, and this is a distinction that attends him from the outset of the work to its conclusion. Regardless of what we might think of Lanzelet's behaviour, within the work he is called *der beste* from the beginning to the end (L:1346, 2161, 2260, 7811, 7921). Gwigalois is distinguished from the moment of his arrival at Arthur's court – both by the stone on which he dismounts (W:1489–563) and by the testimony of the narrator, 'sin muot ie nach dem besten streit' (W:1494). Der Pleiaere uses the same words to praise the twelve-year-old Meleranz (M:178), 'des pris mit wirdekeit wart ganz' (M:164). These heroes, like the majority of the others, enter the romance with the highest praise and maintain their position throughout.

But what of Erec, Iwein, and Parzival? Are they not celebrated for their mistakes? Indeed, and Gauriel and Tandareis might enjoy the same notoriety were they better known. Can one say of them as of Gwigalois that they maintain their supereminence throughout the romance? We should begin by noting that there is hardly a soul within the works who dares to criticize the seemingly flawed heroes. Hartman, in introducing Erec, maintains that his is a hero 'der vrümekeit und saelden phlac' (E:3). And Crestiens, comparing the same hero to the rest of the Round Table, claims, 'n'i ot chevalier si loé' (CE:86). Having listed Erec's virtues, he concludes his introduction, 'onques nus hom de son aage ne fu de si grant vaselage; que diroie de ses bontez?' (CE:91–3). Surely Hartman and Crestiens know, when they pronounce their laudatory prologues, of the crisis that is in store. In the unorthodox prologues to *Yvain* and *Iwein* the narrators contrive to evade mention of their imperfect hero altogether: mention would require praise or, unthinkable in a prologue, blame. Even at the moment of crisis, however, Hartman cannot bring himself to criticize either Erec or Iwein. At the analogous moment in *Parzival*, Wolfram steps forward to defend his hero: he attributes to Parzival 'küenes herzen rat und wariu zuht bi manheit' – although he doubts their usefulness under the present circumstances (P:319,4–5).

Who are we to find fault with the canonical heroes when Hartman and Wolfram refuse to utter a word of blame? Arthur's court is just as reticent: after hearing the denunciations of Lunete and Cundrie the court merely feels sadness (I:3239–44; P:319,12–19, 331,10). Besides the accusers and their closest allies, only the heroes themselves seem to recognize the significance of their errors; but their opinion, it turns out, is the one that really matters. By acknowledging and accepting their mistakes Erec, Iwein, and Parzival turn them into a special distinction. They show that they understand more clearly than either court or narrator what is required of them (just what the romance needs: more adventure) and thereby acquire for themselves more glory.

Arthurian heroes, then, fall into two classes: on the one hand are the majority, those who never err; on the other are those whose recognition of error sets them apart. These latter are not flawless, they are better than flawless. As Wolfram remarks at Parzival's moment of disgrace: 'schame git pris ze lone und ist doch der sele krone' (P:319,9–10). Even in his moment of disgrace the Arthurian hero remains supereminent; even when he seems most threatened he is assured the crown.

The Mediator (M)

It is one of the essential myths of Arthurian romance that there exists somewhere a true story and that this true story is transmitted to the hearer by a faithful storyteller. In the telling the true story, *daz buoch, diu aventiure*, is transformed; it exists now only in the form of its performance, *daz liet, daz maere*. According to our scheme, the true story is constructed from the first four functions, while the figure of the faithful storyteller is a manifestation of the fifth function, the mediator. We recognize this function most easily in the figure of the narrator: contentious Wolfram, moralizing Wirnt, good-natured Hartman.

Émile Benveniste distinguishes, on the basis of their use of pronouns and French verb tenses, two types of utterance which parallel the Arthurian distinction between the true story and the faithful storyteller.[49] According to Benveniste, the historian will never say *je* or *tu* or *maintenant*, nor will he employ more than three verb tenses – the aorist, the imperfect, and the pluperfect. This type of utterance Benveniste names *histoire*. Every utterance that assumes a speaker and a listener, on the other hand, is *discours*; it admits all tenses except the aorist, although it prefers the present, the future, and the perfect.

We notice a similar distribution in Arthurian romance. Uolrich, for instance, as he completes his description of the castle at Dodone and returns to the adventures of Lanzelet, tells us:

> ouch horte man der glocken schal
> in der burc über al,
> so man an den zimbel sluoc,
> da von ich e han genuoc
> gesaget, ob irz hant vernomen.
> nu ist unser ritter komen.
> als er kom zuo der linden,
> sin ros begund er binden
> zuo des boumes aste. (L:4185–93)

When he relates the events of his story or describes its situation, Uolrich uses the preterite (*horte, sluoc, kom*). Notice his use of *begund* plus the infinitive to paraphrase the preterite.[50] When he speaks in the first person to his audience in the second person, Uolrich employs the perfect (*han gesaget, hant vernomen*). Note his use of the perfect in line 4190, perhaps because, even though he is relating an event of his story, he has, by calling Lanzelet 'unser ritter,' introduced him into the *discours*. The linguistic distinction between *histoire* and *discours* helps us isolate the two aspects of M: one faces the first four functions and is realized when the narrator, speaking primarily in the preterite, relates the events of the story; the other faces the sixth function, the recipient, and is realized when the narrator, speaking primarily in the perfect or the present, addresses his audience directly.[51]

An Arthurian narrator is not impartial, even when he speaks historically, for the terms in which he relates his story are bound to colour our reception of it. For instance, just after Heinrich has settled Gawein and Amurfina in the same bed, he says:

ir rede diu was linde
under in und lobesam.
Vrowe Minne hete alle scham
ir von dem herzen gesniten,
sie enhet sin anders niht erliten,
daz sie so eine waren.   (C:8328–33)

Where he might simply have said that the two talked, Heinrich instead characterizes their speech in a way that reflects on their relationship (*linde*) and judges their speech in a way that is bound to affect our judgment of them (*lobesam*). Where Heinrich might simply have said that Amurfina felt no shame, he instead attributes her feeling to Vrowe Minne. Since we all know that the power of Vrowe Minne is irresistible, her appearance serves to justify Amurfina. At the same time, the introduction of a traditional literary device, personified *minne*, acts independent of the context as a signal that Heinrich is composing a self-consciously literary work. Thus we see that merely by the choice of the terms in which he relates his narrative Heinrich prejudices the reception of the story he pretends to be transmitting faithfully. There is, after all, no access to this story except through the terms in which the narrator presents it.

At times the narrator will abandon the historical mode, however, and by addressing his audience discursively attempt to influence directly their reaction to his tale. The passage just cited continues:

swie Minne wil gebaren,
wer mac ir des wider sin?
daz ist an manigem ende schin,
daz wir sin vinden bilde.
nieman ist so wilde,
sie habe in schiere gezamt.   (C:8334–9)

Heinrich poses a rhetorical question, introduces our own experience (*wir vinden*), and states a conventional truth. Here he involves his listeners directly in the story he is relating, in an attempt to make them sanction Amurfina's behaviour on their own account. By the terms in which he speaks historically, the narrator subtly prejudices his auditors' reception of the tale; by the way in which he directly engages them in *discours*, he overtly tries to mould their reaction.

There are other cases, however, in which the narrator will abandon his story altogether to express a personal opinion. Thus, after Gawein has, by various questionable means, been installed as lord of Amurfina's kingdom, Heinrich pauses for a few words on bad hosts: they ask how long you're staying; as you leave they calculate how much you've eaten; they delay meals so long that you'd gladly buy your dinner if you could, rather than wait any longer (C:8747–66). Heinrich continues:

> ich rate, daz man anderswa
> von solhen wirten kere
> und laze sie mit unere
> ir guot aleine niezen,
> die des niht kan verdriezen,
> sie wehseln guot umb ere.
> daz da von ein man kere,
> daz ist min, Heinriches, rat.   (C:8767–74)

Here the narrator steps forward with an opinion of his own that is only tangentially related to the story: he was explaining what a *good* host Gawein was. Why does he do this? What do Heinrich's personal opinions on hosts have to do with Gawein's adventures?

Heinrich's personal opinions on hosts are related to Gawein's adventures only in so far as a detail of these adventures prompts him to offer his opinions. That is a relatively weak connection. They figure much more importantly as a part of the narrator's relation to his audience. When Heinrich abandons his tale to offer his own remarks he ceases to function as active mediator and draws our attention to his personal relation to his audience. Of course he would not enjoy this personal relation were he not primarily a storyteller, yet we might lose sight of the character of the narrator if he did not occasionally draw our attention away from the story to himself. Heinrich's remarks on hosts, then, derive almost entirely from that aspect of the function M that faces the recipient and that requires the narrator to sustain, even while apparently absorbed in telling his story, a direct personal contact with his audience. By concluding his remarks with his own name Heinrich indicates quite clearly that they have a different source from the French story he is telling.

We find then that Heinrich's role as narrator allows him a considerable range of behaviour. For brief stretches he may report his story quite neutrally; over any longer period, however, the terms in which he presents his tale are bound to colour its reception. Sometimes he will intervene more boldly, explaining particular points to his audience or trying to engage them directly in the action; occasionally he will abandon his story altogether and offer his listeners his own personal opinions. Although Heinrich's behaviour can vary considerably, all the variations derive from the double aspect of the function M. Sometimes he will stress his relation to the tale, other times his relation to the audience; always he mediates between them.

Of course Heinrich is not the only narrator in *Diu Crone*: Giwanet tells Gawein about the events at Alverne (C:5694–729); Riwalin relates many of Gawein's past and future adventures (C:6095–131); the ferryman explains how the castle at Salie was built (C:20380–451). In each case a character in the story – Giwanet, Riwalin, the ferryman – turns narrator and presents his own short account. The technique by which a character can turn narrator is simply the partial transfer of the function M from the principal narrator to a deputy in the story.

The delegation of the function M to a character within the story is very popular among Arthurian authors as a way of providing background information. Hartman does not tell his audience about Ascalon's magic spring, Kalogrenant tells members of Arthur's court (I:600–762); Wolfram does not tell us what's going on at Bearosche, a stray page tells Gawan (P:343,19–349,16); Uolrich does not inform us that Ginover has been abducted, an errant page reports the tidings to Lanzelet and his fellows (L:6708–51). In each of these cases the direct exchange of information takes place not between the narrator and his audience but between characters in the narrator's story. Here one can observe, incidentally, the tendency of the romance narrator to limit his perspective to that of the hero. Wolfram acts as if he were no better informed than Gawan; Uolrich, as if he were as surprised by the news as Lanzelet. It is as if the narrator's access to the events of his story were limited to the perceptions of his hero. One might note as well that the various internal narrators often serve, by the secondary stories they relate, to motivate the hero. Their stories provide the ostensible reasons for the hero's subsequent combat.

Sometimes the secondary narrator does not deliver his or her message until long after we might have wanted it. Wolfram refuses to elucidate the grail ceremony for us (P:241,1–30); we must wait for some hints from Sigune (P:250,17–255,29) and the full story from Trevrizent (P:468,23 –471,29, 476,24–484,30). Hartman will not tell us why Guivreiz is so upset by the sight of Brandigan (E:7822–30); we learn the reason piecemeal from Guivreiz himself (E:7997–8027), from the lord of the castle (E:8474–519), and finally from Mabonagrin (E:9443–621). Der Strickaere neglects to explain the mystery of the abandoned tent that Daniel discovers filled with good food (D:2418–30); we must wait for a few scraps of information from those who deliver the food (D:2631–66) and a lengthy explanation by the Frouwe von der Grüenen Ouwe (D:4244–562). In each case the narrator withholds important information so that it can be disclosed later, often much later, by a character within the story. In this way the author generates suspense (when will we learn about the grail mysteries?) and at the same time establishes connections between distant parts of the narrative (books five and nine of *Parzival*).

Even though narrators occur at all levels of a romance, there can be no question but that the principal narrator is of a different kind from those who are also actors in the romance story. Within the works themselves the difference in kind between the first-level narrator and those at other levels is marked by a consistent linguistic fiction: Wolfram and his audience speak German while Cundrie and Arthur talk 'en franzois' (P:314,20, 779,11; cf. C:1006–7, 1637). To remind us that we know them only in translation the characters like from time to time to sneak in a few words in their mother tongue, especially in greetings: the messenger of the queen of France addresses Gahmuret, 'bien sei venuz, bea sir' (P:76,11); the 'Ritter mit dem boc' greets Arthur, 'Artus fier, gentil rois' (C:24792); Parzival thinks his name is 'bon fiz, scher fiz, bea fiz' (P:140,6). The narrators themselves are diligent in drawing attention to their role as translators: Hartman has *Erec* from 'Crestiens' (E:4629[12]); Uolrich got his tale from a 'welschez buoch' (L:9324); Kiot, though Provençal, spoke 'en franzois' (P:416,28); Heinrich first read his story, which he attributes to 'meister Cristian' (C:16941; cf. C:23046, 23982), 'en franzois' (C:8146, 23260); der Strickaere translated 'uzer welscher zungen' (D:9); der Pleiaere found *Tandareis* 'an einem buoche ... in wälhischem getihtet' (T: 4066–7) and translated *Meleranz* 'von welschem' (M:103).[52] There is in fact no reason to believe that any of the later works actually had a French source, and yet the narrators feel compelled to pretend that they did. They do so because the role of the narrator is a bilingual position; only thus can he mediate between the French story and his German-speaking audience. At the same time his knowledge of two languages distinguishes him from the actors within his story – among them the secondary narrators – who know only French.[53] Thus, in spite of the presence of secondary narrators, the principal narrator never relinquishes his function. Even a surrogate like Kalogrenant, who dominates the narrative stage for a long stretch of *Iwein*, remains dependent on the translation and transmission of his superior, Hartman.

Just as the continuous presence of the hero helps unite the paratactic series of episodes that constitute the romance story, so the continuous activity of the narrator guarantees the coherence of the level on which he functions, and this increases the coherence of the romance as a whole. In spite of this similarity, however, hero and narrator are actors of different kinds. One can distinguish them according to the categories of Greimas: the hero, as we have seen, is a *sujet puissant*; the narrator, however, is a *sujet savant*. The former accomplishes his tasks by physical strength, the latter by strength of mind. Thus the *pouvoir-faire* and *savoir-faire* that Greimas distributes along the narrative axis are, in Arthurian romance, distributed on two different levels of the work.

And what if the narrator's mind should not be equal to the task? What if Hartman should translate wrong? An idle question, even in the case of romances where the sources are known, but it points up the importance of the narrator's position. We have no way of judging the accuracy of the narrator's translation because we have no access to the world of the romance story except through his words. Generally the narrator is eager to advertise his devotion to the truth, and we have no reason to doubt the accuracy of his story; but occasionally he will feign ignorance – Hartman claims not to know the details of Iwein's fight with Ascalon (I: 1029–50) – or pretend to be able to influence the direction of his story – Wolfram intercedes with Vrou Minne on Parzival's behalf (P:294, 21–30). In cases like these, which we will consider later in detail, the narrator even while pretending ignorance draws attention to our complete dependence on him: if *he* doesn't know, then *we* don't know either. He draws attention, that is, to the importance of the mediator, the function that transmits the true story to its audience.

The Recipient (R)

The existence of a narrator implies, at least, the presence of an audience: Kalogrenant in relating his story will not be talking to himself. And indeed, seated around him are a select company of Arthurian knights, the queen, and, later, King Arthur himself. At every level on which we can isolate a narrator we can also find a recipient: Kalogrenant listens to the *waltman*; the Arthurian court listens to Kalogrenant; and there is as well an audience for the narrator Hartman.

Since Kalogrenant and the Arthurian court, besides providing an audience for the *waltman* and Kalogrenant, are also themselves characters in a story, we know a certain amount about them. We owe this information to the narrator of the story in which they figure; he, from his vantage point at a superior level, puts them in perspective. Hartman's own audience, however, is much more elusive. It exists, along with

Hartman, only at the level of the text, where there is no superior narrator. One might say that Arthurian romance at this primary level is more
like drama than narrative. We learn about its characters only what they
themselves reveal or what is revealed by other actors on the same level.

Curiously, this first-level audience is most active in the earliest German Arthurian romance. In *Erec* it repeatedly poses questions to Hartman, and at one point one of its number tries to take over the narration
himself: he attempts a description of the saddle of Enite's horse (E:
7493–525). But he fails, as he necessarily must, for the audience, isolated
at the level of the narration, is not privy to the events of the story. It
depends on the mediation of the narrator, the only one able to translate
the French of the story into German, the only language that the audience
understands.[54] The active role of the audience in *Erec* is an innovation of
the German version. In none of the many cases in which Hartman
responds to a question from the audience (E:4150–2, 6554, 7106, 7145,
7826, 8946) does Crestiens's audience have anything to say. Audience
participation in *Iwein*, which is much less than in *Erec*, is, on the other
hand, a reflection of audience activity in *Yvain*. Just before Yvain and
Gauvain fight, someone asks Crestiens, 'et or donc ne s'antr'ainment
il?' (CY:5995). His answer, 'oïl, vos respong, et nenil,' introduces a dialogue that lasts 104 lines. The corresponding passage in *Iwein* begins
even more boldly. One of the audience directly challenges Hartman to
defend his metaphor, 'ich waene, vriunt Hartman, du missedenkest dar
an' (I:7027–8).

In romances other than *Erec* and *Iwein*, however, we know the audience only from what the narrator says about it: Uolrich describes his
public in the prologue to *Lanzelet* (L:14–26); Wolfram rebukes those of
his listeners who press him for information ahead of time (P:241,21–30)
and poses rhetorical questions that seem to originate with his audience
(P:241,1, 584,5); from time to time Wirnt portrays the collapse of standards among his listeners (W:2320–48, 2358–95). Most often, however,
the recipient appears, by implication only, in the narrator's formulaic *nu
hoeret* or *ich sage iu vür war*.

Why does the audience play such an active role in *Erec*, only to grow
more reticent in the subsequent romances? Perhaps Walter Ong can help
provide an answer. He wonders if the frame device in the *Canterbury
Tales* was not 'demanded by the literary economy of the time,' a time in
which 'audience readjustment was a major feature.' By providing an
internal audience, Ong states, 'Chaucer simply tells his readers how they
are to fictionalize themselves.'[55] *Erec* was the first Arthurian romance in

Germany, and the real audience that first received the work had no way of knowing what sort of role they were expected to assume with regard to it. To help them the author sketched in unusual detail the behaviour of a surrogate recipient, the internal audience, on whose behaviour the real audience could model its own. They would learn that although they might ask questions the narrator was free to dismiss them if he chose, and that if they attempted to usurp his role they were bound to fail – for the twelfth-century German audience, even though it might have direct access to native materials, was entirely dependent on the mediator for these new French stories. As the real audience made its adjustment to this new material its need for instruction diminished, and as a result the internal audience has less to do in the later romances. As Michael Curschmann has shown, Wolfram, too, uses an imaginary audience 'to create a live audience that will respond more readily to the intricacies of a highly involved narrative.'[56] This is certainly true. Yet when we consider the general tendency in *Parzival* to give every function a more distinctive profile than in other romances – consider the narrator, for instance – we cannot but be struck by the relative inactivity of its audience in comparison with the audience in *Erec*.

If my hypothesis is correct, then it can explain the historical variation in the role of the audience in Arthurian romance. And yet, no matter how retiring, the internal audience is clearly present in all the works of the genre. We must recognize that Arthurian romance belongs to the small group of narrative genres that explicitly incorporate a counterpart for the narrator within the text itself.

Summary Remarks on the System of Functions

If we assemble in one place the functions about which we have been talking, we get the following list:

Function		Primary Realization in Arthurian Romance
the world	W	forests, meadows, divine order, magic
the society	S	courtly society, Arthur's court
the other	O	opponents, companions, women
the individual	I	hero
the mediator	M	narrator
the recipient	R	audience

Todorov maintains: 'any theory of genres is based on a conception of the work, on an image of the work, which involves on one hand a certain number of abstract properties, on the other a certain number of laws governing the relation of these properties.'[57] The system of six functions is my attempt to isolate the abstract properties that define the genre of Arthurian romance. To be sure, a great deal more could be said (and has been said) about the nature of these properties; each one is itself a semantic category, a collection of traditional props and meanings, a collection of signs. One could very well investigate the semantic principles according to which each function is organized: what do magic fountains and dragons signify? what did the appearance of a castle mean to a twelfth-century audience? One could investigate the semantic composition of each category, but I have chosen not to for I am concerned not primarily with the functions themselves but with the relations they sustain with one another. I have attempted therefore simply to determine the essential outline of each functional category and to establish those features of its internal structure that will be important in our later analysis. We have considered the 'abstract properties' themselves only in order to be able to talk about 'the laws governing the relation of these properties.' Before going on to discuss these laws, however, two observations should be made on the list of functions as it stands above.

First, the functions are not characters or settings or themes. We regard Lanzelet, in the first instance, as the hero of *Lanzelet* (I), but he is also a member of courtly society (S) whose life is in large measure determined by a water fay (W). We think of Uolrich primarily as narrator (M), yet he upholds the tenets of courtly society (S), he is the first recipient of the story (R), and at the level of the narration he is himself the main character (I). Since there are no 'pure' realizations of the functions, it will be necessary in investigating functional structure to choose examples on the basis of their primary allegiance: I will talk of Lanzelet as I and of Uolrich as M; sometimes I will seem to consider W and S as locations. Although this simplification cannot be avoided, it should be recognized for what it is: a distortion required by the decision to talk about function rather than character or setting or theme. The functions themselves are abstractions and are seldom realized without contamination.

Second, the functions form combinations of two kinds. On the one hand are static combinations; combinations of this kind define romance space and generate characters and themes. On the other hand are dynamic combinations; the progression of dynamic combinations produces episodes and ultimately the linear shape of entire romances. Although the chief concern of the second and third chapters will be with the episodic structure of romances and thus with the dynamic combinations of functions, we should first investigate briefly the ways in which static combinations of functions determine romance space, romance characters, and romance themes.

ROMANCE SPACE

The six functions of Arthurian romance divide naturally into three pairs. W and S together define the causal and ideological space in which romance exists. The interaction of O and I generates the linear form of the romance story. M transmits and interprets this story for R, thereby generating the surface of the text we know. The first pair of functions defines an axis of causality; the second, an axis of plot action; the third, an axis of communication. The pairs, or axes, are clearly of altogether different kinds, yet they interact to determine the nature of romance space.

The World of the Hero

The functions W and S, as we have considered them, are realized in two ways: first, tangibly – the settings, characters, and conventional actions associated with each function; second, causally – the kinds of explanations and motivations that each provides. Within each group the citizens of S and W oppose each other systematically. The organized social setting of the Arthurian court opposes the scattered natural settings of W; the dependable figures of Gawein and Keie oppose a varied assortment of giants, dwarfs, apostate knights, water fays, and monsters; the coherent ideology of courtly society opposes the incomprehensible workings of fate, chance, and providence. In every case a familiar, cohesive order opposes a collection of unknown, unpredictable threats.

The systematic distinction between W and S is clearly articulated by the knight whose lands have been ravaged by the giant Harpin. He laments, 'mir hat gemachet ein rise mine huobe zeiner wise' (I:4463–4); the *huobe* had a social function, the *wise* is part of the landscape. It is of course the same piece of land, the distinction depending entirely on the position of the boundary between W and S. If this boundary runs between the knight and the plot of the land, then the plot lies outside his jurisdiction; it is *wise*, part of W. If the boundary runs between the giant and the plot of land, then the land belongs to the knight; it is *huobe*, part of S.

At first glance the position of the W/S boundary may seem of importance only to the heirs of Harpin's victim. Actually this boundary is the crucial determinant of romance space, for, depending on which side of the boundary we find ourselves on, we can expect to encounter there the settings, characters, and causality typical of W or those typical of S. The boundary between W and S runs throughout the romance world. It takes concrete form as a castle wall or the edge of the Walt Aventuros, but these are only material reminders of the general opposition of W and S.

That Harpin and Iwein can move the boundary between W and S back and forth across a single piece of land shows that this boundary does not occupy a fixed position in the Arthurian landscape. When Daniel rescues the Frouwe von dem Liehten Brunnen he, like Iwein in his combat with Harpin, pushes back the boundary with W and secures an endangered territory for the realm of S. When Erec wins the 'joie de la curt' he restores to S an adjacent piece of land that had been taken from it. When Lanzelet defeats Galagandreiz he liberates the land from the domination of W and establishes a new colony of S. With each victory the map of romance landscape is redrawn; and in each case the happy teleology of Arthurian romance ensures that the new boundaries will always represent an increase in area or population for the realm of S.

For most characters the boundary between W and S remains impassable: Harpin's victim cannot leave his castle and Harpin cannot enter it. Only Iwein is able to enter and depart at will. This mobility is the consequence of Iwein's functional allegiance. In Arthurian romance only the actor who fills the function I can freely cross the boundary between W and S. Of course the six sons of Harpin's victim preceded Iwein across this boundary; in doing so they too filled the function I, although their present captivity reveals them to have been false heroes, a category to which we will return later.

Occasionally a member of Arthur's court will desert the realm of S, which is by definition his natural home, and venture into the realm of W. When Gawan sets out in *Parzival* or Arthur in *Diu Crone*, he fills the function I and behaves like a genuine hero. But when Keie or a lesser knight (Segramors, Urjans) crosses the boundary between W and S, he usually assumes the function O. Such a figure, on his own, can only cross the boundary once and then only in the direction of apostasy. His return is accomplished by the prowess of the hero, who defeats the apostate, transforms him into O^+, and sends him back where he belongs, to the realm of S. Thus we see that, although various members of courtly society can cross the W/S boundary and enter the woods either as heroes, false heroes, or opponents, only the hero can cross this boundary freely in either direction, and only the hero, incarnation of the function I, can cause another function, O, to cross the boundary.

Some of the most memorable episodes in Arthurian romance depend on irregularities in the position of the W/S boundary. In the scenes of challenge and accusation (Valerin in *Lanzelet*, the giants in *Daniel* and *Garel*), the boundary between W and S has been moved right into Arthur's court. Although the hero, by the end of such an episode, will have moved across the boundary into the realm of W, the challenger, even when he or she is talking directly to King Arthur, cannot by the constraints of the function O cross into the realm of S. Thus Arthur is never physically attacked in his court and Ginover is never actually seized. Arthur or the hero ventures forth to meet the challenger, and the queen is freely handed over to her abductor.[58] Even though O^- cannot enter S, the threatening incursions of W into the realm of S that these challenge scenes represent severely shock the very heart of courtly society. At its most extreme, in the *Charrete*, the shock is sufficient to dissolve S into W; when the court disperses, the spatial axis on which we depend to get our bearings dissolves as well, and as a consequence we can hardly predict, for much of the romance, whether we ought to expect the causes and characters of S or those of W.

Although the German romances will not accommodate the extreme spatial ambiguity of the *Charrete*, they do include episodes in which a less severe ambiguity plays an important role. Keie's fight with Iwein, for example, will be read in different ways depending on whose perspective we adopt in drawing the boundary between W and S. On the one hand, Arthur's court, as it moves to Lunete's fountain, assumes that it is expanding the borders of S into the territory of W; and Keie, its champion, believes that he is venturing across the W/S boundary as I, that his victory will bring O^- across the boundary as a defeated O^+, and that he will thereby incorporate the land of the magic fountain into the realm of S. Iwein at first actually does behave like O^-, a knight eager to attack the champion of King Arthur. On the other hand, Iwein's victory over Ascalon has already effected the incorporation of Ascalon's land into the sphere of S. Thus Keie, in opposing Iwein, ventures across the W/S boundary not as I but as O^-, thereby guaranteeing his certain defeat. It is of course characteristic of Keie to think he is the hero when he is really the opponent.

The fateful implications of an attack by an Arthurian knight on the courtly social order (the attacker is Iwein or Keie, depending on the perspective) are diffused by turning the combat into a personal affair. Since it is precisely Keie who opposes Iwein, Iwein's charge, which began as an assault on Arthur's champion, is transformed *in mid-career* (I:2551–64) into an act of personal revenge for Keie's earlier insults. As soon as Iwein has unhorsed Keie, he presents his attack as a joke at Keie's expense (I:2587–600): look, he says, you thought I was the enemy of society, but I am only the foe of Keie. When Iwein reveals his name to Arthur he functions as his own messenger and reveals to the king that the land of Ascalon has already been conquered by a champion of S. When the court joins Iwein in mocking Keie (I:2643–5), they show their willingness to abandon their original perspective and adopt his. And just before everyone sets off for Iwein's castle to celebrate, the narrator adds his voice in a one-line summary, 'sus het erz *umb si alle* braht' (I:2652). All agree: Iwein had conquered the fountain for the sake of S; Keie must have been the one to step across the boundary and champion W. At last the original position of the W/S boundary is clear.

The author of *Parzival* apparently did not consider the W/S boundary a sufficient challenge for his hero, for he complicated the spatial system of his romance by the addition of a second, entirely new boundary. While the other romances get by with oppositions on a horizontal axis (W vs S; Harpin vs Iwein; non-court vs Arthur's court; outside vs inside), *Parzival* has added oppositions on a vertical axis (Arthur's court vs Munsalvaesche; Gawan vs Parzival; secular vs sacred; down vs up). Both Parzival and Gawan are able to cross the boundaries of the space defined by W and S. Only Parzival, however, and other members of the grail family can cross the boundaries of vertical space. Just as the kinds of cause and character differ between W and S, so they differ between the world of Munsalvaesche and the world below. When Anfortas and Sigune acted in the regular romance world they are said to have behaved like other knights and ladies, but on Munsalvaesche they are penitents. In the 'lower' world Parzival transforms his opponents by fighting them, but in the 'upper' world he transforms an Other by asking a question. In one realm transformation is defeat while in the other it is a cure. Even though the spatial system of Parzival is richer than that of other romances, the principles of spatial organization nevertheless remain the same. We would no more expect Parzival to run Anfortas through with a spear than we would expect Iwein to ask Ascalon about his health or Harpin to offer his victims a courtly welcome. Each division of romance space has its own characteristic logic, its own verisimilitude.

The World of the Narrator

So far we have considered only one kind of romance space, that determined by the boundary between W and S. There is, however, another
equally important variety, that in which the mediator faces the recipient,
and that space too is defined by a particular kind of boundary. We have
already noted the convention by which the true story – strung together
out of operations along the W/S boundary – is said to be in French, while
the account that we get from the narrator is in German. The narrator
must translate this story from one side of the French-German boundary
to the other. Reformulating this convention in my terms, the function M
transforms the plot material – the series of encounters between O and I
within the space defined by W and S – from a sequence of events into a
coherent account and presents this account to the function R. In doing so
M transfers the romance material from the realm of actions into the
realm of words, from the realm of plot events into that of spoken narrative.

The world of Arthurian romance then is divided into two different
kinds of space. There is first of all that space defined by the W/S boundary, the space in which I, passing freely across that boundary, transforms O^- into O^+ or rearranges the boundary to the advantage of S.
Then there is the space defined by the boundary between the true story
and the narrator's account, the space in which M draws material from
the world of actions, transforms it into narrative, and presents it for the
delight and edification of R.

Just as functions in the first space are defined by their ability to cross
the W/S boundary, so functions in the second space are defined by their
ability to cross the boundary between story and narrative: M can cross
the boundary, R cannot. Thus Hartman's auditor fails when he attempts
the description of the saddle on Enite's horse (E:7493–525), just as the
Parzival audience remains frustrated in its attempt to divine the story's
conclusion (P:734,1–3). Only the narrator can penetrate the boundary
between story and narrative; only he can tell what actually happened.
The audience knows no more than what it is told; it knows only the
narrative. Hartman has this distinction in mind when he tells his upstart
listener, 'ir sult michz iu sagen lan' (E:7525); and Wolfram says the same
in promising to relieve the frustration of his audience: 'ich tuonz iu kunt
mit rehter sage, wande ich in dem munde trage daz sloz dirre aventiure'
(P:734,5–7).

The ability to cross boundaries is not the only similarity between I and M. Both have a natural allegiance on one side of the boundary: I with S, M with R. Both accomplish transformations: I of O, M of the story. By this transformation both are able to introduce something foreign into their own society: O becomes part of S, the French tale is given to the German audience. Finally both, by virtue of their continuous presence throughout the romance, help unify the work: the single hero counteracts the fragmentary tendencies of the romance's episodic skeleton; the figure of the single narrator guarantees a more or less coherent perspective in his narrative. Of all the Middle High German Arthurian narrators, Wolfram seems most aggressively conscious of his affinity with a romance hero – as we see in his famous assertion, 'schildes ambet ist min art' (P:115,11). Hartman also calls himself 'ein riter' (I:21); and Heinrich, speaking metaphorically, says of himself, 'ich trage daz wafen bi mir da, daz valschen man versnidet' (C:10449–50). Although Wolfram does not fight the same sort of battles as Parzival – polemics aside – their activities are, as we have seen, analogous. Parzival, one might say, is the hero of romance action; Wolfram is the hero of romance narration. Parzival is the hero of *res*, Wolfram of *verba*.

The Three Levels of Arthurian Romance

The narration of which Wolfram is the hero is spoken narration addressed to an audience present within the romance. Before we have access to this narrative, the romance material must pass yet another boundary; it must pass from the world of the narrator Wolfram to our own world, and to do so it must be written down. This of course is the job of the author. His material is not just the romance story. In fact it is not the romance story at all, except second hand. Nor is his material limited to the narrator's account of the story. It is, rather, the entire act of narration: the narrator composing his narrative as well as its reception by his audience. In order to make this act of narration accessible to us, the author must move the romance material across the boundary between literature and life; he must transform the fictional, oral relation of narrator and audience into a concrete, written text that we can read or have read to us.

Just as at the levels of the hero and the narrator, the parties at the level of the text itself are distinguished by their differing ability to cross the boundary that defines that level. At the level of the text the author himself is the only one who can cross the crucial boundary; he is the only one who can enter the closed literary world of romance. We are isolated in the real world and have access to the romance only through his mediation. As a consequence we are no more able to compose the prologue to *Erec* than Hartman's listener was able to describe Enite's saddle. Only the author of *Erec* knew how Hartman introduced his account of the story, and since he has died and his written account has been lost the lines with which Arthurian romance was first introduced to a German-speaking audience have been lost forever.

Clearly the author's activities along his boundary are congruous with the narrator's activities along his and, by a principle of Euclid's, must be congruous with those of the hero as well. We have then three different kinds of romance space, each defined by its own boundary yet all organized on a single pattern. The similarities can be seen in the following diagram.

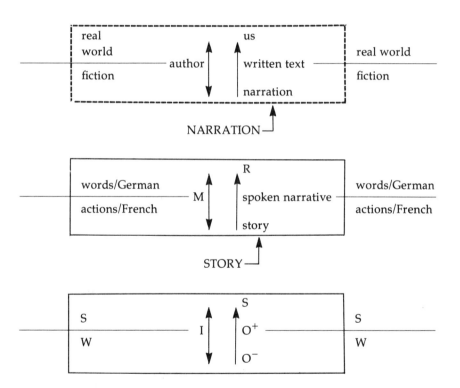

I moves freely across the W/S boundary, transforming O^- to O^+ and transferring it from the realm of W to that of S; this activity generates the romance story. M moves freely across the boundary between the story and the audience, translating a series of actions into a spoken narrative and transmitting it to R; this activity is narration. The author moves freely across the boundary between the realm of fiction and the real world, giving a written account of the romance narration and transmitting it to us; his activity generates the text. In every case an agent moves an object across a boundary, thereby changing the nature of the object. In each case, however, the boundary is of a different kind and requires a different kind of activity to move objects across it: fighting at the W/S boundary; speaking at the next; writing at the last. These three kinds of activity define the characteristic event at each level of Arthurian romance.

The three levels of romance, in spite of their distinctive boundaries and characteristic events, form a single system. First, the several levels are interdependent: the highest level, the text, depends for its matter on transferrals from both subordinate levels, and each of the lower levels depends for its existence on its translation into the text. Further, the distinctive boundary that defines each particular level is valid for the whole system of romance space; in other words, each can be defined not only by its constitutive boundary but also by its position in relation to the other boundaries. The level of the story falls entirely within the realm of fiction and the realm of (French) action. The level of the narration falls within the realm of fiction and that of S. The level of the text falls entirely within the realm of (German) words and the realm of S: the author's audience is assumed to be courtly. The three levels and the three boundaries taken together constitute the system of romance space.[59]

In distinguishing between story and narration I have abstracted somewhat the situation as it occurs in the romances themselves. Hartman claims to be translating not from the realm of action to the realm of words but from the French of 'Crestiens' (E:4629[12]) to the German of his audience; and the French from which he translates is itself based not on a series of actions but on a verbal account, a 'conte d'avanture' (CE:13). One could move backwards across innumerable boundaries of verbal transformations before getting to the action itself, but actually this is unnecessary. For, whatever the narrator's source, whether written – a 'welschez buoch' (L:9324), 'le livre' (CP:67; cf. CCl:20) – or oral – the words of a 'knappe' (W:11687–90), a 'conte d'avanture' (CE:13) – this verbal source is hidden from us by the figure of the narrator. The words that the romance audience hears and that we receive indirectly are not the words of this source but the words of the narrator. Whatever form of

verbal organization is claimed for the source, this verbal form is decom-
posed by the narrator into a body of narrative material – actions – and
re-formed by him as spoken narrative. Although this transformation is
most clearly expressed in the German convention of translation from one
language to another, it is the essential activity of the narrator Crestïens
no less than of the narrator Hartman. For any narrator, his source is the
source of plot organization, not the source of verbal organization. By
calling the first level of romance the level of the story I hope to reflect
both the claims of the romance narrator and the actual function of that
level. In its general meaning, *story* can well refer to the *aventiure* or *conte*
that the narrators claim as their source. Yet *story* in its more technical
sense, 'events arranged in their time sequence,' defines the kind of
material – events, actions – that constitutes the level of the story and distinguishes it from the level of the narration.[60]

Of course narration occurs within the story itself through assumption
of the function M by one of the actors in the story – Kalogrenant, for
instance; and even writing occurs occasionally, as in the hands of the
maiden in the 'pesme aventure,' 'diu vil wol ... wälhisch lesen kunde'
(I:6456–7). In these cases the entire system of transferences is incorporated into the story itself: Kalogrenant narrates a story; the maiden reads
a written account of a narrator's spoken account of a story. From the
larger perspective, however, the speaking and reading are actions in the
story and, like the other actions in the story, are subject to the regular
transformations before they reach us as text.[61]

Students of Arthurian romance are affected by the boundaries of
romance space no less than romance heroes or narrators. I, for instance,
having set out to investigate the internal structure of a genre, am concerned only with the world of fiction – only, that is, with what falls
below the uppermost boundary in my diagram. If I wanted to analyse the
relations between author, text, and reader, I would need altogether
different tools: archives, history books, theories of reading and reception.
As it is I am concerned only with what can be found in the texts. Occasionally we will in fact refer to relations involving the author, his text,
and his audience, but only when it seems clear that these relations are
reflected within the fictional world of romance itself.

NAME, ROLE, CHARACTER

We first hear the name Iwein at line 88 of *Iwein*, when he is sitting among
a group of knights listening to Kalogrenant; but we must wait more than
seven hundred lines before he distinguishes himself from his compan-

ions in any way. While in many romances a character becomes active much sooner after the first mention of his name, all romance characters are at first simply names. In the case of Lanzelet, 'der ungenande' (L: 1287), a series of nominal designations substitutes for his unknown name: 'daz kint' (L:98); 'unser helt' (L:3365). In the case of the narrator, the pronoun *ich* (W:33) stands in for the inevitable proper name: Wirnt von Gravenberc (W:141). In every case the character appears first simply as a point of focus, identified sooner or later by a proper name. Throughout the romance the name itself – rather than any possible psychological consistency, for example – remains the principal means by which the coherence of an Arthurian character is assured. As we follow this name through a series of actions, however, we collect various impressions and attach them to the name. The name turns into a character as these impressions – in effect interpretations, attempts to name the meaning of an action – collect about the single point of a name.[62]

The first bit of meaning we attach to the name Iwein, the one thing we do know about him even at line 88, is that he is a member of courtly society. We deduce this from his presence at Arthur's Pentecostal *hochzit*. Every Arthurian character has a necessary allegiance to one of the two causal-ideological functions, W or S; there is no mistaking Gwigalois's courtly opponent 'der werde künic Schaffilun' (W:9095) for 'Ruel diu ungehiure' (W:6406). In addition to the necessary allegiance to either W or S many courtly characters will reveal an optional, secondary functional tie to W: Lanzelet and Gwigalois had 'magical' childhoods; there is no mistaking them for the sensible Daniel.

No sooner does a name become involved in an action – does a name become the subject of a predicate, in Todorov's terms[63] – than we connect it with one of the Arthurian roles. Each of our last four functions corresponds to a traditional role: O⁻ is opponent; O⁺, companion; I, hero; M, narrator; R, audience. As readers of Arthurian romance, we are familiar with the repertory of roles and automatically seek to match the names we learn with the roles we expect. It is hard to know at line 945 of *Iwein* what sort of adventure will be next, but we already know whose side we are on for we have already identified the hero.

Yet roles are not characters; they, like the functions from which they are derived, are merely abstractions. Thus on the one hand a single role can be filled by many characters: Gawein, Aliers, and Harpin are all opponents of Iwein.[64] On the other hand one character can fill several roles: Gawein is opponent, companion, and narrator.[65] Certain of the roles are more prone to unstable alliances than others. The roles of opponent and companion, for instance, tend to alternate frequently in a single character – they are, after all, both derived from the same function. These same two roles are filled by many characters, and this succession delineates the sequence of episodes. The hero's role, on the other hand, is seldom transferred. Similarly the role of the narrator remains the property of the principal narrator, even when he enlists the aid of a deputy from within the story: we receive Kalogrenant's account only second hand, translated and transmitted by the voice of Hartman.

A character is located by his or her name and achieves differentiation according to the roles he or she plays and the camp, W or S, into which he or she falls; but this tells us very little. Laudine is the only name I can think of identified primarily with S, with a secondary allegiance to W, who fills, in this order, the roles: opponent, companion, opponent, companion. Would this help me recognize her? Hartman tells us that Laudine is very beautiful (I:1308–9, 1331–4), but what use is this? All Arthurian women are beautiful. In fact I would be able to distinguish Laudine from, say, Condwiramurs only if I saw her near her fountain or debating with Lunete. I would recognize her, that is, either by a prop with which she is associated or by an action I know her to have performed. We will discuss below the two techniques by which this identification is accomplished – static differentiation and active differentiation. Let us for the moment simply note that all Laudine's distinguishing traits are external. Arthurian characters, that is, are not Jamesian but Aristotelian.[66] They do not exist as coherent psyches of which the plot is a consequent revelation; they are born, rather, out of the needs of the plot, and we know them only by the actions to which they owe their existence. In Arthurian romance plot comes first, character second.

The hegemony of action has as its consequence the inconsistency of the characters. Anyone, for instance, who seeks some essential coherence in the character of Laudine – her 'personality' – will soon come across insuperable contradictions. Why, if she loves Iwein, does she let him go off with Gawein for a year? Why, if she is still angry with him, does she allow herself to be reconciled in the end by Lunete's trick? There is no inner coherence to Laudine; she is merely a proper name that adopts certain standard roles and that, in these several roles, serves the narrative in whatever way is necessary. The same is true of Lunete. At one moment she is Iwein's warmest advocate; at another she denounces him bitterly. She too is simply a series of actions united by their attribution to a single name.[67]

We might note here that the author of *Iwein* shows a greater interest in names and the coherence they bring to the romance than does his source. If we follow the version of Guiot, then Laudine has no name in French; and although Lunete is named, the 'dameisele' (CY:2707, 2778) who denounces Yvain before Arthur remains anonymous. By turning this 'dameisele' into Lunete the German adaptor introduces a greater coherence into the dramatis personae of the work, but he does so at the expense of the coherence of Lunete's character. The difference between the French and German attitudes to proper names and the unifying ties of consanguinity that they can generate is even more striking if one compares the German *Parzival* with its French source.

We will not find any greater coherence in the behaviour of an Arthurian narrator than in that of the characters at the level of the story. Der Pleiaere, addressing his audience in the prologue to *Tandareis*, maintains that he is unlucky in love (T:119–26) and that he writes the epic 'durch ein reinez wip' (T:161); yet later, in what amounts to a second prologue, he forgets his earlier devotion and claims to write 'durch kurzwile' (T:4076). Michael Curschmann has shown the variety of poses that Wolfram assumes in the first half of *Parzival*;[68] and we should note now, as we will see in greater detail later, that some of these poses can actually undermine the narrator's official role as the conscientious transmitter of a true story. When Wolfram intercedes with Vrou Minne on Parzival's behalf he pretends that his own action might somehow affect the course of the tale (P:294,21–30), but how can he presume to alter Kiot's tale?

Reto Bezzola has drawn the most radical conclusion from the endemic inconsistency of Arthurian characters and has declared with regard to the heroine of *Erec*, 'in effect, the Enide of the first part and the Enide of the second are two different women.' But surely this is overstated.[69] The author of *Erec* gives its heroine only one name and assigns her only one role. She is by definition a single individual. Faced with a single name that performs contradictory actions, we, in analysing romance structure, have a relatively easy task: we need only note that our genre admits apparent inconsistencies. The interpreter of Arthurian romance has a more difficult task. He or she must justify and give meaning to the seeming contradictions that surround and define the single name.

We might say then that, while the author thinks up the names for the various actors in a romance and determines how they will behave, the creation of an Arthurian *character* is the work of the reader, for only when the reader has discovered some single viewpoint from which the various contradictions can be explained and reconciled can the name and the behaviour ascribed to it be understood as a coherent character. The creation of an Arthurian character, then, is not an act of composition but an act of interpretation.[70]

THE SYSTEM OF THEMES

When two functions sustain a relation with one another without sacrificing any of their individuality, an Arthurian theme is born. The theme lives in the field of tension of which the functions establish the boundaries. One would suspect then that there would be an Arthurian theme for every possible pair of functions, but this is not so. I is the focus of the romance story and M of its narration; themes exist only in relation to these functions. The functions W and I delimit the theme 'individual and the world around him,' which is usually considered under the heading *aventiure*. The functions S and I establish the theme 'individual and society,' which is realized most often in the relation between the hero and Arthur's court. The functions O and I generate the theme 'individual and other,' which reveals two aspects corresponding to the two aspects of O. O^- and I generate the ever-present theme of combat and contest; O^+ and I, the most frequently articulated theme of all, *minne*.

M establishes a thematic relation both with the story that is transmitted (that is, with the first four functions together) and with the recipient. The theme that exists between M and the first four functions might be called 'the narrator as custodian of the tale.'[71] The thematic space between M and R is the most highly charged of all. At its tamest it has to do with the definition of the conditions of reception: who is the audience? At its most subversive it can undermine the act of communication itself.

These thematic axes are implicit in the functional structure of the Arthurian romance and thus constitute the thematic substructure of the genre. They are realized at every possible level. The theme *minne* in *Erec*, for example, is developed as it affects the individual character Erec, as it affects his relation with Enite, as it affects his relation to courtly society, and as it is the subject of remarks by the narrator. Should we undertake to investigate the theme *minne* in *Erec*, we would have to consider its effect not only on Erec and Enite but on all the levels of the romance.

The Arthurian themes, as fields of tension between paired functions, derive from the functional structure of the genre, yet the various romances realize these implicit themes in various ways, depending on the character the individual functions assume in different works. The themes of mediator and recipient have a clearer profile in *Erec*, with its active audience,

than in *Lanzelet*. The themes of individual and world are more promi-
nent in *Parzival* than in *Erec*. In *Daniel*, where the women are quite
faintly drawn, *minne* plays hardly any role at all.

TRADITION AND THE INDIVIDUAL AUTHOR

We have isolated the six constituent functions of Arthurian romance and
have investigated the relations implicit in the system they form. We have
seen that these functions imply a series of roles essential for the existence
of characters and that they generate as well the set of thematic axes that
underlie the genre. In all this we have considered Arthurian romance as
if it existed only as a genre. Of course the opposite is true; it exists only as
a group of individual works. We have sought those features common to
all the works so that we might speak with justification of the 'characteristics of the genre'; yet we have access to the genre only through its
various representatives. What is the relation of the six functions to the
individual Arthurian romance?

Clearly the six functions and the static relations of character and
theme they generate serve the romance author as a repertory of traditional material. We have discussed the essential role played by King
Arthur and the members of his court. We have noted as well the significance of magic springs (L:3889–909; I:553–97), the function of a traditional episode like the abduction of Ginover (L:6725–51; I:4530–726;
G:31–90), and the effect a narrator creates when he interrupts his tale to
reproach Vrou Minne (P:291,1–293,17; M:1383–418). By introducing
such well-known patterns an author proclaims his allegiance to the traditional conventions of Arthurian romance and at the same time draws
on the constituents of that tradition in the interests of his own work.

Yet the six functions supply the romance author with more than an
assortment of hand-me-down characters and a few familiar patterns of
behaviour: they allow as well for the creation of new heroes and the
composition of new romances. Just as I can invent a new English word
– Arthurianism, for instance – the author of *Daniel* can invent a *buchloser
valant* (D:2026); you recognize the monster in *Daniel* as an opponent
because of its relation to Daniel and as a creature of W because it comes
out of the sea. In each case formal properties enable you to place the
innovation in its proper class. We need not rely on our own judgment,
however, to determine that the author of *Daniel*, in creating his new
monster, has acted in accordance with the rules of the genre; we can
introduce as well the testimony of the author of *Garel*, who incorporated

this same monster into his own work under the name of Vulganus. The later author recognized *Daniel*'s *buchloser valant* as a legitimate Arthurianism, grammatical according to the rules of the genre.

Each of the functions, it turns out, is an open class. New items can be added, just as they can to the class of English nouns, provided they are formed and can function according to the requirements of the class. Thus we find that each romance has its own hero, its own narrator, and its own audience; we find as well that the functions W and S can vary considerably from one work to another and that the function O can include both familiar and unfamiliar faces. And yet in no case do we have any difficulty placing the newcomers in the traditional categories, for romance authors are very careful to tailor their innovations to the traditional specifications. They do so out of respect for the genre in which they have chosen to write, a genre of which these traditional specifications are essential determinants. We see then that the six functions confront the individual author in two ways: on the one hand they offer a collection of well-known props and topoi; on the other they require the invention of new elements according to traditional patterns. On the one hand Arthurian tradition is concrete and static; on the other it is creative and dynamic.[72]

In the composition of a romance the author transforms the dynamic aspect of Arthurian tradition into its static aspect, for in the act of writing he must satisfy the creative requirements of tradition with concrete realizations. At the end of the romance these concrete realizations enter the repertory of traditional characters and familiar patterns available to later authors. We just noted that the author of *Garel* took up a *buchloser valant* from *Daniel*; we have already considered at length how the heroes of earlier romances became permanent members of Arthur's court; we will see later how authors like to cite Erec's *verligen* as an example of unacceptable behaviour. In every case the later authors testify to the orthodoxy of the feature they adopt. At the same time, they transform that feature from an isolated instance into a constituent of the tradition.[73] Thus the substantiation of Arthurian tradition depends as much on the reception by the later authors as it does on the innovations of their more illustrious forebears.

This has important consequences for the investigation of romance structure. The early, widely celebrated romances introduced a wealth of possible models into Germany. Some of these possibilities were accepted as binding and came to constitute the tradition (the role of Arthur's court, the myth of the French source, the bugaboo of *verligen*). Others, however, were ignored and, no matter how much we might miss them, cannot be considered among the determinants of the genre (a crisis generated by the hero, a prologue as in *Iwein*, a coherent world beyond courtly society as in *Parzival*). It is true that without *Erec* there might not have been any Middle High German Arthurian romance at all, and yet the possibilities offered by *Erec* do not by themselves constitute a tradition. In a sense, then, our investigation must be prejudiced in favour of the later works. If we want to study the structure of a genre we must consult those who were aware of writing in the tradition of that genre; what the later authors accepted as Arthurian we are bound to accept as well. This refers not only to the concrete bits and pieces they imported from earlier works but – much more important from our point of view – to the structural principles they regarded as binding. Thus, whereas we can talk about the structure of *Erec* by consulting that work alone and about the structure of the canonical works by including *Iwein* and *Parzival*, we can only speak accurately of the structure of the entire genre if we consult the works of later authors as well. They are the ones who, by selecting elements from their models, established these elements as constituents of the Arthurian tradition.

CHAPTER TWO

Episodes:
The Functions as a Dynamic System

We began in the Arthurian theatre. Standing in the back door we observed the activity within the theatre and were able to isolate six areas and kinds of actor or activity; these we called functions. We turned away from the activity that had at first attracted our attention and investigated the six functions both individually and in the static relations they maintain among themselves. In doing so we acted as if Arthurian romance were architecture. Each function became a certain kind of space with a certain kind of internal structure and these spaces all stood in hierarchical and static relation to each other.

But if you turn back to the Arthurian theatre you will find that the activity of which we first caught a glimpse has not stopped. The hero is still under way, and the spotlight keeps your eye focused on him. The narrator is talking nonstop, and you don't lose track of him either. At first every movement, every remark seems unique, but soon you begin to recognize certain patterns: whenever a stranger appears on stage, the narrator will describe her dress or his armour; whenever the hero enters the woods, he will find some sort of combat. If you watch several different performances at the Arthurian theatre you will begin to recognize certain recurring features: the narrator begins each evening with a speech to the audience and ends it by briefly sketching the hero's rosy future; near the end of each performance the hero will make an appearance at Arthur's court.

No, Arthurian romance is not architecture. It is narrative and exists in time as well as space. Indeed, the linear, narrative organization of the genre is much easier to perceive than its static, functional structure. Anyone can see that Lanzelet fights Iwaret to win Iblis, but that Iblis and Iwaret are two aspects of the same function is not so easily recognized. But how are we to describe the linear organization of the narrative? How are we to account for those recurring patterns we observed in our model theatre? Our first job, it seems to me, must be to discover the natural divisions of the narrative line. Only then will we be able, by examining the relation of these line segments to one another, to discuss the larger patterns of the linear structure.

The natural divisions of an Arthurian narrative? Clearly they are episodes. It seems more than likely that an audience in 1200 perceived a romance as a succession of episodes. Certainly this is true of the scribes of the following centuries – who indicate as much by their placement of initials – and of the editors and scholars of the last hundred and fifty years. But what are the criteria on which this perception rests? What *is* an episode? I think, at bottom, it is any single encounter between the Individual and the Other. Since there are only a few possible ways such an encounter can turn out, there are only a few skeletal forms for an Arthurian episode. These skeletons come to life only when their constituent functions are given substance. In the process of substantiation each potential episode acquires the distinctive profile that differentiates it both from its skeletal scheme and from other similar episodes. And yet we do not see this profile through our own eyes but hear it described in the voice of the narrator. In portraying an episode he draws our attention to this or that feature, colouring the surface and inevitably influencing our perception. There are, then, three levels at which one can analyse an Arthurian episode: (1) the encounter of the hero and the other, which has only a few skeletal forms; (2) the realization of this skeleton, which reveals many varieties of shape and substance; (3) the narrator's portrayal of this substantial episode, by which the surface we perceive is created. The first level isolates the syntactic aspect of an episode, while the second accounts for those ways in which the syntactic skeleton is realized by specific semantic content. Together they delineate the possibilities according to which the six functions can combine to generate a romance story. The third level isolates the verbal aspect of an episode; it accounts for the ways in which elements of the story are transformed and modified in narration, the written record of which we have before us as text.

SKELETONS

The Archetypical Episode

After his second rescue of Ginover and the subsequent rescue of Erec and Walwein, Lanzelet returns to Arthur's court for a large celebration.

When the partying has ended he goes off to bed with Iblis and asks her for the latest news. She tells him of a serpent in a nearby woods that implores every passing knight to kiss it; but it is so fearsome – 'der was gebart, daz nie tier so vreislich wart' (L:7847–8) – that they flee instead. Lanzelet resolves, despite Iblis's entreaties, to enter the woods and kiss the serpent himself. He does so, and the serpent turns into a beautiful woman: 'er wart daz schoeneste wip, die ieman ie da vor gesach' (L: 7938–9). After this transformation Lanzelet and 'diu schoene Elidia' (L:7990) return to Arthur's, where she becomes a judge of love-disputes. This episode shows in a very concise form the stages of the archetypical Arthurian episode: the hero, at home in society (S/I), hears of an opponent (S/O$^-$/I); he travels through the woods (W/I); by his action the opponent is transformed into a companion (W/O$^-$/I $\rightarrow$ W/O$^+$/I); the hero and his companion return to court (S/O$^+$/I).

S/I $\rightarrow$ S/O$^-$/I

In telling Lanzelet about the serpent, Iblis performs a crucial function: she introduces the hero and the opponent. Yet Lanzelet, who naturally wants to fight every opponent of whom he hears, cannot fight the serpent at court, since the serpent is not there, so he sets out at once to find it. Thus the result of Iblis's news is to separate Lanzelet from society and get him into the woods.

There are many scenes in Arthurian romance that are similar in type to the bedtime talk between Iblis and Lanzelet: Erec is en route to King Arthur's and hears of the 'joie de la curt' – he determines to fight Mabonagrin; Iwein is enjoying Arthur's *hochzit* when he hears Kalogrenant's story – he resolves to fight Ascalon; Parzival has just been welcomed into the Round Table when Cundrie arrives and denounces him – he immediately leaves court; Gwigalois has just been knighted when Nereja appears with her entreaty – he requests and receives permission to defend her mistress; Daniel has just been installed as king of Cluse when an old man appears and runs off with King Arthur – now Daniel must figure out how to rescue him; Garel arrives at Arthur's just in time to hear Malseron challenge the king – Garel sets out to organize Arthur's defence. In every case the hero has just been integrated, or reintegrated, into society, often at a *hochzit*, and is in danger of losing his individual features; he is more nearly a member of society than an individual. Suddenly an opponent – more often a messenger of the opponent or news of the opponent – appears, issues a challenge, and the hero rides off to fight.

There is of course a crucial difference between Cundrie's denunciation of Parzival, which is elicited by his own previous behaviour, and the completely unprovoked challenge of Malseron, and this difference in motivation would certainly lead us to differing interpretations of these two episodes. From a rigorously functional perspective, however, the two episodes are identical: each serves to separate the hero from society and launch him on an essentially unrelated series of adventures. What Walter Haug says of Parzival's first visit to Arthur's court is true of all scenes of the type S/I → S/O⁻/I: 'Viewed from the point of view of structure, this is a provocation motif, that is, an introductory situation that sets the plot in motion and that acquires its significance from this function.'[1]

We can observe from the examples just given that, in scenes of the type S/I → S/O⁻/I, O⁻ can take a great variety of forms. The opponent himself can appear, as in the case of the old man in *Daniel*. More often the opponent will send a messenger, like the giants in the opening scenes of *Daniel* and *Garel* or like Lunete when she accuses Iwein before the court. In many cases, however, the hero merely hears tell of an opponent, as when Iblis tells Lanzelet about the serpent or when Iwein hears about Ascalon. Sometimes news of the opponent is not specific, like the promise of 'groze ritterschaft' (C:3215) that attracts Gawein and most of the rest of Arthur's knights to the tournament at Jaschune. Finally, the opponent can exist simply as an abstraction: Lanzelet leaves the water fay 'durch niht wan umb ere' (L:351); Gawein entices Iwein away from Laudine by telling him, 'nu hat ir des erste reht daz sich iuwer ere breite unde mere' (I:2902–4); young Gwigalois leaves his mother because he knows he should not lie about (W:1299–1301). Although Lanzelet, Iwein, and Gwigalois are not challenged by a specific opponent, they all feel challenged to increase their *ere*, and they know that to do so they must leave society and seek opponents. Thus the generalized obligation to seek adventure (that is, increase *ere*) can function in just the same way as a direct challenge before the court. It separates the hero from society and leads him into the woods.

There is one final, uncommon but very famous form of S/I → S/O⁻/I, that in which the hero is separated from society without being challenged at all, not even to increase his fame. The clearest example is Parzival's departure from Munsalvaesche. He leaves because of something he did *not* do. Erec's departure from Karnant is similar. One might say that he has been challenged by Enite to prove himself as a knight; one could also say that Erec leaves society to compensate for what he has not done, just like Parzival. The analogous scene in *Iwein* might have turned out the same: even before Lunete arrives at court Iwein recalls that he has overstayed his leave, with the result 'daz er sin selbes vergaz' (I:3091). Had he left court at once he would have resembled Parzival, separated from society for what he did not do. But in this case the opponent does materialize, like Cundrie at Arthur's, and gives the episode a more orthodox form. Finally, one should mention Tandareis and Flordibel, who separate *themselves* from Arthur's court; they fall in love and run off, causing Arthur to pursue them. Here the hero takes an active role, as opposed to Parzival and Erec, but like them he is not separated from society by any opponent, even the most abstract. Perhaps Tandareis gives us the key to the other episodes. Through his own actions he causes the separation from court; Parzival causes the same by his inaction. In both cases the hero is the agent of separation; he is his own opponent.

Had Lanzelet, Iwein, or Gwigalois *not* left in search of adventure, he would have been guilty of *verligen*. Erec is the only hero to have actually commited this sin, but his example traumatized all his successors: Gawein is able to pry Iwein away from Laudine by conjuring up the shame of the one 'der sich ... durch vrouwen Eniten verlac' (I:2793–4); Wolfram asks Vrou Aventiure if Parzival 'hat ... sider sich verlegen' (P:434,9); young Gwigalois already knows that he must not 'verligen in disem lande hie' (W:1301); Gawein refuses the crown of King Flois because 'ern ... wolte sich so niht verlegen' (C:10106–7); Tandareis is disconsolate in the care of Antonie 'wan ich han mich hie verlegen' (T: 12153; cf. T:12169); Erec himself recalls his own mistake when he tries to convince Gauriel to leave his lady (GM:2884–905). That the spectre of *verligen* is so frightening in romance has nothing to do with the real world. There is no reason to think that Landgraf Hermann wanted his vassals to go off alone, wandering about the forests of Thuringia; medieval society did not depend on knights errant. But romance society does. Arthur refuses to serve breakfast until his knights scrounge up news of some adventure; he does so because his very existence depends on adventures. If the knights were to lie about court all day there would be no adventures; if there were no adventures there would be no romances; and without romances Arthur would not exist. *Verligen* is the original sin of romance: introduced by the first romance hero, it threatens death to the world of romance. Yet for all that it is a purely literary sin.

The constellation S/O⁻/I is the structural equivalent to the courtly injunction against *verligen*; it is the mechanism by which the romance itself generates episodes – which are the structural equivalent of adventures. Of course, you will say, we expect the structure to accommodate itself to the meaning. But to say this is to see things backwards, for whenever the structural needs of the romance conflict with the dictates of courtly ideology, the romance wins. We can see this in the scene cited from *Lanzelet*. Iblis ends her tale about the serpent by entreating Lanzelet not to go off in search of it (L:7862–7); but no sooner does she finish than he starts out for the woods. Just two episodes earlier Lanzelet had applauded the example of Gilimar, who remained silent for years at the bidding of his lady (L:6639–72), but now he has no use for such devotion: 'im wart zer aventiure gach' (L:7874). One might say more accurately, 'dem maere wart zer aventiure gach.' Iblis, with courtly ideology and Lanzelet's recent opinion on her side, wants Lanzelet to stay home; but the romance wants him off on another adventure, and the romance wins.

The German romances are much stricter on this point – the hero must prove himself regardless of what the lady says – than the French. In the *Charrete*, Guenievre twice requires Lancelot to fight badly and he obeys without hesitation (CCh:5638–56, 5836–57); and twice, when he overhears the queen accede to Bademagu's request that she allow Lancelot to stop fighting, he stops at once (CCh:3788–812, 5016–23). When Iblis wants Lanzelet to stay at home, however, he immediately does just the opposite; and when Nereja suggests that Gwigalois pass up a fight he refuses outright:

> er sprach 'vrouwe, nein, durch got!
> ich wil allez iuwer gebot
> leisten an andern dingen;
> mir muoz hie gelingen,
> od ich verliuse swaz ich han.'   (W:1958–62)

There are cases in which a knight is *suspected* of riding poorly on account of his lady's command, but the suspicion is always mistaken. Gurnemanz believes that Parzival rides so poorly and wears fool's clothes 'durch wibe gebot' (P:164,28), and Johfrit suspects the same of young Lanzelet (L:504–5); but in both cases the hero's strange behaviour results only from his lack of proper training. Gurnemanz and Johfrit base their reaction on a convention of French romance that does not obtain in Germany. Women in German romances never request a hero to forgo a battle or to fight badly, or if the request is made it is brushed aside. As the young Gwigalois says, 'swer sinen rat laet an diu wip, dern ist niht ein wiser man' (W:1358–9).

And why does Gwigalois dismiss women's opinions so cavalierly? Because the romance needs adventures.[2] We see a similar conflict between official courtly ideology and the needs of romance in Arthur's breakfast custom. Theoretically a host should never keep his guests waiting for food, as Heinrich reminds us (C:8759–66); but the romance wants adventure, so Arthur is made to engineer S/I → S/O⁻/I. Here again ideology comes in conflict with romance, and again romance wins. It always does.

W/I

As soon as Iblis finishes her story Lanzelet sets out for the woods, and once in the woods he finds the serpent. This was not to be avoided; whenever an Arthurian knight finds himself in the woods he is bound to come upon some adventure. Gwigalois, for example, after defending the dog he captured and gave to Nereja (W:2207–318), comes upon a lamenting woman; in order to comfort her he must win back a horse of which she has been robbed. Garel is engaged in a long-range project recruiting forces to defend King Arthur when he comes upon a knight with upraised spear, 'also er tjostieren wolt' (G:2153). Lanzelet is in the woods because of S/I → S/O⁻/I; Gwigalois, because he has just completed an adventure in the woods; Garel, because he has a long-range goal: no matter what has gotten him into the forest an Arthurian hero, once there, is certain to come across a knight with upraised spear or the equivalent. The function W, although it might seem threatening and unpredictable to the romance population, is from a literary point of view entirely predictable: it always produces adventure.

We should note that W/I is the prerequisite not only for a combat that occurs in the woods (Garel's fight) but also for one that takes place before a courtly assembly (Gwigalois's recapture of the stolen horse). There does not seem to be any logical reason why an opponent should not appear at Arthur's court while Iwein, say, is in residence and why Iwein could not defeat him at once in clear view of the entire company, but this never happens. When the opponent himself appears at court (the giants' father in *Daniel*) he must be overcome elsewhere. When the hero does fight before a courtly company (Iwein fights Gawein) he invariably approaches from the woods. There are a number of cases in which Arthur's knights hear of a challenger and meet him in view of the court; yet the challenger is always the hero (or the hero's father, *Wigalois*), and he approaches from the woods (Parzival in book six; Joram, Daniel, and Gauriel when they first arrive at court). There does not seem to be any logical reason why an opponent should not appear at court and be defeated by the hero then and there, but the genre apparently does not allow this possibility. The hero must pass through the woods between episodes.

The author of *Diu Crone* is especially careful to note each time his hero enters or leaves the forest, and in one particularly graphic passage (C:6782–816) he reveals quite clearly why. Passing between the homes of Riwalin and Blandukors, Gawein enters 'ein vinster tan' (C:6784). Heinrich describes at some length the difficulties of riding through the forest, then turns to the reaction of Gawein, who laments, 'ich enkunde mir nie sanfte geleben' (C:6805–6). The narrator assures us that Gawein is actually praising himself, 'wan er wolt, daz ime vergalt solch arbeit hohen pris' (C:6813–14). From an ideological point of view *arbeit* is the prerequisite for *pris*, and Gawein recognizes this. The structure of a romance episode reflects the ideological importance of *arbeit* and always begins with 'ein vinster tan.' It stands as an emblem for *arbeit*, a reminder that the way to *pris* leads necessarily through *arbeit*.

This emblematic function of the woods is peculiar to Arthurian romance and is not matched even in the closely related Tristan tradition. In Eilhart the woods of the 'Waldleben' episode are indeed the scene of 'arbeit' (ETr:4739), but without any hope of *pris*; in Gottfried they are allegory. Occasionally the Tristan authors show themselves closer to the Arthurian tradition. The Gilan episode in Gottfried resembles an Arthurian adventure more nearly than most of Tristan's other adventures (a single knight defeats a giant, liberates the surrounding countryside, and sends a token to his lady back at court); and here for once the hero approaches his opponent through 'einen harte wilden walt' (GTr: 15965). In Eilhart's version, when Tristrant leaves Cornwall after having returned Isalde to Marke, he rides off to King Arthur's (ETr:5016–20); and, after having visited Isalde in Arthur's company, Tristrant rides on to Karahes (ETr:5488–90). This is surprising. Later it becomes clear that one can only travel between Karahes and Tintanjol by ship (ETr:6269, 8210–11, 8723–59, 9355–9, 9498–9, 9502–3), yet Tristrant first arrives at Karahes by land. It seems that Eilhart is more susceptible to the immediate claims of literary convention (knights must come and go from Arthur's through the woods) than to the overall claims of topographical consistency.

Tristrant's ride away from Arthur's court is all the more striking if one recalls that the articulating function of the Arthurian woods is usually filled in the Tristan tradition by the sea. This is clear in the last part of Eilhart and in the first part of both Middle High German versions. In

Eilhart the voyages to Ireland seem to be guided by the same providence that watches over the Arthurian woods. In both cases the hero has no fixed goal yet is led ineluctably to the only possible goal. Gotfrit disapproves of such sailing about 'nach wane' (GTr:8618), and his hero sets out with his destination clearly in mind. Yet Gotfrit himself makes God responsible for the outcome of Tristan's first sea voyage, at the hands of his kidnappers (GTr:2406–10, 2442). To the extent that the sea is an instrument of an inscrutable fate it is related to the symbolic system of the Tristan romances (to the potion and thus to the love of the hero and heroine). Thus it functions structurally, in articulating the episodes, and symbolically, in relation to a central idea, in ways analogous to those of the Arthurian woods. Yet in spite of the functional analogy the meaning is different: the fate of which the sea is an instrument shatters the social order, while the *arbeit* of which the woods are an emblem is the keystone of courtly ideology. Once again we can observe how the elements of the Tristan tradition foster disintegration while the analogous elements of Arthurian romance serve to integrate.[3]

$O^-/I \rightarrow O^+/I$

When Lanzelet comes upon the serpent he kisses it, and at once it is transformed into a beautiful woman. This transformation of O from a threat into an ally forms the heart of the archetypical Arthurian episode. In spite of its concision, however, the scene from *Lanzelet* is atypical in several ways. First, the transformation is usually accomplished not by a kiss but by a fight: Gwigalois must defeat in armed combat the knight who claims the dog; Garel attacks Gilan, the knight with upraised spear. Second, the change from O^- to O^+ is seldom as graphic as it is in *Lanzelet*: when Garel defeats Gilan and the latter gives *sicherheit*, Gilan is transformed from an enemy into a devoted friend, not from a monster into a woman. Third, O^- and O^+ are most commonly represented by different characters: Gwigalois kills the knight and wins the dog. Most often O^- will be a hostile knight and O^+ a woman: Lanzelet kills Iwaret and wins Iblis. Finally, O^- and O^+ are often present together for a time: Gwigalois defeats the knight because he has already determined to keep the dog; Lanzelet commits himself to Iblis even before Iwaret appears (L:4280–6). Yet in spite of the variety of forms the transformation $O^- \rightarrow O^+$ can take, the scene from *Lanzelet* presents the change with magical concision: the hero by his intervention (a kiss) transforms O^- (a serpent) into O^+ (a beautiful woman).

Lanzelet's fight with Iwaret, his kissing of the serpent, Gwigalois's defence of the dog, Garel's fight with Gilan – these adventures all take place in the woods. Yet fighting in the woods has certain drawbacks. As a page tells Lanzelet and Walwein, whom he is trying to dissuade from fighting, 'maezic lob da von geschiht, so ez niht wan einer siht in dirre wilden wüeste' (L:2607–9). What is his alternative? That they attend the tournament he is advertising, for it is 'ein lobelich getat, swa man iht guotes begat, daz ez wol mugent schouwen ritter unde vrouwen' (L: 2619–22). It is better, according to the page, that society witness the hero's victory.

There are many cases in which the transformation $O^- \rightarrow O^+$ before society is not essentially different from the same transformation out in the woods. Ade loves Lanzelet, Lanzelet kills Linier in a fixed contest, Lanzelet wins the hand of Ade as well as the kingdom of Limors. At this stage of reduction the episode is identical to the combat with Iwaret, fought in the woods. Yet there are other cases where the presence of courtly onlookers is essential. Trial by combat, by which for example the controversy over the estate of the Grave von dem Swarzen Dorne is to be settled, *must* take place before an assembled court. Society must be able to observe the outcome, or in case of doubt to hear the decision of the king (I:7690, 7718). In other instances Arthurian combat is socialized even more thoroughly. The winner of the 'Sperberkampf' in *Erec*, for instance, wins for himself nothing but praise and for his lady the distinction of being acknowledged the most beautiful woman present (E:200–2). In the special case of Erec the hero's victory wins him his heroine, Enite, but while this is crucial to the romance, it is purely coincidental to the pre-scriptions of the combat itself. According to these the reward for victory at the 'Sperberkampf' is intangible: praise for the victor and his lady. In contests like this the transformation $O^- \rightarrow O^+$ has been abstracted one notch: the potential humiliation of defeat – the social equivalent of death – is transformed into general acclaim – the greatest social victory. Because this abstraction depends on the presence of society, I distinguish two forms of the transformation $O^- \rightarrow O^+$: the one takes place in the forest $(W/O^-/I \rightarrow W/O^+/I)$, the other occurs in the presence of courtly society $(S/O^-/I \rightarrow S/O^+/I)$.

We ought to note that the most common form of $O^-/I \rightarrow O^+/I$ is the one in which the hero defeats an opponent (rather than kisses a serpent) and wins a woman (rather than a friend or a dog). Now the undertaking by which a hero approaches an opponent is called *aventiure,* and the relationship he sustains with a woman implies *minne.* To be sure, not every episode that includes a woman leads to love: Lanzelet does not wed Ginover, nor does Gauriel desire the daughter of Asterian. Yet the possibility of a union is often mentioned: the Vrouwe von Narison offers her hand to Iwein; the Frouwe von dem Trüeben Berge offers her hand to Daniel. Both Iwein and Daniel decline the offers, but Lanzelet is not so reticent. He lives with four women in the course of the romance. Sometimes, even if a combat does not involve a woman at all, it will be one of a series of episodes fought in the presence of a single woman, who is, in effect, gradually won by the repeated demonstration of the hero's prowess; this is certainly true of Nereja in *Wigalois* and Orgeluse in *Parzival* and, in a special sense, of Enite in *Erec*. Ilse Nolting-Hauff maintains – correctly, I suspect – that marriage forms the natural conclusion of an Arthurian episode but that in many cases this marriage is negated for thematic reasons. Adultery was after all a sin, and the author of *Iwein* is clearly more concerned with the regulation virtue of his hero than is the author of *Lanzelet*.[4] In spite of those cases in which the hero's virtue thwarts the terminal marriage, every episode in which O^+ is a woman implies, at least, a *minne*-relation between that woman and the hero. Thus, since O^-/I implies *aventiure* and O^+/I (where O^+ is a woman) implies *minne*, we see that the structural core of an Arthurian episode, the transformation of O^- to O^+, parallels the thematic pair, *aventiure* and *minne*, that is so often invoked as the very heart of Arthurian romance.[5]

$S/O^+/I$

After Lanzelet's kiss transforms the fearsome serpent into the beautiful Elidia, the two set off at once for Arthur's court: 'do nam Lanzelet du Lac die vrowen also wol getan und fuorte si ze Kardigan' (L:7962–4). There Elidia becomes an adjudicator of love disputes. Thus the threatening creature of the forest is incorporated into society and the hero is praised by the court: $W/O^-/I \rightarrow W/O^+/I \rightarrow S/O^+/I$. Not by any means all Arthurian episodes end with a trip back to court. In those cases where the combat is fought before a courtly audience (Iwein's fight with Gawein; Gwigalois's recapture of the horse from Hojir) there can of course be no return to society. And often in the case of combats fought in the woods the hero will simply move on to another adventure in the woods: after Erec defeats the first group of robbers he comes upon the next; after Gwigalois defends the dog he meets the woman who has lost her horse. Yet in many cases the constellation that results from combat, O^+/I, will seek recognition by and integration into society: Lanzelet and Iblis, after sending a message back to Dodone (L:4637–55), set out for King Arthur's (L:4960–3); after Garel defeats Gilan, they are reconciled and set off for Pergalt, the castle of Gilan's brother-in-law (G:2482–4, 2778–803).

Although $S/O^+/I$ can simply signify return and integration, as in the case of Lanzelet and Elidia, in its more elaborate realization $S/O^+/I$ becomes a courtly *hochzit*. After Erec has won Enite they both return to Arthur's court to celebrate their marriage. Arthur plans a *hochzit* at Pentecost that is attended by dignitaries from all over the world. After the *hochzit* a tournament is arranged at which Erec distinguishes himself above all others. The presence of the hero with his lady in society – often at Arthur's court – is the most stable situation in Arthurian romance. $S/O^+/I$ is the state of equilibrium towards which the genre strives, the constellation that occasions courtly *vreude*. It appears at the end of *Lanzelet*, *Daniel*, and *Diu Crone*, virtually at the end of *Erec*, *Garel*, *Meleranz*, and *Tandareis*, and at the conclusion of important episodes: after Lanzelet's rescue of Ginover; after Iwein wins Laudine; after Erec vanquishes Mabonagrin.

If we reassemble those constituent elements of an Arthurian episode that we have just isolated, we will produce the following sequence:

$$S/I \rightarrow S/O^-/I \rightarrow W/I \Big\langle \begin{array}{l} S/O^-/I \rightarrow S/O^+/I \\ W/O^-/I \rightarrow W/O^+/I \rightarrow S/O^+/I \end{array}$$

As we have already observed, the transformation $S/O^-/I \rightarrow S/O^+/I$ or $W/O^-/I \rightarrow W/O^+/I$ is at the heart of the episode and this transformation is necessarily preceded by W/I. We have also noted that many episodes omit the initial $S/I \rightarrow S/O^-/I$ or the final return to society, $W/O^-/I \rightarrow S/O^+/I$. The scheme given above, then, represents the most elaborate form of the transformation episode.

The Three Types of Episode

The initial definition of an episode, however, required only the encounter between O and I, not the transformation; and indeed, there are episodes in which the encounter occurs but in which the transformation $O^-/I \rightarrow O^+/I$ is not realized. This includes some that have already been mentioned. The scenes in which Cundrie denounces Parzival before Arthur or in which Malseron challenges Arthur and motivates Garel are examples of $S/O^-/I$, as are those in which Iblis tells Lanzelet of the serpent, or in which the giants' father snatches Arthur away from Daniel's coronation feast. Yet, while the second pair of encounters leads directly to a transformation (Lanzelet kisses the serpent; Daniel rescues Arthur), the first pair introduces a series of adventures essentially unrelated to the encounters that initiate them. Parzival disappears for most of thirteen thousand lines before he is reconciled with Cundrie; Garel fights half a dozen adventures before he can finally respond to Malseron's challenge. In the case of Cundrie and Malseron one must speak of an independent $S/O^-/I$ episode, while in the case of Iblis's serpent and the abduction of Arthur, $S/O^-/I$ is merely the introduction to a transformation.

Similarly $S/O^+/I$ can be detached from the transformation episode and become an episode in its own right. The difference between the dependent and independent versions can be easily seen in *Lanzelet*, where they appear close together. After Elidia regains human shape she returns with Lanzelet to Arthur's court, where she becomes the object of great interest (L:7965). Here the return to society is simply the conclusion to the encounter in which Elidia was transformed from a serpent into a woman. Two episodes later Lanzelet and Iblis, accompanied by Arthur and his court, journey to Dodone to assume their throne. Here O^+ appears not as the result of a transformation just achieved – Iblis was won four thousand lines ago – but figures as O^+ from the beginning of the encounter. As the entire episode takes place in society and as there is no transformation, the coronation must be considered an independent $S/O^+/I$ episode.

Todorov states: 'The elementary narrative thus includes two types of episodes: those which describe a state of equilibrium or disequilibrium, and those which describe the transition from one to the other.'[6] I prefer to rearrange Todorov's categories a bit and say that Arthurian romance has three types of episode: one that describes the transition from equilibrium to disequilibrium ($S/I \rightarrow S/O^-/I$); one that describes the transition from disequilibrium to equilibrium ($W/I \rightarrow S/O^-/I \rightarrow S/O^+/I$ or $W/I \rightarrow W/O^-/I \rightarrow W/O^+/I$); and one that describes a state of equilibrium ($S/O^+/I$).[7] If we revise the scheme given above to accommodate these three episode types, we will come up with the following:

$$^1S/I \rightarrow S/O^-/I. \rightarrow {}^2W/I \rightarrow \begin{matrix} S/O^-/I & S/O^+/I. \\ W/O^-/I & W/O^+/I. \end{matrix} \rightarrow {}^3S/O^+/I.$$

Since an episode is any encounter between O and I, an episode can begin at any Arabic numeral and end at the next period. Yet a period may be ignored if the functions continue to be filled in the same way, creating an episode that might include all three stages of the encounter O/I.

Skeletal Action

Although the same transformation, $O^- \rightarrow O^+$, forms the heart of most Arthurian episodes, anyone who has read even a single romance will recognize that this transformation can be realized by episodes that appear quite different: the scene in which Daniel fights Gawein is not at all the same as the one in which he overcomes the monster who bathes in blood. Yet in spite of the great range of Arthurian episodes, most of them do fall into relatively few categories, and the episodes in any category will reveal a surprising degree of uniformity. For example, the armed combat between two knights, probably the most common form of the transformation $O^- \rightarrow O^+$, has the same outline from its first appearance in *Erec* to its much later occurrence in *Garel*: first the combatants approach and exchange a challenge; then they joust, after which they dismount and fight with swords; after a while the hero seems in danger of defeat, but suddenly he pulls himself together and brings his opponent to his knees; the hero is about to kill his victim but the latter begs for mercy, which is granted in exchange for a pledge of surety.

In order to show the remarkable constancy of this pattern, I have abstracted and give below those lines from two episodes – Erec's fight with Guivreiz and Garel's fight with Eskilabon – that establish the skeletal pattern. I have included as well those lines that contain straightforward description – the lines, that is, to which we will return shortly in discussing the techniques of static and active differentiation – but I have set these lines off by indenting them. Although it has not always been easy to distinguish those lines that outline the action from those that describe the action, a few changes of category will not upset my observations.

from *Erec* (E:4321–2, 4368–477; Er = Erec; Gu = Guivreiz)

from *Garel* (G:3384–5, 3526–812; Ga = Garel; Es = Eskilabon):

nu sahen si also drate
in [Gu] dort zuo riten.
...
er [Gu] sprach:
'wert iuch durch iuwer schoenez
   wip.'
sin ros er [Er] wider kerte.
zesamene riten zwene man
   der ietweder nie gewan
   zageheit dehein teil.

diu sper si uf stachen
   daz si gar zebrachen.

der [sparwaere] braht diu niwen maere
uf des wirtes [Es] palas.
...

ietwederhalp wart widerseit.

Garel mit einem grozen sper
der staphte ritterlichen her.
der manlich Eskilabon,
   der ie nach prislichem lon
   ranc mit ganzer wirdicheit,
mit einem sper gein im [Ga] reit,
   daz was groz und unbesniten,

diu tjost wart krefteclich.
do muosten si lazen
die zoume von den handen.

si erbeizten beide geliche
vil unmüezecliche
und ervuorten diu swert.
nu begunden si vehten.
diz huop sich umbe einen mitten
tac.

mit unverzagetlichen siten.
langer si do niht beliben;
diu ors mit sporn si do triben
von rabin hurticlichen dar.
ir ietwederr sin sper
gar verstach unz an die hant.
uf gein den lüften wart gesant
trunzune von ietweders sper.
ir ietwederr gahte her,
(da man) diu sper dort stecken (sach).
sus verstachen si snellen
diu sper in kurzen stunden,
swaz si der da funden;
dannoch was ez ungescheiden.
nach ir swerten beiden
wart gegriffen sa zehant.
ietwederr daz sin bereit vant.
werte sich der werde man [Ga]

also ritterlichen gar.
ze orsse si noch beide striten
mit unverzagetlichen siten.
si erbeizten nider uf daz gras.
dise zwene küene man
die liefen beid einander an
mit starken slegen ungezalt.
Eskilabon, der degen balt,
des slege waren starc genuoc.
Garel ouch mit kreften sluoc.
diu swert vil lute erklungen.
von ir schilden sprungen
die spaen.
uz ir helmen draeten
fiwers vanken uf daz gras.
kraft und ellen an in was.
Eskilabon, der degen klar,
werte wol sin bluomen lieht.
ze striten im [Ga] geschach
mit dem allerküensten man,
der ritter namen ie gewan.
daz wart wol schin an dem tage

mit manegem ellenthaften slage,
den er uf minen hern Garelen sluoc.

den schilt er [Er] im dar bot
[Gu] sluoc im von der hant
den schilt
  unz an den riemen.
zuo der siten ern [Gu, Er] erriet
und sluoc im eine wunden.

den schilt, den er [Ga] ze scherme truoc,
den howet er [Es] im ze stucken gar.

der wirt sluoc den gast her
  über den anger mit gewalt.
uf des angers wite
  si einander umbe triben.
der schilt was in niht ganz beliben,
  den ietwederr dar bot
  ze scherme für sich.
  die helde ellens riche
  striten gar an zageheit.
Garel

ein wenic trat er [Er] vürbaz:
  niht langer er im vertruoc,
uf den helm er in sluoc
daz der wenige man
da durch ein wunden gewan

  der stolze helt gemeit
nam mit slegen für sich
den wirt.
unz daz der wirt der wer vergaz.
  Garel von dem blüenden tal
  des slege mit kreften gaben schal,
  da von dem wirte der helm erdoz.
  die slege waren also groz,
  daz er kum da vor gestuont.
  sin slege waren swaere,
  des wart der wirt betoubet.

und daz er vor im gelac.

da von der gast den sic erranc.
Garel in da nider swanc.
daz swert er im uz der hende brach
und den helm ab.
  do daz geschach
  daz houbet im entwapent wart.

er [Er] wolde in erslagen han.
'nein' sprach er [Gu]
'la mir den lip.'
  nu hete gewert dirre strit
  unz an die nonezit,
  den sumertac also lanc.
die genade er [Er] an im begie

[Ga] sprach 'din lip [wirt] niht gespart.'
'Neina helt, la mich genesen'
sprach der wilde Eskilabon.

uf zuhte er in bi der hant:
den helm er im abe bant.
er [Er] sprach: Er [Ga] sprach hinz im 'wilt du genesen,
'nennet iuwern namen.'   so suln din gevangen wesen
er [Gu] sprach: ledic'
'ich bin künec über Irlant
Guivreiz le pitiz genant.'   'swaz du gebiutest, daz ist getan:
                                         die gevangen suln ledic sin.'

There are several points to be noted from the comparison of these two outlines. First, in both cases the lines given above account for about one third of that part of the episode devoted to the fight itself (E: 44 lines out of 112; G: 89 out of 289). Second, the number of lines required for the outline of the action is practically the same in both cases (E: 31; G: 30), and these lines are strikingly similar. Third, der Pleiaere indulges in a great deal more straightforward description than does Hartman, much of it repetitive. Finally, of the straightforward description, that in *Erec* is more distinctive than that in *Garel*. That Erec stops fighting for a spell, that Guivreiz actually wounds Erec, that the fight lasts three hours – these are more vivid than the description in *Garel*, which consists chiefly of the traditional splinters from spears and shields. The large amount of redundant material, much of it quite unimaginative description, is one of the stylistic hallmarks of *Garel*.

Yet without wanting to discount the differences between the excerpts given above, one recognizes that the skeletal action pattern that underlies them is the same. It is the same pattern that forms the basis of Erec's fights with Iders and with Mabonagrin, of Gwigalois's rescue of the stolen horse, and of Iwein's combat with the wicked steward who would burn Lunete. In every case sight or news of the opponent leads to a challenge followed by a joust and a sword fight; after a bit the hero seems to be losing, but then he gains strength, defeats his opponent, and exacts *sicherheit*.

The pattern that underlies Erec's fight with Guivreiz appears in alternate forms in other episodes. The fights with Gawein in *Lanzelet*, *Iwein*, and *Parzival* end undecided. When Eumenides has been vanquished by Gawein he commits suicide (C:6599–616). In some cases (Iwein's fight with Ascalon; Garel's fight with Gilan; Lanzelet's fight with Valerin) the hero's increase in strength is not mentioned. The most abbreviated form of knightly combat goes no farther than a single joust, which can end in a simple defeat (Iwein's fight with Keie or Parzival's with several Arthurian knights out in the snow) or in death (Gwigalois's joust with the knight who might have offered dinner or with the knight who claimed the dog).

Although readers of Arthurian romance may regard fights on this pattern as the only possibility, this is not the case. Tristan's fight with Morolt, among the most Arthurian of his combats (compare his premeditated murder of Morgan), differs from the Arthurian pattern in a number of ways. The boat trip to the place of combat (ETr:787–90; GTr:6753–86); Morolt's attempt to dissuade Tristan from fighting (GTr: 6807–19), even offering him a bribe (ETr:810–30); Tristan's cutting off Morolt's hand (ETr:904–6; GTr:7046–9); Morolt's flight (ETr:909–11) – these are all quite unlikely in the standard knightly contest of Arthurian romance.

Other types of scene also follow strict patterns. A proper courtly welcome, for instance, consists of a certain series of events – indeed, if the formula is not observed the welcome cannot serve its function. Courtly festivals also reveal a strong family resemblance.[8] Non-courtly opponents come in greater variety than courtly ones, and therefore fighting with them takes many different forms; yet here too certain standard patterns emerge. Giants, for instance, wield clubs and are customarily defeated by cutting off their limbs, usually their legs (E:5549–54; C: 9439–63, 10062–9; D:2784–839, 3814–24; GM:2632–43, 2657–71; G: 5634–52, 5774–91; T:5869–936, 6287–99, 6662–727).

Essentially the Arthurian functions can combine in only a very few ways. If an author wants to construct a grammatical episode he must respect these limited combinational possibilities. Although he enjoys a certain latitude in realizing the three basic episode types, here too his hand will be guided by tradition. In most cases he will construct his episode on the basis of one of a limited number of skeletal action patterns.[9]

Excursus: A Word on Others' Skeletons

Since Vladímir Propp's study of Russian fairy tales became known in the West a considerable number of scholars, inspired by his example, have set out to accomplish similar kinds of analysis on other bodies of literature. These range from Ilse Nolting-Hauff's reverent projection of Propp's own categories onto *Yvain* to A.J. Greimas's bold attempt to found a universal grammar of narrative based on semantic theory. Having just proposed yet another highly reductive model for analysing narrative structure, I feel obligated to explain why I could not simply have adopted one of these ready-made systems. I will limit myself to four examples.

Ilse Nolting-Hauff, taking up Propp's observation that 'certain novels of chivalry' exhibit the same structure as Russian fairy tales,[10] investigates *Yvain* according to the Proppian system, but in doing so she does violence both to Propp and to *Yvain*.[11] On the one hand she overlooks many features of Propp's system. He finds, for instance, that 'difficult tasks' and 'fights' never occur in the same 'move'; this is the only case of complementary distribution in his system.[12] Yet, according to Nolting-Hauff, these two types merge in the Arthurian episode; accomplishment of the difficult task coincides with the victory over the opponent (pp. 154–5). Since Nolting-Hauff believes that Arthurian episodes are derived from the minimal form of the fairy tale (p. 147), she works with Propp's system in its most reduced form; yet even at this stage of reduction she is unable to observe the minimal rules of distribution that that system requires.

Not only does Nolting-Hauff ignore much of Propp; she ignores as well many of what she herself calls the 'most important of those characteristics of the *Chevalier au lion* peculiar to romance' (p. 175). She dismisses the return to Arthur's court, which she says quickly became a romance convention (p. 174), by calling it 'an artificial conclusion' (p. 173). This seems mistaken on two counts. First, only a few of the Middle High German Arthurian romances actually do end at Arthur's court; how can we speak of a convention when it is so seldom observed? Second, if we substitute $S/O^+/I$ for Arthur's court in her formulation, then we can hardly call an episode of this type an artificial conclusion; it is rather the essential conclusion of any romance and must not be dismissed. But the necessary conclusion with $S/O^+/I$ is only one of many romance features that Nolting-Hauff overlooks. She lists a number of other characteristics that distinguish an Arthurian episode from a fairy tale (dialogue, descriptive insertions, narrator activity) but does not investigate them since, she says, they cannot be accommodated in the method she has chosen to employ (p. 175)! I do not see how our understanding of Arthurian romance will be advanced by a method that can register only those features that romance shares with the Russian fairy tale – and the simplest form of Russian fairy tale at that.[13]

If Nolting-Hauff ignores most of the distinguishing features of Arthurian romance, at least she recognizes the episode as the fundamental unit. Eugene Dorfman does not even do that.[14] The substructural unit or 'nareme' into which he resolves French and Spanish heroic epic along with the romances of Chrétien has no relation at all to the episode. Of the four narremes out of which he fabricates the 'Core System' of *Erec*, the first two fall within a single episode, the crisis of *verligen*, and the third includes all the episodes up to the fourth narreme, the reunion of hero and heroine (p. 50). Yet in spite of the extreme desiccation of his model and his frequent references to linguistics, Dorfman bases his isolation of any particular narreme on nothing more concrete than his own interpretative understanding of the characters' motives and the authors' themes. The second narreme of the 'Core System' of *Erec*, for instance, owes its existence to Dorfman's understanding of Enide's intentions – he calls it 'the insult, the challenge to his [Erec's] sovereignty' (p. 50). One recognizes this same fondness for radically reductive interpretation in Dorfman's compression of the *Chanson de Roland* and the *Cid* to the same single theme, 'treachery' (pp. 8–9, 14–15). This kind of wilful simplifying culminates in Dorfman's assertion that French *chanson de geste*, Spanish heroic epic, and the romances of Chrétien all show the same essential pattern (pp. 70–5). A system of narrative analysis that ignores the unit of the episode and that, at its most abstract level, rests upon the crudest interpretation of motives and themes will not be of much use to us in the structural analysis of Arthurian romance. Nor will our understanding of Arthurian romance be much advanced if we cannot distinguish Erec from Roland.

While Dorfman's analytic procedure is inspired by linguistic theory, the model that Tzvetan Todorov develops in his *Grammaire du Décaméron* is based on concrete linguistic categories: the parts of speech and the moods of the verb. Given the familiar clarity of this terminology as well as the clear definition of his corpus and the nature of the stories in the *Decameron*, one might expect Todorov's model to be more useful in our analysis of Arthurian romance than Dorfman's. Unfortunately this is not the case. Todorov reduces all the stories of the *Decameron* to propositions, each of which hinges on a verb; by far the most common verb is the one he labels *a*: 'to change the situation' (p. 34). Would this verb *a* not include my transformation $O^- \rightarrow O^+$? Perhaps it might. But unfortunately Todorov's verb never stands alone. Every verb is characterized by a mood (indicative, optative, obligatory, predicative, conditional), and this mood usually implies volition on the part of the character. The organization of Arthurian romance, however, does not as I understand it depend on the free will of the characters: everybody wants to modify the situation by fighting because the genre depends on that activity. If, as Todorov mentions at the end of his investigation (pp. 81–2), the *Decameron* reflects the importance of individual initiative in early capitalism, then the motivations attributed to a character may be an important structuring element in the work. In Arthurian romance, however, a character's motivation does not affect the structure of a work; it merely colours the way that structure is realized in a given romance. Todorov's model is unsuitable for our purposes for other reasons as well. First, since the *Decameron* is not an episodic work, Todorov's formulas do not easily accommodate series of episodes; yet our description of Arthurian romance must reflect its episodic construction. Second, Todorov establishes a category of adjectives that, in conjunction with a noun (i.e. character), establish a state. The character will want to modify a state or to preserve it. Yet how are we to define these adjectives and states for Arthurian romance? What does the hero want to preserve? to modify? To answer such questions we must consider the motivations attributed to a character. And what if no motivation is given, as for instance when Garel automatically attacks Gilan at first sight (G:2148–217)? Then we will be forced to interpret: Garel's attack means that he is searching for *ere*, or that he is accepting the *aventiure* that providence has ordained. I feel, however, that our structural model will be the more useful the less it relies on interpretative decisions.[15]

Todorov bases his narrative model on the parts of speech. A.J. Greimas, in his 'Éléments d'une grammaire narrative,' develops a model based on semantic theory. In this regard, as in several others, he stands closer to my own model of Arthurian romance than any of the theorists already mentioned. Greimas's semantic model is a static system of oppositions whose essential structure determines the dynamic series of narrative sequence (pp. 160–4) much as the static oppositions among my six functions generate the dynamic series of constellations that constitute an episode. Further, to the extent that Greimas's model rests on a theory of communication (pp. 175–8) it can, like my own system, accommodate both the events of the story (episodes) and the single event of the narration – although Greimas himself is not interested in this latter possibility. Finally, Greimas's three types of narrative statement ('énoncé narratif') are closely analogous to the three stages of the Arthurian episode (confrontation: $W/O^-/I$ or $S/O^-/I$; domination: $W/O^-/I \rightarrow W/O^+/I$ or $S/O^-/I \rightarrow S/O^+/I$; attribution: $S/O^+/I$) (pp. 172–3). The series of three narrative statements in the canonical order ('suites syntagmatiques d'énoncés narratifs') Greimas calls 'la performance' (pp. 173–4). In Arthurian romance we would call it an episode.

In spite of these striking parallels, however, Greimas's model makes claims much different from my own. Greimas is attempting a universal narrative grammar as part of a general semantic story (pp. 157, 163). As a result his system is more abstract than mine: while his 'actants' can be either hero or traitor and the 'performance' can result in a gain for either of the two, the structure of an Arthurian episode requires that the values I and O^- be clearly assigned and that the episode end with the victory of I. Here as elsewhere my system might seem to be merely a specific form of Greimas's as it appears in a particular genre: where he distinguishes between 'performances' accomplished by the requisite knowledge ('savoir-faire') and those accomplished by the requisite ability ('pouvoir-faire') (pp. 174–5, 178–80), Arthurian stories with very few exceptions admit only episodes of the second type; where he distinguishes 'performances' in which the canonical series of 'énoncés narratifs' is explicit from those in which it is implied (p. 174), Arthurian romance knows only the explicit variety. In each case Arthurian romance seems to be defined by the particular choices it makes among the various possibilities of the universal scheme.

Yet my Arthurian model is not merely a particular form of Greimas's universal scheme, and that is because, as others have already pointed out, Greimas's claims of universality are much overstated.[16] The few concrete examples that he gives are drawn from Propp's corpus of Russian fairy tales, and this is clearly the corpus that determines his sytem. Yet the transfer of values that he, prompted by his sources, puts at the core of a 'performance' (pp. 176–8) is not at the core of an Arthurian episode; indeed, an Arthurian combat can just as well be fought to prevent the transfer of values (ere, damsel) to O^-. Further, one should stress that the question of value, beyond the clear and fundamental assignment of negative and positive values to O^-, O^+, and I, does not affect the skeletal structure of an Arthurian episode at all. Whether the hero acts to rob an opponent of ere or to prevent the abduction of a damsel are questions of motivation, questions of how the skeletal episode acquires substance, which will be considered in the following section. The fundamental structure of the Arthurian episode is based not on the transfer of value nor even on the prevention of that transfer but on the transformation of the single function O. In many of its more abstract formulations Greimas's model parallels important features of my own; in its particulars, however, it turns out to have been tailored on another corpus and, as a consequence, not to fit Arthurian romance particularly well. Therefore, while happy to draw support from Greimas's example, I have preferred to develop a new model, one that reflects the skeletal structure of Arthurian romance with as much precision as possible.[17]

In the end, my system of skeletal analysis is bound to differ from these others because I have set different goals. They are concerned to analyse narrative at its most basic level and are content when they feel they have done so. For the analysis of Arthurian romance, however, we need a structural model that not only will do justice to Arthurian romance at this skeletal level but also will serve as the basis for a much more elaborate model of narrative structure. The skeletal pattern of the episode must reflect the structure of the episode, but it must also serve as the basis for the skeletal analysis of entire romances. The semantic categories that constitute the skeletal model must at the same time reflect the relation of narrator and audience at the surface of the romance. And the same few categories that define the episodic skeleton must be capable of transformation into more subtly articulated categories capable of accommodating a variety of non-skeletal but nevertheless important romance features. It is to this problem, how the bare bones of the episodic skeleton can be transformed into something one might recognize as a romance, that we must now turn.

SUBSTANCE: THE TECHNIQUES OF DIFFERENTIATION

If my skeleton were set next to your skeleton, it is quite likely that we could not tell ourselves apart; yet in real life we suffer no more than the normal confusion. The same is true of Arthurian episodes. Parzival's fight with Clamide and Lanzelet's fight with Iwaret, for example, are transformation encounters with identical skeletal action, yet we do not confuse them. Parzival is not Lanzelet; Clamide is not Iwaret; and Condwiramurs is not Iblis. When the skeletal episode is given substance it becomes tangible and acquires those distinctive contours by which we recognize it.[18]

Middle High German has its own term for this transformation: *schin werden*. After Iwein and Gawein stop fighting, Hartman advances the principle that a proper knight will not harbour a grudge against another with whom he has fought unless the blows were exchanged from pure wilfulness. Then he announces, 'daz wart wol schin an in zwein' (I: 7369) and reports the amicable conversation that leads to the revelation of their identities. The general principle is realized, *wirt schin*, in the specific action that follows. Yet obviously each time a skeletal episode is realized it is realized differently; otherwise all episodes of one type would look alike.

The processes by which a skeletal episode is realized, those processes that account for the differences among episodes, I call techniques of differentiation, both because it is through them that an episode or a function is differentiated from the abstract episode or ideal function, and also because their effect enables us to differentiate one episode from another. The techniques of differentiation fall into three main categories: static differentiation, in which elements of the episodic skeleton acquire durative attributes by virtue of the things with which they maintain static relations; active differentiation, in which elements of the skeleton are defined by the actions they perform; and differentiation by multiplication, in which an episode acquires special characteristics through the replication of features it already possesses.[19]

Static Differentiation

Names are the most elementary form of static differentiation. The episodic skeleton says 'I,' and I implies a particular role: the hero; but we do not feel we have a secure grasp on our hero until we know his name. 'Erec,' we hear in line 2, and that is a very important bit of information. The whole effect of withholding the names of the heroes in *Lanzelet*, *Parzival*, and the *Charrete* depends on the insecurity we feel when forced to get along without this elementary designation. The opponent too will be baptized, even if only generically: 'der rise,' 'der riter.' The elementary determination of setting parallels the naming of a role. The episodic skeleton says 'S'; will this be Arthur's court or one of its offshoots? The skeleton says 'W'; will this be a forest path or a pleasant meadow? Names and places do not seem much, but they are the prerequisites for any of the techniques of differentiation; they provide fixed points to which all these techniques refer.

One might expect the first step in the differentiation of a name or place to be some sort of basic description, but straightforward description is surprisingly rare in Arthurian romance. What does Erec look like? We aren't told. And what of Oringles? He is 'ein edel herre, ein grave' (E:6118–19); we know no more. Who could describe the setting where Kalogrenant tells his story? All we know is that there must be a chamber nearby to which the king and queen can retire. This extreme degree of descriptive reticence seems to be a particularly Arthurian trait. When Tristan enters the court of King Marke, Gotfrit pauses to paint his portrait: we learn among other things that Tristan has curly brown hair and unusually shapely legs and feet (GTr:3332–50).

Ordinarily, straightforward description of characters and settings in Arthurian romance is limited to those cases where the person or place described differs from the courtly norm. We do not know what Lanzelet and Parzival look like, but we are told what sort of figure they cut before they learn to ride properly (L:489–505; P:144,17–145,5). The same is true of opponents. We do not know what Oringles looks like, but Guivreiz is described in some detail (E:4282–92). One expects to come upon noble lords; one does not expect a valiant and courteous knight to be the size of a dwarf. Consistent with the principle by which only abnormal characters are portrayed, most of the lengthy, straightforward descriptions in our romances are accorded freaks and monsters: Cundrie, for instance (P:313,17–314,10), or the *waltman* in *Iwein* (I:425–64), or Ruel (W:6285–306, 6314–24). In a few cases, Arthurian women are described at some length: Iblis (L:4018–63), for instance, or Florie (W:863–949). But such descriptions are by no means the rule. Larie (W:4131–5), Laudine (I:1333–4), and Condwiramurs (P:187,12–23) are praised for their beauty but they are not described at all. The general principle applies as well to settings. When they are unusual, like the Wahsendiu Warte or the Schriendez Mos (L:5124–41, 7044–78), they are described for us, but otherwise we know virtually nothing: the tourney at Djofle takes place on a field that is 'breit unde sleht' (L:2685). The gratuitous inclusion of detail for mimetic effect is unusual in Arthurian romance.

Yet if Arthurian romance does not regularly include straightforward description, how is it that we do have a feeling for what Erec is like? Notice how Guivreiz sizes up his opponent when he comes across Erec and Enite riding in the woods. He greets Erec and says:

mich bedunket ane strit,
ir muget wol ein degen sin.
daz ist an zwein dingen schin:
ir vüeret, sam mir min lip,
daz aller schoeniste wip
der ich ie künde gewan:
wer gaebe die einem boesen man?
dar zuo sit ir gewafent wol,
als ein guot ritter sol
der ze deheinen stunden
werlos wil werden vunden
und der aventiure suochet.   (E:4329–40)

Guivreiz automatically does what we are repeatedly expected to do: he interprets the props that accompany a character or the situation in which he or she is found as an index of the nature of the character. Erec cannot be *ein boeser man* because he is with a beautiful woman. Erec must be seeking a fight because he is well armed.[20]

Clothing is the most obvious of the props used to differentiate a character in Arthurian romance. Its description, however, is never an end in itself but rather a reflection of the character wearing it. Florie's clothes include among other rich and exotic elements an image of 'herre Amor' (W:831) and a ruby that dispels sadness (W:792–800); these are suitable for a princess in a magical kingdom who is about to marry Gawein. The clothes of the five hundred *juncfrouwen* who attend Daniel's coronation are described at some length (D:6564–95); this explains how they contributed so noticeably to the 'fröuden' (D:6563) of the occasion. Lest we mistake the worth of Blandukors, we are told even before we learn his name of the wonderful scarlet cloth from which his clothes were made (C:6832–57). Poor clothes also appear in Arthurian romance, and they, just like rich clothes, serve primarily a symbolic function. Enite's threadbare garments reflect her poverty (E:324–8); the same is true of the hapless souls at the bottom of the wheel of Fortune (C:15845, 15862–4) and of the prisoners of Karedoz (T:7084–112). Hartman explicitly equates clothing and condition in describing the mad Iwein, saying, 'er lief nu nacket beider, der sinne unde der cleider' (I:3359–60).

One indication of the essential connection between clothing and character is the great importance attached to changing clothes. Florie's outfit is described only once, since she is a character who never varies. When Enite moves out of her poverty and into Arthur's court, however, we are given all the details of her new outfit (E:1537–77). The last stage of Iwein's recovery from insanity is to put on the courtly clothes that had been left near him. We are told, 'als er bedahte die swarzen lich, do wart er einem riter glich' (I:3595–6). Regaining his knightly identity *depends* on his getting into the proper clothes. The same is true of Lanzelet when he is released from Schatel le Mort (L:3749–59).

The most elaborate system of clothing changes is to be found in *Parzival*, where a new outfit marks each new stage in the hero's progress. When Parzival leaves his mother he wears 'toren kleit' (P:127,5); after killing Ither he covers his fool's outfit with Ither's 'ritters kleit' (P:156, 27); at Gurnemanz's he exchanges the fool's clothing for rich, courtly garments (P:168,1–20). Before meeting Condwiramurs, Parzival is given a rich cloak (P:186,7–10); and just after he arrives at Munsalvaesche, Repanse de Schoie lends him her cloak (P:228,8–20) – a sign, Trevrizent later reveals, of the eminence he was expected to attain (P:500,23–30). While at the grail castle Parzival is given Anfortas's sword (P:239,18–240,2), yet in leaving he bears both the new sword and the one he won from Ither (P:246,26). None of these changes is accidental or arbitrary;

all indicate something about Parzival's relation to the world around him at a particular moment in the romance. The conventional correspondence of essential worth and outward appearance is so firmly rooted in Arthurian romance that romance authors can capitalize on violations of the system without having first to explain it. At first Enite's own beauty and virtue are not matched by her clothing; Hartman notes the disjuncture (E:333–5) and Duke Imain twice tries to remedy the situation (E:637–40, 1407–9). But Erec refuses: Enite shall be praised as the result of his prowess alone (E:650–6); the task of finding and fitting suitable garments for Enite will be reserved for Ginover herself (E:1532–78). By frustrating for over a thousand lines our expectation that clothing will correspond to character, the author of *Erec* heightens our interest in his story and underscores the significance of the moment when our expectations are finally met, the moment when Erec and Enite arrive at court. This would be impossible if we did not already accept the conventional correspondence of inner worth and outward appearance. Once Enite has been suitably invested and our expectations have thereby been satisfied, Hartman marks the restoration of equilibrium in the conventional system with the summary observation, 'ir kleit was rich, si selbe guot' (E: 1578).[21]

Although the conventional correspondence of clothing and character obtains for most medieval literature, various traditions exploit this convention in different ways. In Arthurian romance clothing is a natural reflection of a character's social or interior condition. In the *Nibelungenlied*, however, clothing is an expression of wealth and power, and this meaning is consciously manipulated by the characters. Sifrit (Nbl:64–6) and Rüedeger (Nbl:1155) both insist on taking good clothes with them to Worms 'daz wir's ere vor fürsten mügen han' (Nbl:1155,3). Kriemhilt is more calculating: before her quarrel with Prünhilt she requires her attendants to dress in their richest clothes, 'ze leide Prünhilde' (Nbl:837,4); when Rüedeger comes to woo her she wears everyday clothes, to display her mourning, while her attendants wear their finest, to display her wealth (Nbl:1225).

Tristan and Isolt also exploit the political effect of clothing. When Tristan appears before the Irish court he is very careful that his clothing, as well as that of Marke's barons, should make a splendid impression (GTr:10747–55, 10839–44). When Isolt endures her ordeal she dons the garb of a penitent; we recognize this as yet another aspect of her deception, but the crowd accepts the clothing as an accurate indication of her spiritual condition and is moved to pity (GTr:15656–67). This same kind of calculation is employed by the narrator as well: he does not provide the full-scale description of Tristan's and Isolt's clothes when we first see them, as we might expect, but saves this for their first appearance together in public, just before they set sail for Cornwall (GTr:10900–85, 11098–141). This calculating use of clothing is foreign to Arthurian romance; were it admissible it would have to be considered below under multiplication of cause. Instead we find in our works a straightforward correspondence between the clothing and the essential condition of a character. What Wirnt says of Florie – 'so was diu juncvrouwe gekleit nach ir rehte harte wol' (W:743–4) – can in fact be assumed for all Arthurian characters. They are clothed strictly according to their nature. The only exceptions (Enite, for example) reflect the compositional or thematic designs of the romance itself not the conscious intentions of the characters within the romance story.

But assigning an outfit or another material accessory is not the only technique by which a character can be differentiated in Arthurian romance. Often someone will be set in surroundings that, like clothing, visualize some of his or her essential qualities: from the portrayal of Lanzelet's childhood with the water fay we learn that he, by nature, can never be sad (L:234–40); when Iwein goes mad, this is made graphic by placing him helpless in the forest; the same is true when Gwigalois suffers a moment of self-doubt (W:5791–840). These scenes are exceptional, for the hero is seldom passive out in the woods. Much more common are those scenes in which the hero is shown as part of society, either just before the opponent appears with a challenge or at a concluding celebration. These are reminders that society is the hero's true home. The Other, however, *is* at home in the woods, and some mention of his or her natural habitat almost invariably accompanies him or her. Before Parzival speaks with Sigune for the last time, he comes upon 'eine klosen niuwes buwes' (P:435,7); the recluse is set in her hermitage. Before Erec fights Mabonagrin, he sees a large circle of stakes with heads upon them (E:8769–74); the fierce opponent is surrounded by his trophies. Malduc lives in the middle of the Genibeleter Se (L:7158–65); the magician is surrounded by his magic. The narrator too can achieve differentiation from the environment in which he is placed. Wolfram, for instance, reveals his own poverty by mentioning the situation in his own home, where even the mice must steal their food (P:185,3).

Not only characters but whole episodes are differentiated by the background in which they are set. The conditions of Lanzelet's captivity and release from Schatel le Mort are determined by its nature, which is explained to us just before Lanzelet enters (L:3542–9). The major part of *Wigalois* is determined by the magical topography of the land of Korntin. These are episodes in magical surroundings. The 'Sperberkampf' in *Erec* on the other hand must, according to its specifications, take place before a large crowd (E:191–9). Similarly a good deal of the effect of Cundrie's attack on Parzival derives from its being delivered before society; indeed she first addresses Arthur himself. We should note that the differentiation of characters, setting, and event is reciprocal. The nature of Schatel le Mort reflects on Mabuz and determines the behaviour of Lanzelet when he enters it; yet the castle itself is differentiated by the peculiar nature of its lord and by the example of Lanzelet's behaviour. Similarly Cundrie's denunciation depends for its effect on the presence of Arthur and his court; yet the court itself is differentiated by the way in which it reacts to such a denunciation.

Just as a change of clothing will mark a change in the nature of a character, so a change of venue will signal the beginning of a new episode. Lanzelet wins Iblis by fighting Iwaret at a spring with a gong that has to be struck three times: those are the conditions, as we were told in advance by the abbot (L:3884–909), of the *aventiure* by which Iblis is to be won. Iblis and Lanzelet declare their love immediately after the combat, but their love is not consummated until they move off to another location. This is the spot to which the messenger of Lanzelet's foster mother brings a magic tent, richly ornamented with jewels, marvellous images, and citations from Ovid. The new location, beautiful in its own right, and the magic tent characterize the new episode, in which Lanzelet and Iblis are united and in which Lanzelet learns his name. Such changes of scenery regularly mark episodic divisions. Each setting determines the action that takes place within it, and the different effects of different settings make for episodes of different character.

In some cases placing a character in a setting begins a process of regressive differentiation. A giant appears at King Arthur's and delivers a challenge from King Matur (D:440–810), about whom we know nothing except through the description of the land he rules. This land, Cluse, contains many wonderful features, among them the parasol-bird, *babian* (D:550–74), and elephants who bear *feste* on their backs (D:585–634). Thus Matur is differentiated by his land, which is differentiated by its elephants, which are differentiated by the *feste* they bear. Each particular description is itself a signifier that adds meaning to the feature of which it is a component,[22] and the cumulative effect of this regressive differentiation adds meaning to the challenge itself: Matur is an opponent to be reckoned with.

The same techniques are employed in the battle scenes from *Erec* and *Garel* that we just considered. Erec's fight with Guivreiz lasts three hours; this fact reflects back on the combatants who are able to sustain such a fight. Garel's speak 'was groz und unbesniten' (G:3571); the size of the spear reflects the strength of the knight who wields it. In every case the description is offered not for its own sake but for what it reveals of something else. As Edmond Faral puts it: 'The idea seems to be secondary; in fact, it is of considerable importance. This explains why, throughout medieval literature, description aims only very rarely at depicting people or things objectively and why it is always dominated by an affective intent that fluctuates between praise and blame.'[23] Or, as Paul Zumthor writes, 'The descriptive intent is not – at least is not primarily – to "imitate reality" but to suggest the significance of things.'[24]

To be sure, 'the significance of things' is sometimes presented in straightforward ways: Oringles is 'ein edel herre' (E:6118); Laudamie is 'diu schoenste und diu beste' (G:7347). This is also static differentiation. But such attributions are so vague as to be almost meaningless. Since virtually all of Arthurian manhood is noble and virtually all of Arthurian womanhood is beautiful and good, calling someone noble or beautiful differentiates him or her in no way from other realizations of the functions O^- or O^+. More distinct differentiation is accomplished, as we have seen, by contiguity. We remember Florie not because of her 'groziu schoene' (W:951) or because she 'was riche' (W:953) but because of her unusually rich clothing, in which her beauty and wealth are made manifest. As we have seen, differentiation by contiguity is active at many levels: the woman is defined by the dress she wears; the knight by the place where he was born; the encounter by the space in which it takes place. In every case characters, settings, and material props reflect on one another and reveal to us something of their significance by the static relations they sustain with each other. Differentiation by contiguity is differentiation in the long run. It tends to establish an unchanging quality of that which is differentiated: we learn the nature of Florie or the nature of the events that occur in Schatel le Mort. Guivreiz's choice of words in the passage cited above reflects this static quality of differentiation by contiguity: he does not say that Erec's nature '*wirt* an zwein dingen schin' but that it '*ist* an zwein dingen schin.'

Active Differentiation

In the midst of Garel's fight with Eskilabon, the narrator pauses to reflect on the trouble that Garel has caused himself by picking the flowers in Eskilabon's garden:

> da von ze striten im geschach
> mit dem allerküensten man,
> der ritter namen ie gewan.
> daz wart wol schin an dem tage
> mit manegem ellenthaften slage,
> den er uf minen hern Garelen sluoc.
> den schilt, den er ze scherme truoc,
> den howet er im ze stucken gar. 					(G:3670–7)

Such scenes, in which a character is differentiated by what he or she does, are common in Arthurian romance. True, der Pleiaere tells us some things in a straightforward way: to fight with Eskilabon is to fight 'mit dem allerküensten man, der ritter namen ie gewan,' but this is no more useful than knowing that Laudamie was 'diu schoenste und diu beste.' Eskilabon's valour is not tangible for us until we can perceive its effect on Garel's shield.

Differentiation of character on the basis of an action he or she performs can take several forms. In the example just given from *Garel*, Eskilabon is characterized by a single action. He is defined as well by a customary action: he fights anyone who breaks the flowers in his garden. In *Daniel*, Matur is also differentiated by a customary action: he has divided his entire country into seven groups each of which jousts one day per week (D:648–68). Our admiration for Matur is increased by his custom of daily tourneys. Mabuz kills one of his captives whenever he is angry (L:3560–3); Trevrizent eats only raw roots (P:485,21–486,12); a knight in *Wigalois* will only offer hospitality to those who have defeated him in battle (W:1940–53): in each case a character is differentiated by a customary action.

Finally, a character can achieve differentiation by performing a traditional symbolic action. Iwein, for example, rode up to a castle

> und vant beslozzen daz tor,
> und einen knappen da vor.

der erkande wol sins herren muot:
sin herre was biderbe unde guot,
daz wart wol an dem knappen schin:
er hiez in willekomen sin
ze guoter handelunge.   (I:5579–85)

There follows a description of the *guotiu handelunge*, the welcome by the lord of the castle and the disarming of Iwein. We can assume that, had Iwein not been gravely wounded, he would have been invited *vrouwen schouwen*, feted at dinner, and accompanied to bed. We feel free to make this assumption because we have witnessed so many proper welcomes, and we have learned of what they are composed.

We have witnessed so many welcomes not because the series of actions itself is so fascinating but because of what the actions as a group signify. When Enite's father welcomes Erec, or when Galagandreiz welcomes Lanzelet, or Gurnemanz Parzival, the host shows by his proper welcome that he is a worthy member of courtly society and that he takes his guest for the same. By the questionable welcome that Vergulaht offers Gawan (P:399,25–403,9) he shows himself a less worthy member of courtly society. We read Vergulaht's welcome as a sign that we can expect, within the romance, a less-than-courtly sequel and, from another level, that the author has tired of the conventional formula and turned to parody.

In every case, whether a character is differentiated by a single action, a customary action, or a symbolic action, we are dealing with a system that has two levels. On one level the actions can be of interest in their own right: the welcome Gurnemanz accords Parzival is unusually rich and gracious. Here the action is the signified. On another level, however, the actions themselves are of interest only to the extent that the whole action differentiates character: Gurnemanz shows by his welcome that he is an estimable and courteous man. Here the action is the signifier. The two levels work together to give substance to the elements of the episodic skeleton. An action of the type we have been considering reveals a relatively stable quality of a character, rather like static differentiation, yet at the same time this significant action becomes part of the plot of the episode.[25]

Differentiation by Multiplication

Erec's fight with Guivreiz and Garel's fight with Eskilabon are both episodes of the same basic type ($W/I \rightarrow W/O^-/I \rightarrow W/O^+/I \rightarrow S/O^+/I$ or W/I

→ S/O⁻/I → S/O⁺/I → S/O⁺/I), and, as we have seen, both fights follow
the same skeletal action pattern; yet the two episodes cannot be confused. To a certain extent we distinguish them on the basis of the static
and active differentiation of the characters involved: Guivreiz is a valiant
dwarf; Eskilabon customarily fights anyone who picks the flowers in his
garden. To a greater extent, however, we find the episodes different
because of various additions to the skeletal patterns. The number of
actors can be increased: Erec is accompanied by Enite, Garel by Gilan.
Additional points of view can be introduced: Enite watches Erec and
Guivreiz; Garel and Eskilabon fight before an audience of four hundred
captives. Finally, the characters are said to have particular motivations:
Guivreiz fights first because he is out looking for a fight and then
because Erec impugns his *triuwe*; Eskilabon fights because Garel has
picked his flowers. The technique by which the essential elements of an
Arthurian episode are expanded I call differentiation by multiplication.
There are three sorts: multiplication of actor, multiplication of perspective, and multiplication of cause.

Multiplication of Actor

By Outrider: Midway through his fight with Eskilabon, Garel cuts off the
decorative eagle from atop his opponent's helmet:

> der ar wart ouch gerüeret,
> der uf des wirtes helme stuont.
> dem wart ein slac mit ellen kunt,
> daz er muost rumen den helm.
> er viel verhowen in den melm.
> sin gevider wart verschroten gar.   (G:3648–53)

Since the eagle is merely an extension of Eskilabon, incapable of independent action, it hardly seems to qualify as an actor at all. Yet the eagle's
overthrow prefigures Eskilabon's defeat, and thus the two are at least
symbolically equivalent; the eagle, which might have been merely a synecdoche, momentarily draws our attention away from Eskilabon and in
so doing enriches and differentiates the fight. The eagle, however, even
though it has a short life of its own, cannot sustain any independent
action; bound to suffer Eskilabon's fate along with him, it is merely an
outrider of the principal character.

Outriders – often, unlike Eskilabon's eagle, they are animate creatures – are common in Arthurian romance. Iwein's lion is one, as are
Gauriel's ram and the two leopards that fight alongside Kurion (T:
9105–16, 9254–328). The dwarfs of Iders fil Niut and the Künegin von
Pluris also function as outriders. In such cases, as so often, static and
active differentiation work hand in hand. By virtue of the traditional
meanings associated with the various kinds of outrider (lion, eagle,
dwarf), their mere presence serves to differentiate the nature of the principal (static differentiation, by contiguity); in this sense, attaching a lion
to Iwein differs little from dressing him in armour. The lion differs from
the armour, however, in that the lion in addition to the traditional
meaning it bears also generates action (active differentiation), while the
armour does not. That the action of the outrider is completely dependent
on the will of the principal and cannot take place outside his or her
immediate proximity facilitates the transfer of meaning from the one to
the other. Thus the presence of an outrider reflects, both by its nature
and by its actions, on the character and the actions of the principal,
differentiating him or her from other similar characters.

By Proxy: Garel does not arrive alone at Eskilabon's garden, but in the
company of Gilan von Galis. Gilan had meant to fight Eskilabon himself,
but he came across Garel first, who defeated him, after which the two
became friends. Now, as Eskilabon appears to fight Garel, Eskilabon's
marshal, followed by two others, takes on Gilan. Gilan and 'des wirtes
ritter' are hero and opponent by proxy, and their fight, described just as
the main event is getting underway (G:3586–603), is a miniature version
of that between Garel and Eskilabon. Through the description of the
lesser fight the greater one is summarized and Garel's victory is fore-
shadowed:

> uz Galis der fürste Gilan
> gewalticlichen uf in reit,
> unz er im bot sin sicherheit.
> die nam er und liez im den lip. (G:3588–91)

Although Gilan's defeat of 'des wirtes ritter' and Garel's cutting off the
eagle on Eskilabon's helmet both prefigure Garel's victory over his opponent, Eskilabon's marshal and his eagle are not auxiliaries of the same
type. The eagle, as we have noted, is simply an extension of the knight
who wears the helmet, but the marshal takes the place of Eskilabon and

fights just as his lord would have. The function O⁻ has been temporarily transferred from Eskilabon to the marshal, just as the function I has for the moment been delegated to Gilan.

In this instance from *Garel* both the hero and his opponent have proxies, but this is not always the case. In the fight for Pelrapeire, for instance, a single hero, Parzival, must do battle with both Clamide and his auxiliary, Kingrun. In *Tandareis* the multiplication is carried further. In connection with his defeat of the giant Karedoz the single hero must overcome four auxiliaries of his opponent: a series of three gigantic gate-keepers before the main engagement and one normal-sized gatekeeper afterwards. In other cases a single opponent must fight both the hero and his auxiliaries: in *Iwein* Ascalon fights both the true hero, Iwein, and his forerunner, Kalogrenant. Kalogrenant is one of the class of 'false heroes,' those who fail in the attempt to do that which the hero later achieves; their failure serves to heighten the effect of the hero's success. This device is used quite extravagantly in the episode from *Garel* where, we are told, Eskilabon has already defeated and imprisoned four hundred. Report of the failures of false heroes can be condensed until it verges on simple description, as in the introductory remarks about Guivreiz:

[Guivreiz] hate unverzaget
den pris an manegem man bejaget:
dar umbe man noch von im seit
daz im an siner manheit
unz an den tac nie misselanc.   (E:4306–10)

A proxy for a hero or an opponent is always able to generate some action of his or her own. This might be a scene in a longer episode (Gilan), or an entire episode (Kalogrenant), or even, as hero in his own right, a series of episodes (Gawan in *Parzival*).[26] Invariably these auxiliary scenes and episodes illuminate the activities of the hero. In *Lanzelet*, for instance, Galagandreiz's daughter, before turning to Lanzelet himself, offers her love to Kuraus and Orphilet. Her speeches to them and their rejections present all of the issues involved: her burning desire, Galagandreiz's treatment of her, their obligations to their host. Thus when she turns to Lanzelet and he accepts her proposal even before she utters it we lose nothing, since the implications of the action have been spelled out for us in advance. The false heroes differentiate the action of the hero.

Multiplication of actor by proxy provides the means by which two standard Arthurian episode types, tournament and battle, are generated.

Full-scale tournaments occur in six romances: once in *Erec* (E:2222–851), once in *Lanzelet* (L:2595–694, 2760–3501), twice in *Parzival* (P:59,1–97,12, 339,12–391,4), once in *Diu Crone* (C:17522–18585), in a series of three in *Tandareis* (T:12740–13222, 13496–990, 14084–428), and twice in *Wigamur* (Wm:1974–2457, 4656–5310). (The anonymous 'schefte brechen und ritterliche stechen' [D:8183–4] that usually accompany a courtly celebration do not constitute a tourney but are merely a necessary component of a proper *hochzit*.) A tournament seems to imply a particular skeletal action. First it is agreed upon, then announced by pages wandering through the countryside. When the hero arrives he lodges apart from the rest of the knights. He is either unknown to the rest (Lanzelet, Gahmuret, Gawein) or to himself (Wigamur [Wm:2261]), disguised (Tandareis), or untried as a jouster (Erec). Considerable attention is given the hero's armour (Lanzelet, Erec, and Tandareis, like Cligés, each have three sets in different colours). The hero is the champion of a lady, but this fact is kept hidden. The contest itself usually consists of a *vesperie* (a kind of narrative proxy of the tournament itself) and at least one day of the tourney proper (in *Lanzelet* and *Parzival* the tournament is cut short because the hero's great valour has rendered further fighting senseless). After the fighting the hero rejoins or is joined by his lady in the presence of a large company. The revelation of that for which the hero has been fighting (or his refusal of that for which he was ostensibly fighting, *Wigamur*) occasions considerable surprise (except in *Erec*) or dismay.

From the perspective of romance society a tournament consists of a contest between two large groups of knights, each of which wants to capture as many as possible of the opposition or drive it from the field. From the perspective of the romance itself, however, a tournament is fought so that the hero can distinguish himself both against a collection of opponents (multiplication of actor: opponents by proxy) and in comparison with his allies (multiplication of actor: false heroes). Notice that whenever the real hero pauses to rest, his compatriots are pushed to the brink of defeat (E:2630–50; L:3260–82; P:78,25–9; C:18476–90; T:13890–8). Thus we see that a tourney, even though jousts in which the hero does not take part are often mentioned, exists solely for the hero. He arrives unknown or untried, wins the admiration of all, and is united with his lady. As Hartman says of Erec: 'si namen alle sin eines war' (E:2470).

Battles, like tournaments, also depend for their realization on the extravagant multiplication of actor: here O⁻ and I each turn into a huge army. Although there are a number of near battles in Arthurian romance – Lanzelet assembles an army but does not need to employ it (L:8050–

105); Iwein (I:3703–77) and Meleranz (M:8501–631) lead armies, but we are scarcely aware of them; Arthur's forces must defend themselves from attack while passing Logrois (P:664,18–665,24); Gahmuret (P:36,3–42,6) and Tandareis (T:2124–882) achieve victories over beseiging armies by a number of individual combats – the corpus includes only four full-scale battles: in *Wigalois* (W:9799–11284), in *Daniel* (D:2969–3858, 5000–807), in *Garel* (G:10797–15989), and in *Wigamur* (Wm:2540–3328). A battle differs from a tournament and from other types of episode in many ways: it is an affair of state rather than a service of love;[27] jousts serve only as introduction to the fighting rather than as the principal form of engagement; one seeks to kill his opponent, not merely to exact *sicherheit*;[28] there is no courtly audience; the leaders of each army regularly solicit advice from their deputies; the preparation for the engagement can be described at great length; each side is organized into units that are paired off one against the other.[29]

   With regard to the technique of multiplication of actor, battles reveal one particularly surprising feature: the number of other actors becomes so great that the hero himself tends to disappear. The portrayal of a battle regularly alternates between the description of individual combats and mass fighting; since the hero will not be the only individual fighter portrayed, this alternation necessarily restricts the amount of time he is before our eyes. Some authors, however, go beyond this necessary restriction and reduce the hero's importance to such an extent that his role is undermined altogether. In *Daniel*, for example, King Arthur fights the first joust with the opposing king, Matur, and kills him at once; this begins a four-day engagement in which both Arthur and Daniel distinguish themselves but which is finally won by a trick thought up by Daniel; Daniel receives the kingdom and Matur's widow, but they are bestowed on him by Arthur acting on the advice of his council. The importance of Arthur and Daniel is so evenly matched that one could not say with any assurance whether Arthur or Daniel is the hero of the battle. In *Wigalois* the hero's role is even further reduced. As soon as preparations for the campaign against Lion get under way Gwigalois delegates responsibility to Gawein (W:10424–37): Gawein determines what is needed; he deploys the forces; and he fights the crucial battle with Lion. Gwigalois merely takes the first resolve, appears a few times in battle, and watches one of the enemy portals – along with Gawein!

   Battles, then, turn out to be the precise opposite of tournaments. Although both are generated by multiplication of actor, the large number of extras in a tournament serves to highlight the hero's prowess, while in a battle the masses tend to force the hero off into the wings. Such a formulation reveals that, although tournaments are a natural elaboration of the skeletal Arthurian episode, battles are foreign imports. Ordinarily we expect the hero to dominate each episode; indeed the connection of one episode to another, and thus the coherence of the whole romance, depends on the hero's constant pre-eminence. Whereas in tournaments this pre-eminence is exaggerated, in battles the hero tends to disappear. As a result, battles undermine one of the conventional functions of the hero.

Battle episodes, atypical from a strictly Arthurian standpoint, have doubtless been strongly influenced by the traditions of heroic poetry: in *Garel*, the lists of heroes on both sides that precede the battle remind one of similar scenes in *Das Buch von Bern*; in *Wigalois*, the role of 'her Gawein, der des heres pflac' (W:10764) resembles that of Rüedeger in the *Rabenschlacht*, who organizes Dietrich's forces and even gives orders to Dietrich himself.[30] Helmut Brall has these relations in mind when he says of *Daniel*, 'The peculiarity of Stricker's Arthurian romance lies primarily in his combination of heterogeneous kinds of representation, taken from genres that are traditionally kept strictly differentiated: the heroic epic and the courtly romance of adventure.'[31] These same generic distinctions are familiar to Lion, whose outrage against Amire and Liamere leads to the battle in *Wigalois*. When he hears that an army led by Gwigalois and a selection of famous Arthurian heroes is marching against him, he retorts, 'hie enist niht aventiure' (W:10182); here, he means to say, the Arthurian heroes will not find that artificial kind of encounter they are used to. Indeed they do not; they find a full-scale battle. Yet they manage to win the battle none the less, and Lion is killed in the process. Let us not make Lion's mistake and underestimate the flexibility of our heroes; nor should we join those scholars who prescribe generic restrictions that Arthurian authors clearly did not acknowledge.[32] Battles are unusual in Arthurian romance and differ essentially from other kinds of Arthurian episode, yet they are liable to turn up nevertheless.

One final variety of proxy is of considerable importance in Arthurian romance, that by which the principal narrator delegates his function to a character in the story itself. Ivreins tells Erec about the 'joie de la curt'; Kalogrenant narrates his adventure at Ascalon's well; Lanzelet learns about Iwaret's *aventiure* from a 'wizzic abbas' (L:3832); Trevrizent explains a number of crucial points to Parzival; Lar tells Gwigalois about the land of Korntin; the Frouwe von der Grüenen Ouwe recounts to Daniel the history of her land: in every case a character relates a story or relays information, and we, rather than hearing this information from the perspective of the principal narrator, hear it from that of the characters in the story. Often these secondary narrators serve to multiply perspective or cause, yet the precondition for these services is their existence as multiples of the principal narrator. To be sure, the relation between the principal narrator and his auxiliaries does not exactly parallel that between a character and his or her proxy: Hartman and Kalogrenant are isolated at different levels of the story and could not possibly talk with one another, while Garel and Gilan are friends and undertake adventures together. Still the possibility of introducing auxiliary narrators provides an important technique by which one episode is differentiated from another.

In spite of their various relations to the principal actors (Trevrizent is Parzival's uncle; Lar is Gwigalois's father-in-law), the auxiliary narrators listed above exist primarily to convey information. Their stories are not meant to serve the interests of a particular party but merely to inform. We must distinguish these disinterested proxies from the large and important group who actively serve the interests of the major actors. A messenger from his foster mother reveals Lanzelet's name; Lunete accuses Iwein at Arthur's court; Nereja solicits aid for the dispossessed Larie; a giant delivers to Arthur the demands of Matur, and another, Karabin, the challenge of Ekunaver: in each case the messenger delivers information but does so as partisan proxy, fully identified with the interests of his or her principal.

Arthurian romance loves auxiliary narrators and partisan messengers and relies on them for the transmission of much crucial information. In this it differs from works in the Tristan tradition. Morolt delivers his challenge himself; Eilhart's Tristrant serves as his own messenger at the conclusion of the 'Waldleben.' Gottfried's Tristan knows directly from Morolt that his wound must be cured in Ireland and from his own experience that Marke's wife must be sought there; in Eilhart the trips to Ireland are accomplished by fate working through the agency of bad weather. In no case is motivating information conveyed by an auxiliary character. In Gottfried such information comes to Queen Isolt and Marjodo in dreams (GTr:9298–305, 13511–36) and to Tristan via an anonymous 'lantmaere' (GTr:18443–5, 18714–19). Gottfried's Rual functions as messenger when he arrives at Tintajel, as do Marke's hunter when he reports his discovery of the lovers' cave and Curvenal when he conveys the king's pardon to them; yet Rual is more than a mere proxy, the hunter is messenger by accident, and Curvenal's embassy is reported but not portrayed (GTr:17682–93). In all versions Tristan serves as Marke's messenger in wooing Isolt; yet his essential role as hero prevails and subverts his temporary function as proxy. Perhaps it was the example of this famous subversive messenger that made the Tristan tradition so chary of messengers in general.

As we have seen before, the Tristan tradition approaches Arthurian romance most closely in the episodic second half of Eilhart's work. Here a priest named Michel tells Tristrant about the sad fate of Havelin (ETr:5505–82), Piloise is sent as messenger by Isalde to effect a reconciliation with Tristrant (ETr:7127–437), and a merchant is dispatched by the dying Tristrant to fetch his beloved (ETr:9256–335). Yet these few instances are not enough to upset the basic distinction: the communications network of Arthurian romance relies in large part on the kind offices of auxiliary narrators and messengers; in the Tristan romances information is conveyed by the principal characters themselves, arrives in dreams and by anonymous word of mouth, or is rendered unnecessary by the inscrutable workings of fate.

In the examples of Arthurian multiplication of actor that we have considered – the fall of Eskilabon's eagle, the presence of Gilan, battles, tournaments, messengers, and narrators by proxy – a role that is derived from one of the essential functional components of the episodic skeleton (O⁻: opponent; I: hero; and, at another level, M: narrator) is filled by more than one character: the principal actor is accompanied by one or more auxiliaries. The presence of these auxiliaries reflects on the character of the principal and, perhaps more important, gives each episode a distinctive profile.

Multiplication of Perspective

Immediately after Garel and Eskilabon exchange challenges we leave the battlefield:

> von dem palas daz man sach,
> waz von den helden da geschach.
> ritter unde vrowen
> die wolten gerne schowen,
> wer da bejaget hohen pris.
> Alexander und Floris
> die pruoften dise beide,

die man uf der heide
so ritterlichen halden sach.
...
die ritter alle jahen,
daz si nie gesahen
zwen man so schone ze velde komen.
von al den frowen wart vernomen,
daz si des selben jahen,
do si die ritter sahen.
nu sach man dise viere
zesamen komen schiere.   (G:3527–35, 3547–54)

Such shifts of perspective are frequent in *Garel*. Often, as in the last two lines cited above, the formula *man sach* seems superfluous (G:3560, 3563, 3585, 3592, etc.): that the four knights were *seen* approaching one another tells us little more than that they approached. Frequently, however, the change in perspective adds an extra dimension to the main event. We learn in the lines given above, for instance, of the active involvement of the prisoners, especially of those we know most about, Alexander and Floris. In addition we get their testimony as to the praiseworthiness of Garel and Eskilabon. Later the intensity of the fight is mirrored in the expectation of the onlookers that one of the contestants will surely be killed (G:3710–11).

When we join the captives in Eskilabon's castle we gain a second perspective on the fight: to the ever-present point of view of the narrator has been added that of an internal onlooker. A bit later we are enabled to witness the fight from a third point of view as well, that of the participants. Of Eskilabon we are told, 'der want, er solt den sic bejagen' (G:3691); and near the end of the fight Garel says, 'ich waene dich ze lange her geheien han' (G:3720–1): in each case we get an evaluation of the fight from one of the combatants. In *Erec*, after the hero tries to evade Guivreiz's challenge on the basis of his long ride and great exertions, Guivreiz thinks to himself, 'er ist verzaget, sit er sine arbeit klaget' (E:4366–7). This is the way Guivreiz interprets Erec's reaction, but thanks to the narrator we know otherwise: Erec reacted as he did not from cowardice but 'durch sinen spot' (E:4348). The point is not that Guivreiz was wrong – as was Eskilabon in expecting to win – but that the action increases in meaning as we witness it from various points of view.[33]

Although the number of basic Arthurian situations is quite small, the participants view these situations in different ways, and we, as a result, also perceive them differently. Gauriel, for instance, establishes himself on the outskirts of Arthur's camp and hopes thereby to entice the knights of the Round Table to come out and fight him. Daniel does the same thing, as do Joram in *Wigalois* and, in spite of himself, Parzival while entranced by the blood drops in the snow. In *Daniel* and *Wigalois* we know nothing about these challengers until we watch them defeat, one by one, the most celebrated Arthurian heroes. In *Gauriel*, however, one of Arthur's knights has seen the challenger before and tells of his great prowess. The knight was so impressed that he refuses to accept Gauriel's challenge: 'nu lat mich sin einen zagen unt vart hin zuo dem selben man' (GM:679–80). A hundred lines later, however, this 'zage' jousts five times with Gauriel without being unseated, and they fight with swords until darkness forces them to stop – which is doing a good deal better than those who ridiculed him. The knight's earlier speech turns out not to have been a sign of cowardice at all but merely a device by which our estimation of Gauriel's valour is increased. That a brave knight can be temporarily transformed into a coward simply in order to multiply the perspective shows again how the needs of the romance take precedence over the dictates of courtly ideology or latter-day notions of consistency.

While the perspective of a single participant can be revealed in a monologue (D:3960–76), conflicting points of view in Arthurian romance are most often expressed in dialogue. By comparing the actual challenge in our two test scenes we will be able to see the effect of such multiple-perspective dialogues. In *Garel* the challenge is reported in the simplest way possible: 'ietwederhalp wart widerseit' (G:3526). We do not hear the combatants exchange a word until near the end of their fight when Garel expresses his impatience with the length of time it is taking for him to win. In *Erec*, on the other hand, the challenge is expanded into a dialogue nearly as long as the fight itself. Strictly speaking this dialogue is superfluous, for Erec and Guivreiz, like Garel and Eskilabon, are going to fight regardless of what is said. This is required by the functional structure of an Arthurian episode or, if you prefer, by the obligation of knights off in search of adventure to take on all comers. Yet the words that Erec and Guivreiz exchange give their fight an ostensible motivation that differentiates it from other similar contests. The passage begins with Guivreiz's perception of Erec, in which, as we saw above, he classifies Erec according to his clothes and his companion (E:4326–40). This leads directly into the formal challenge (E:4341–7). From Guivreiz's point of view the situation is unambiguous: since Erec is a knight they must fight.

But Erec refuses the challenge, thereby blocking the expected continuation of the scene. Instead he accuses Guivreiz of violating his *triuwe* by wanting to fight a man he has just greeted. Furthermore, Erec doesn't see any need to fight since he hasn't done a thing to Guivreiz and is exhausted besides. Erec here wilfully – the narrator's 'durch sinen spot' (E:4348) is a crucial bit of information for understanding the perspective – assumes a surprising, unorthodox position. He pretends to believe that two knights need not, indeed should not, necessarily fight. Guivreiz, not privy to Erec's intent as we are, interprets Erec's remarks from his own perspective as a sign of cowardice – which, according to normal courtly standards, they are. Indeed Guivreiz defines the assumption of his courtly perspective – the greeting is merely ancillary to the challenge – and sharpens the challenge in two ways: by objecting to Erec's impugnation of his *triuwe* and by mentioning Enite. The dialogue then is carried on from two contrary perspectives: the 'standard,' courtly one of Guivreiz and the capricious, individual one of Erec. From the opposition of these two points of view a secondary, ostensible motivation for their fight is developed, the affront to Guivreiz's *triuwe*.

There are many memorable dialogues in Arthurian romance: Lunete and Laudine debate marriage with Iwein; Trevrizent instructs Parzival; Walwein tries to convince Lanzelet to come to Arthur's court. In none of them does anything really happen. What seems like an essential furthering of the action – persuasion, instruction, invitation – in fact *retards* the inevitable result. The Arthurian form *requires* Laudine to marry Iwein; Parzival *must* return to God if he is to attain the grail; Walwein and Lanzelet are *bound* to fight. These dialogues arrest the forward movement of the narrative so that a given situation (constellation of functions) can be viewed from several points of view, each of which reveals a different aspect of the situation. In effect such a scene has more than the minimal number of dimensions. The different features we see from each of these several perspectives give a scene its own special contours and differentiate it from other similar scenes.[34]

Multiplication of Cause

The dialogue between Guivreiz and Erec produces an ostensible reason to fight – Erec's disparagement of Guivreiz's *triuwe* – but at the same time disguises the real reason. This real reason, rooted in the nature of the genre, is simply that Arthurian episodes are formed around the transformation $O^- \rightarrow O^+$ and that therefore the hero will fight and defeat any opponent he comes across. Guivreiz himself understands the redundancy of all other motivation, maintaining that his greeting and the rest of his speech were merely expedients: 'daz enhan ich anders niht getan wan uf ritterschefte wan' (E:4370–1). Essentially all Arthurian combats are like the one between Parzival and Gramoflanz: they spot one another and begin their joust 'e daz deweder ie wort zem andern gespraeche' (P:703,30–704,1). Their fight, an involuntary reflex triggered by the sight of another armed knight, is the simple reflection of the generic necessity, $O^-/I \rightarrow O^+/I$.[35]

Yet most Arthurian combats, unlike the fight between Parzival and Gramoflanz, include some explanation for what is going on that is credible to our everyday logic. In some cases this ostensible cause functions as mechanically as Parzival's reaction to Gramoflanz. The fight with Eskilabon, for instance, is occasioned by Garel's picking the flowers in Eskilabon's garden. This, as we have already been told three times (G:2692–752, 3181–92, 3342–49), is the way to challenge Eskilabon. Lanzelet's adventure at Pluris and Iwein's fight with Ascalon are triggered by similar mechanisms. This automatic trigger can be reduced to a single phrase, as when Guivreiz says to Erec, 'wert iuch durch iuwer schoenez wip' (E:4376). Theoretically the mere mention of a knight's lady will cause him to do whatever you wish. Later, when Guivreiz begs for mercy, he again invokes Erec's lady (E:4444).

In many cases the apparent motivation is internalized, thereby making the characters seem to act of their own free will: Erec answers Guivreiz 'durch sinen spot' (E:4348) and holds his shield up 'mit listen' (E:4410); after Eskilabon begs for mercy, Garel reasons to himself for sixteen lines before deciding to grant the request (G:3767–82). Intent and desire are also attributed to Arthurian characters: after Erec defeats Guivreiz 'er wolde in erslagen han' (E:4441); in fighting Garel, Eskilabon 'wolt erwerben ... ein phant für sin liehten bluomen glanz' (G:3644–5); Erec and Guivreiz are said to have long sought as taxing an opponent as they now find in each other (E:4399–403).

Often some courtly precept will be given as the ostensible motivation for a character's action: Gauriel goes off into the woods 'durch aventiure spehen' (GM:3149); Iwein defends Lunete out of *triuwe* (I:4342); Guivreiz challenges Erec with the phrase, 'durch iuwer schoenez wip' (E: 4376). The obligation to seek adventure, to demonstrate *triuwe*, and to abide by the conventions of romance love are all part of the official Arthurian ideology. Among the various types of multiplication of cause derived from Arthurian ideology, those related to women have the greatest effect on the substance of the story. The presence of Enite at every one of Erec's adventures; the contempt of Nereja for Gwigalois during his long trip to Roimunt; the love that Orgeluse sparks in Gawan in spite of her mockery: these all function as ostensible causes for a series of adventures. At the same time the presence of these women (incarnate causes) in episodes in which they are not directly involved significantly expands the essential structural composition of the episode. Multiplication of cause and multiplication of actor work together.

We have already discussed a number of instances where the dictates of courtly ideology are sacrificed to the needs of romance (Lanzelet disobeys Iblis; Arthur will not serve breakfast; the brave knight appears cowardly), yet we cannot overlook the much more frequent coincidence of an ostensible motivation with the Arthurian precepts. Indeed, scholars could not have posited a 'ritterliches Tugendsystem' had not a small number of related ideas been so often advanced. Jonathan Culler, in discussing his 'third level *vraisemblance*,' speaks of 'a set of literary norms to which texts may be related and by virtue of which they become meaningful and coherent.'[36] He maintains further that 'each genre designates certain kinds of action as acceptable and excludes others: ... each genre constitutes a special *vraisemblance* of its own.'[37] The Arthurian ideology establishes the norms according to which our genre becomes coherent, and it designates which actions appear verisimilar. Neither the calculated murder of Sifrit nor the retreat of Tristan and Isolt from society would seem plausible in Arthurian romance. When Gauriel goes off 'durch aventiure spehen,' however, we find it very natural because it accords with the conventions of Arthurian verisimilitude.

A character's free will or the obligations of Arthurian ideology often appear as motivations for particular actions; they are also adduced as causal explanations for entire episodes. Indeed one could easily establish a classification of Arthurian episodes according to the type of cause that is said to initiate them. One would need only about a dozen headings. There are, for example, episodes in which the hero rescues someone (Erec saves Cadoc; Lanzelet saves Ginover; Gauriel rescues the daughter of Asterian) and those in which a hero must himself escape (Lanzelet fights Galagandreiz and Linier; Iwein, the giants at the site of the 'pesme aventure'). There are episodes where a hero wants to right an injustice (Iwein defends the daughter of the Grave von dem Swarzen Dorne; Gwigalois fights the horse thief and attacks Lion) and those in which he makes amends for a wrong he himself has committed (Iwein rescues Lunete; Parzival fights Orilus). There are episodes which the hero undertakes simply because a challenge presents itself, and he, out of knightly principle, cannot refuse (Lanzelet kisses the serpent; Parzival fights Feirefiz; Garel fights Gilan), and episodes in which the hero simply wants something (Parzival wants Ither's armour; Gwigalois fights for dinner and to capture a dog). Note that the class of cause on which the episode is felt to depend has no necessary relation to the type of combat that follows: Erec battles giants to rescue Cadoc; Lanzelet fights a trial by combat to rescue Ginover; Gauriel must overcome all sorts of magic to rescue the daughter of Asterian.

In considering motivation and causality one must distinguish carefully between skeleton and substance. On the level of the episodic skeleton, and in the skeletal action as well, motivation plays absolutely no role. As Propp says: 'One may observe in general that the feelings and intentions of the dramatis personae do not have an effect on the course of action in any instances at all.'[38] Lanzelet seems to recognize the essential irrelevance of his own intentions when he says, 'ez geschiht niht wan daz sol geschehen' (L:6955), a sentiment that is echoed by Gawein and the narrator in Diu Crone (C:7216, 11037).[39] Nothing that a mere character might have in mind can alter the structural determinism of Arthurian romance. Adventures are *bound* to happen regardless of the ways they are explained into existence.

On the level of the realized skeleton, however, at the level of the romance story itself, we have to recognize the importance that the genre accords causal explanations.[40] To be sure, we can recall many instances where the ostensible cause is embarrassingly implausible (why does Iwein overstay the deadline set by Laudine?) or blatantly inconsistent (why doesn't Walwein know where Lanzelet is after Lanzelet explicitly told him he was going to Pluris?). Yet we dare not underestimate the significance of the apparent motivation when one is given. Parzival fights Ither for his armour; he fights Orilus to repair an injustice; and he fights Feirefiz for love of Condwiramurs and devotion to the grail: by virtue of its ostensible motivation each of these combats attains its special significance. If we mean to interpret Parzival – if, that is, we hope to establish the significance of its component parts and their relations – then we must account for the various motivations that are attributed to the hero's actions. The analysis of ostensible motivation will play a crucial role in interpretation. In describing the structure of the Arthurian episode, however, one can limit oneself to defining the general function of romance motivation: by the addition of a secondary, ostensible cause to the generic, hidden cause one Arthurian episode is differentiated from other similar episodes.[41]

It must be evident by now that multiplication of actor, of perspective, and of cause can overlap. In the middle of Erec's fight with Guivreiz, Enite speaks out:

> vil lute schre diu guote:
> 'ouwe, lieber herre min,
> solde ich ez vür iuch sin!
> ja waene ich iuch verlorn han.'   (E:4425–8)

Here all three techniques of differentiation by multiplication are at work: Enite is an outrider (until recently in a very literal sense!) whose fate is entirely dependent on Erec's success; she describes the fight from an additional point of view, letting us know how desperate Erec's situation seemed; and her remarks are ostensibly the immediate cause of Erec's renewed aggressiveness. In Enite's short speech, by means of all three techniques, this one moment of the fight is differentiated from the same moment in Garel's fight with Eskilabon, or in any other similar fight.

The application of these same techniques, incidentally, differentiates the fight between Erec and Guivreiz not only from other fights in other romances; it distinguishes it just as clearly from the equivalent fight in its source. In the French version Enide espies Guivret as he comes careering towards Erec, she warns Erec of the approaching danger, and then Erec

> contre le chevalier s'esmuet
> qui de bataille le semont.
> asanblé sont au chief del pont;
> la s'antre vienent et desfient,
> as fers des lances s'antre anvïent
> anbedui de totes lor forces.   (CE:3756–61)

There is no hint of what the two knights said in challenge and no reason, therefore, to assume that their challenge was anything other than the perfunctory, automatic kind. The multiplication of perspective and cause that Hartmann introduces at this point is entirely lacking in Chrétien. So too is Enite's little speech during the fight, by which Erec is spurred to new vigour. In French she is said to be the very picture of loyal grief, but, though she tears her hair, she utters not a word (CE:3787–94). Thus, from observing her reaction, our view of the fight becomes more differentiated (multiplication of perspective), but since she remains silent the cause of Erec's great bravery remains his secret (no multiplication of cause). Finally, Guivret's submission is motivated in a completely different way: he is overcome only because his sword breaks; he does not invoke Erec's lady; Erec merely pretends to want to kill him (CE:3806–36).

The first fight between Erec and Guivret/Guivreiz occupies the same position in Chrétien's romance as in Hartmann's, and in any structural analysis of the two works it would presumably be found to serve the same function. And yet, because of the very different application of differentiation by multiplication (and I have mentioned only a few of the many differences), we end up with a much different understanding of the episode and its actors when we read it in French than when we read it in German. We see from this example how ostensible cause is irrelevant to the romance skeleton (the two knights are bound to fight) and how it is crucial in the realization of an individual romance (Guivret is not Guivreiz; they act for different reasons).

We began the investigation of episodic syntax with three basic episode types and have continued by noting some of the various ways in which skeletal episodes acquire substance. I suspect that there may be various techniques that I have ignored, and yet I believe mine is a reasonable description both of the skeletal forms of episodes and of the network of techniques by which these skeletal forms become tangible. We have considered so far only those elements that constitute the romance story; we have pursued the investigation, that is, only up to the stage at which everything that can be paraphrased has been included. Now we must move on to the final stage and observe how the narrator transforms the romance story into a narrative and generates the surface we see before us as text.

SURFACE: THE VERBAL FORM OF EPISODES

Consider for a moment the passage that precedes Garel's fight with Gilan (G:2133–204), and compare it with the passage that introduces Parzival's fight with Feirefiz (P:734,1–738,23). In both cases the skeletal action is the same: two knights come upon one another in the woods by chance and, without exchanging a word, begin their joust. And in both cases the same techniques of differentiation are employed: differentiation by contiguity – the knights are characterized by their armour; and multiplication of cause – in the one case they are said to fight out of the desire for *ere*, in the other from devotion to *minne* (and the grail). Yet in spite of these similarities, by the time the jousts begin we have entirely different feelings about, and expectations of, the two episodes. This is due without any doubt to the considerable activity of the narrator in *Parzival* and his reticence in *Garel*: Wolfram is a narrator who makes his presence felt at every opportunity. I propose that we take advantage of Wolfram's forwardness and, by investigating the passage in which he introduces the fight with Feirefiz, try to discover the ways in which a narrator, in transforming an episode as story into narration, moulds our perception of that episode.

The Example of Wolfram (P:734,1–738,23)

The skeletal elements Wolfram has to work with are few: Parzival, riding towards a forest, comes upon Feirefiz; the two see each other and prepare to joust. But Wolfram does not begin with Parzival riding towards the forest. He begins instead with a look forward to the end of the romance and a reminder that he is the only one who can bring us there (P:734,1–9). He recalls thereby his function as mediator and reminds us of his control over the order in which we receive the tale. Wolfram begins his account of Parzival's final combat by claiming full responsibility for what the poeticians call *dispositio*. The assertion of this claim – 'wande ich in dem munde trage daz sloz dirre aventiure' (P:734,6–7) – is all the more telling since it is accompanied by a demonstration. By giving away the end – 'Anfortas wart wol gesunt' (P:734,9) – Wolfram upsets the natural order. In so doing he demonstrates both his control over the disposition of the story and his art in presenting it. Wolfram's behaviour would please Geoffrey of Vinsauf, who holds that it is more artful to begin your narration with the end of the story than with the beginning: 'Nature has placed the end last in order, but art shows deference to it, and, taking up the lowly, raises it on high.'[42]

Having displayed his authority Wolfram might now proceed to the fight, but he does not. Instead he refers a second time to the end of the romance, this time from the point of view of Condwiramurs (P:734,10 –14).[43] At last, in line 16, Wolfram alludes – in general terms – to the coming contest (P:734,16–19), but he turns aside at once (*digressio*) to talk of his own reaction to it and of Parzival's heart. Not until 734,30 –735,8 do we finally receive some concrete information on the promised engagement: Parzival's opponent is a good fighter and a heathen; Parzival comes upon him while riding towards a forest. But Wolfram digresses once again, this time to talk at length about Feirefiz and Parzival and his own difficulties as narrator, before we learn that the two opponents have actually seen each other (P:738,4–5). This news is followed by yet another digression, on hearts and the genetic predisposition to jousting, before Parzival and Feirefiz finally get under way at line 738,24.

One might suppose that the digressions which form such a large part of the passage would be devoted to communicating crucial information about the contestants, but this is true only to a very limited extent. Most of what we hear we have known for thousands of lines: Anfortas is not well; Parzival is brave and chaste; he serves the grail and *minne*; Gahmuret was a fabulous jouster. What we learn about Feirefiz is limited to the following: he is a heathen and an extraordinary fighter; he is devoted to the service of women and rules twenty-five lands; his armour is rich (the *wapenroc* was made at Agremuntin, and he bears an *ezidemon* on his helmet); he has left his army in a harbour and is out looking for adventure. This is all there is to the substance of the episode before Parzival and Feirefiz begin to fight; this, in other words, is the extent to which they are differentiated from other heroes and opponents.

Typically, Wolfram has chosen not to divulge the most important pieces of substantial information about Feirefiz: his name and his relation to Parzival. This is his prerogative as custodian of the *dispositio*, and in spite of appearances his exercise of this prerogative is anything but capricious. We are led to sense Feirefiz's importance in the description of his wealth and power; we suspect something strange is afoot from Wolfram's various laments (P:737,22–4, 738,6–13); yet, although Wolfram comes very close to saying so earlier (P:438,9), it is only after they draw swords that we learn for sure that Parzival and Feirefiz are brothers (P:740,1–6). Although Wolfram's laments interrupt the fight repeatedly (P:739,30–740,6, 740,26–30, 742,14), he never betrays Feirefiz's name; this we learn only after the fight, when Feirefiz reveals it to Parzival (P:745,28). Wolfram could have divulged both Feirefiz's name and his relation to Parzival at the very outset of the episode; the rest of the text, including the laments, could have remained exactly as it is. Yet a good deal of our involvement in the episode would have been lost. By first hinting at and then revealing piece by piece the crucial facts about Feirefiz, that is by carefully exploiting the narrator's control over the order in which we receive information, Wolfram has added considerably to the suspense we feel and thus heightened our participation in the episode.

Analysing Wolfram's Bravura

Geoffrey of Vinsauf distinguishes two stages in poetic composition – first the mental organization of the material, then its poetic realization – that seem to correspond to the distinction between the substance and the sur-face of an Arthurian episode.[44] The skeletal action and the disclosure of substantial information form the backbone of the passage we are investigating; they provide the essential organization. But they account for only a small part of its real effect; this is added at the second stage and derives from the poetry with which Wolfram invests his presentation. Let us try to analyse the constituents of that poetry.

First of all Wolfram considerably expands his material with the help of various rhetorical devices.[45] Much gets said more than once (*expolitio*): that many hadn't learned the end of the story (P:734,1–9); that all depends on Parzival's heart (P:734,24–6); that Feirefiz is a heathen and hasn't been baptized (P:735,3–4). Wolfram introduces comparisons (*collatio*): between this fight and all the others (P:734,18–19); between the value of the stones on Feirefiz's *wapenroc* and the wealth of Arthur's dominions (P:735,15–19). Wolfram sets out to describe Feirefiz's armour (*descriptio*) but exhausts himself in rhetorical evasions (P:735,9–736,24). He offers the well-known circumstances of a lion's birth (*exemplum*) as a parallel to the effect of Gahmuret's jousting on Parzival and Feirefiz (P:738,19–20). He shows off his learning with an explanation of the *ezidemon* (*definitio*) (P:736,10–14). Wolfram interjects himself directly into the narration with his own laments on the proceedings (*exclamatio*) (P:737,22–4) and by his professions of inability to deal adequately with his material (P:734,16–17, 735,9–11, 735,30, 738,1–3).[46]

Often Wolfram expands his material by presenting it in unnecessarily elaborate ways. He sets out with a hyperbaton (*transgressio*) that only modern punctuation can unscramble (P:734,1–9).[47] He tells us where Feirefiz's horse's *kovertiure* does *not* come from (*circumlocutio*) (P:736,15 –19). He indulges in understatement (*diminutio*) (P:734,21) and hyperbole (*superlatio*) (P:735,15–19) and refers to Condwiramurs (P:734,11) and Feirefiz (P:735,2) by circumscription (*circumlocutio*). *Hoher muot* appears as Parzival's companion, and *gelücke* is called on to intervene in the fight (*conformatio* or personification) (P:737,13–16, 738,18).

In addition to the rhetorical devices that Wolfram employs to elaborate his material, he often uses others that serve primarily to ornament. He plays with antithesis (*contentio*): *vreude, truren* (P:738,6–7); *heiden, getoufter* (P:738,11–12); *haz, vreude* (P:738,13–14). He repeats words for emphasis (*traductio*): *rich* (P:735,8, 735,10, 735,14); *mer* (P:735,12–13); *dienest* (P:737,29–30). He draws our attention to the closeness of Parzival and Feirefiz by repeating *ieweder* at the beginning of three lines (*repetitio* or anaphora) (P:738,4, 738,6, 738,9). Nor does Wolfram disdain those devices that are limited to a single word. He plays with the possible meanings of *sloz*: lock; conclusion (*adnominatio*) (P:734,7).[48] He stretches the meaning of *voget* (*abusio* or catachresis) (P:734,30). A single word is made to stand for a more elaborate action with which it is associated (*denominatio* or metonomy): *munt* for the capacity to narrate (P:734,6); *krach* for the joust that produces it (P:738,21). Parzival's *hant* must represent his entire body (*intellectio* or synecdoche) (P:734,18). Finally, lambs and lions appear as metaphors (*translatio*) for the *kiusche* and *vrecheit* that Parzival and Feirefiz both share (P:737,20–1).

Wolfram need not have gone to so much trouble. He might have conveyed the essential information of the story – skeleton and substance – in very few words and gotten us much sooner to the fight itself. Yet he does not. Why? First, Wolfram clearly enjoys showing off. There is no mistaking his delight in drawing attention to himself as a character in his own right, to his own skill, and to our dependence on him. And there is no denying our delight in observing the performance. A good deal of our interest in *Parzival* derives directly from our fascination with the masks Wolfram assumes, the manipulations he practises, and the technical virtuosity he displays. We delight, that is, in the 'literariness' of the work, to which Wolfram constantly calls our attention.

Yet Wolfram is not just showing off. His controlled disclosure of information is calculated to spark our curiosity. His circumlocutions and puns engage our intellect. His comparisons and metaphors increase our understanding. His laments arouse our anxiety, and his professed inability to do justice to his material heightens our awe of what is to come. Wolfram appears to be showing off, and we delight in the display; yet at the same time he is preparing us so that we can properly appreciate the fight to come. Wolfram seems irredeemably self-centred, always drawing attention away from the story to his own performance; yet at the same time he behaves as the most responsible mediator, leading his listeners by the hand and preparing them to receive with greatest interest and understanding the elements of the story that he is about to relate.[49]

The Narrator's Adventure Is the Whole Romance

At first glance Wolfram's two roles would seem to conflict. The attention he attracts to himself as a personality at the level of the narration ought to distract us from the events of the story to which he as the faithful narrator claims to be devoted. Yet the faithful narrator is only one of Wolfram's masks, and the story to which he claims such devotion is an illusion. It exists only in its relation by the narrator; we know it, that is, only from the traces it leaves in his narration. Having looked so closely at Wolfram's bravura performance, we are likely to regard the narration as the work of the narrator and its contents as the record of Parzival's fight with Feirefiz. This is true only within the fictional world of the text. In reality the surface of the text is the work not of the narrator but of the author; its contents do not record the fight between Parzival and Feirefiz but rather how the narrator Wolfram, in transmitting this otherwise unattested contest, interprets his tale, manipulates his audience, and ornaments his performance.

When we focus on the verbal surface of the romance, what we are accustomed to call the episode – the content of the romance story – suddenly disappears: it is subsumed in a much larger undertaking. This larger undertaking, to which we shall return in chapter three, is the story of how Wolfram recounts the adventures of Parzival, what Michael Curschmann calls 'the adventure of narrating.'[50] Note that Parzival's adventures come in the plural while that of Wolfram is singular: the plural adventures of Parzival are the series of episodes; the single adventure of Wolfram is the romance. Exaggerating the distinction, we might say Parzival (Gahmuret, Gawan) is the hero of each episode while Wolfram is the hero of *Parzival*. Of course, Wolfram's performance is not altogether unaffected by differences among the episodes he narrates: he behaves differently in relating Parzival's entry into Munsalvaesche than in relating Gawan's entry into Schanpfanzun. Indeed, he will often explicitly draw our attention to the boundaries between episodes, just as he does before Parzival's fight with Feirefiz. Yet, while the narrator *may* reflect the divisions of his story, he is not bound by them. Wolfram withholds information in book five just as he does in book fifteen. Curschmann has shown that Wolfram establishes his repertory of narrator poses by the end of book six and that his performance in the remaining ten books consists of variations on them.[51] The establishment of these poses and the variations Wolfram plays on them compose a single adventure that encompasses all the separate adventures of his heroes.[52]

We set out to investigate the Arthurian episode but must conclude with the realization that our subject cannot be isolated as thoroughly as we have pretended. We find that if we focus on the hero, Parzival, the episode is of primary importance, but that if we focus on the narrator, Wolfram, its importance is only secondary. The solution seems simple: let us choose to focus on Parzival and thus on the episode. Try to focus on Parzival, however, and you will find Wolfram blocking your view, or, more accurately, creating your view. For the episode exists only as it has been realized by the narrator, and our understanding of it cannot but be prejudiced by the form in which he presents it. The activity of the narrator in presenting his tale is the last stage in the generation of an Arthurian episode: by giving the romance story its verbal form he produces the words of the text which, shaped though it is by the narrator's involvement, is our only access to the world of Arthurian romance.

Having investigated the role of the narrator we have at last completed the final stage of our analysis of an Arthurian episode, the stage in which the surface of the text is generated. Perhaps you are tempted to point out that texts are not so hard to come by, and that you in fact have been holding one in your hands all along; why, you would like to know, if all I wanted was a text, have I adopted such a tortuous procedure for producing one? I could so easily have borrowed your own. My concern, however, has not been to generate a particular text – those we have, indeed, had all along – but to talk about all texts, to talk about the Arthurian episode in a way that is valid for the whole genre.

We have found that in order to define an episode without distortion we have had to frame our definition in the most abstract terms: an encounter between the functions O and I. To have described episodes according to the types of characters that appear in them or the motivations that cause these characters to act would have meant basing our analysis on contingent categories: not all episodes include women; not all episodes have causes. Yet, once having isolated the three basic types of encounter between O and I, the episodic skeleton, we wanted to account for the familiar contours of episodes. Therefore we isolated, between the abstract episode and the real episode, a level at which we could introduce different sorts of characters, descriptions, and causes. We have called this level substance, and the ways in which characters, descriptions, and causes are introduced, techniques of differentiation. These techniques, however, do not *define* an Arthurian episode; they merely account for some of the possible features of Arthurian episodes. Finally, we have wanted to account for the difference between the substance of an episode and the verbal form in which it reaches us; and so we have examined the relation of the narrator to the episode he relates and the effect of his intercession on our perception.

At each of the three levels we have isolated, choices are made that transform *the* Arthurian episode into *an* Arthurian episode: one of the three episode types must be selected; certain techniques of differentiation will be employed in certain ways; the narrator's attitude will colour his presentation. What may have seemed a tortuous procedure is simply my attempt to account systematically for these various choices. I have wanted to do justice both to the Arthurian episode as a single type and to the great variety of individual episodes, to explain why the episode you hold in your hands is like all Arthurian episodes and why it is different from all Arthurian episodes.

CHAPTER THREE

Episodes in Series:
The Whole Romance

If you try to project our discussion of the last chapter into the Arthurian theatre you will produce total confusion: the hero will be caught between several skeletal action patterns; he will be faced with several dozen types of opponents; the narrator will want to describe all this and comment on it at the same time. The reason for this confusion is clear: in discussing the structure of the Arthurian episode I tried to accommodate all possible varieties of episode in one model; but in fact, by the time an episode reaches the Arthurian stage, choices have been made among the many possibilities, choices that transform the polymorphous, potential episode into a real episode with specific contours. The differences I tried to accommodate in that single model actually exist only as they are distributed among the series of particular episodes that constitute a romance.

Who is responsible for choosing among the various possibilities collected in the model episode? And who is responsible for arranging the resultant episodes into a romance? You will answer at once, the author; but this is of little help. Can you tell me who made the essential compositional decisions in *Iwein*? Was it Hartmann von Aue? or Chrétien de Troyes? or was it perhaps some anonymous Welshman? If you settle on any of these your answer is bound to be arbitrary, for we will never be able to determine the formula by which responsibility is to be apportioned among them. And as soon as historical figures are introduced we will want to know the extent to which their compositions were influenced by the fashions of the moment, their place in the social order, and the whims of their patrons. These questions lead us even further into uncertainty. For just these reasons we resolved at the outset to ignore questions of history and to limit this investigation to the romance texts themselves. For us, therefore, the author of an Arthurian romance must remain a mere figure of speech, a conventional term that we prefer to 'Hartmann von Aue,' which is inaccurate, and 'incarnation of the compositional will,' which is impossible. To this abstract author I attribute responsibility for making decisions in all those cases where the genre allows choice. He determines the particular qualities of each real episode, and he establishes the pattern according to which they are arranged in series.

The author, then, is responsible for the overall design of an Arthurian romance. To determine the means by which he realizes this overall design we will have to proceed once again through our three categories: skeleton, substance, surface; but this time we will devote our attention not to the range of possible choices inherent in an Arthurian episode but rather to the consequences that an author's particular choices have for the entire romance. In doing so we move back a step, from the point at which the boundaries of the episode establish the limits of our vision to a point where we can encompass a whole romance. While we were considering the single episode the six functions served as the atomic units of our investigation; the smallest relevant unit from our new perspective is the entire episode. From this new perspective we will be able to observe how the three basic types of episode combine to generate the skeleton for a whole romance; how the particular substance of each episode determines the contours of the entire work; and how qualities of the surface of a romance affect our reception of the whole.

SKELETON: THE ESSENTIAL PROPORTIONS OF A ROMANCE

Perpetual Romance

The general episodic scheme as developed in the last chapter can represent a series of up to three episodes, provided the realization of the functions changes at each numeral:

$$^1S/I \rightarrow S/O^-/I. \rightarrow {}^2W/I \rightarrow \frac{S/O^-/I}{W/O^-/I} \rightarrow \frac{S/O^+/I.}{W/O^+/I.} \rightarrow {}^3S/O^+/I.$$

Yet a romance hero does not simply accept his challenge, fight a single battle, and return to society, where he lives out his days paralysed by courtly *vreude*. Quite the contrary: he takes on adventure after adventure until finally, when their number is too great for a reader to keep them all easily in mind, the hero returns to court for a well-earned celebration.

What are the means by which the three-stage teleology of this episodic scheme is frustrated? How, in other words, can this skeleton be expanded into the formula for an entire romance?

In many cases the hero is not allowed to reach $^3S/O^+/I$. Most commonly this is done by refusing the hero, or having him refuse, the woman he has just won: for Ulrich, at least, there can be no question of Lanzelet's possessing Ginover; Gwigalois sends the maiden he rescues from the giants off to Arthur's and continues on his way; in *Diu Crone* Gawein twice marries off women he won to someone else: Sgoidamur to Gasozein, Clarisanz to Giremelanz; Daniel leaves the Frouwe von dem Trüeben Berge because he wants to try out his new sword, and besides, he doesn't really fancy her anyway (D:1762). If the hero is out in the woods when he refuses or is denied the woman he has just won (Gwigalois and the maiden tormented by giants), then $W/O^+/I$ is changed into W/I; and W/I invariably leads to an adventure, which means a new episode. Should the hero be in society when he is not united with the woman he won (Lanzelet defeats Valerin), then $S/O^+/I$ becomes S/I, which is a highly unstable constellation. Either an opponent will appear in society to challenge the hero, or the hero himself will feel the need to go out seeking adventure; S/I, that is, invariably becomes $S/O^-/I$, and the stage is set for another episode. In some cases (Lanzelet after winning the daughter of Galagandreiz; Iwein after the defeat of Keie and the celebration with Arthur; Parzival at Pelrapeire) the hero does accept the woman he wins but then abandons her for ideological reasons (Lanzelet remembers 'durch waz er uz was geriten' [L:1363]; Gawein convinces Iwein to seek adventure; Parzival wants to seek adventure and to visit his mother [P:223,15–25]); this amounts to the same as refusing the woman outright: as soon as the hero deserts his wife he inaugurates a new episode.

In those cases where O^+ is not a marriageable woman, $^3S/O^+/I$ is impossible. After the fight between Parzival and Feirefiz or that between Garel and Gilan, the combatants become friends and find their way back to society. It seems in these cases that the opponents are transformed into auxiliaries: Feirefiz becomes Parzival's ambassador to India; Gilan assists Garel in the fight with Eskilabon. The same thing happens to Lunete: when Iwein rescues her from the malicious steward he in effect wins her; since he will not marry her, however, she is reduced to the role of auxiliary to Iwein – which is exactly the role in which she appears at the end of the romance. Yet if O^+ is changed into an auxiliary of I (multiplication of actor), then it disappears from the equation and we are left with those two functional pairs $(W/I; S/I)$ that guarantee further adventure.

In a few cases a stable $S/O^+/I$ seems to have been achieved only to be shattered by violence from without. In *Daniel, Wigalois,* and *Wigamur,* a *hochzit* that concludes a long series of adventures – that is, a *hochzit* that might very well have concluded the romance – is interrupted: in *Daniel* by the old man who snatches King Arthur away; in *Wigalois* by news of the calamity at Namur; in *Wigamur* by news of the tournament at Musygrallt, for which the hero departs at once.[1] In these instances as in the others we have considered the constellation $^3S/O^+/I$ is somehow frustrated; it is turned into $S/O^-/I$, which leads us directly into the woods.

If we rewrite our scheme for the Arthurian episode, allowing for episodes with frustrated conclusions (indicated by asterisks), we will turn it into a formula for perpetual romance:

$$
{}^1S/I \rightarrow S/O^-/I. \rightarrow {}^2W/I \left\{
\begin{array}{l}
S/O^-/I \left< \begin{array}{l} {}^*S/O^+/I \;=\; {}^1S/I \rightarrow \\ {}^3S/O^+/I. \end{array} \right. \\[2ex]
\begin{array}{l} S/O^+/I. \\ W/O^+/I. \end{array} \left.\right> \!\!\! \times \\[2ex]
W/O^-/I \left< \begin{array}{l} {}^*S/O^+/I \;=\; {}^1S/I \rightarrow \\ {}^*W/O^+/I \;=\; {}^2W/I \rightarrow \end{array} \right.
\end{array} \right.
$$

Because we are no longer concerned with the internal composition of episodes but only with the different episode types themselves, it is no longer necessary to employ such elaborate notation. In the following I will speak of three types of episodes. Type one includes all those episodes that activate the hero and separate him from society – those episodes that describe the transition from equilibrium to disequilibrium. Type two includes all transformation episodes, whether or not they include an initial $S/I \rightarrow S/O^-/I$ or a final $S/O^+/I$ – those episodes, that is, that describe the transition from disequilibrium to equilibrium. Type three designates only those episodes in which the hero and his lady appear together in society and only in those cases in which this appearance does not follow directly on the transformation encounter in which she was won – those episodes, that is, that describe only a state of equilibrium. All episodes except those of the third type inevitably lead into another episode, and even type three episodes do so in a few cases. They are transformed, that is, into episodes of type one.

The scheme just given indicates that a romance will continue indefinitely as long as type-three episodes are either avoided or frustrated. We see then that the notorious tendency of Arthurian romance to repeat itself endlessly is an inherent feature of the genre. As Northrop Frye remarks, 'At its most naive it [romance] is an endless form in which a central character who never develops or ages goes through one adventure after another until the author himself collapses.'[2] At the same time the concern for local effect at the expense of overall coherence is typical of medieval rhetorical theory. James Murphy reminds us 'that medieval theorists do not worry about what we would today call "composition," that is, a concern for the whole or unified nature of the speech or written document being prepared.'[3] Edmond Faral puts it with admirable terseness: 'As a matter of fact, composition was not the predominating concern of the writers of the Middle Ages.'[4]

The generic tendency to endless repetition is evident also to diachronic observation. Relatively simple works like *Erec* and *Lanzelet* are followed by longer, compound works like *Parzival* and *Diu Crone*; later works, like *Garel*, are strongly derivative and, like *Diu Crone* and *Tandareis*, burdened with numerous references to earlier romances.[5] The tendency to cyclical compilation is evident at the end of *Parzival* and of *Wigalois*, where we are given a capsule preview of the romance to be told of the hero's son (P:824,1–826,30; W:11626–75). Even the most sympathetic readers of romances were in the end offended by their interminable repetitiveness. The canon in *Don Quixote*, for instance, finds the romances 'devoide of all discretion, art and ingenious disposition.' He complains that he has 'not seene in any bookes of Knighthoode, an entire bulke of a fable, so proportioned in all the members thereof, as that the middle may answere the beginning, and the end the beginning and middle. But rather they have composed them of so many members, as it more probably seems, that the authors intended to frame Chimeraes or monsters, then to deliver proportionate figures.'[6]

We must agree with the critics and the canon: essentially Arthurian romance is nothing but a potentially endless string of episodes. Yet the perpetual formula does require of an author certain choices, choices by which he will establish the fundamental proportions of his work. He must decide first of all how he wants to set the perpetual scheme in motion, that is, how he will begin the romance. He must also figure out how he will stop the perpetual scheme once it has gotten going, that is, how he will end the romance. Finally he must determine where he will place episodes of type one, which are the most effective means of organizing the middle of a romance. If an author makes these choices wisely he has taken the first steps in the creation of a work that might satisfy Cervantes's canon, a work, that is, in which 'the middle may answere the beginning, and the end the beginning and middle.'

Beginning a Romance

There are three ways to begin an Arthurian romance: with an episode of type one, with an episode of type two, or with a childhood sequence. The openings of *Parzival, Gauriel, Diu Crone,*[7] and *Garel* find the hero in society (only Gawein and Garel, however, are at Arthur's). An opponent appears (*Garel*); the hero falls into disfavour with his lady (*Gauriel*); he hears of a tournament (Gawein in *Diu Crone*); he is concerned about his *pris* (Gahmuret): thus the hero is separated from society and launched on a series of unrelated episodes. These works, then, begin with episodes of type one.

The first scenes of *Erec, Iwein, Diu Crone,* and *Tandareis* also find the hero in society (all are at Arthur's), and soon an opponent (or news of an opponent: Ascalon; Gasozein) appears to challenge them. But this time the challenge leads directly into the combat that resolves the conflict. These works all begin with episodes of type two in its extended form. The first scenes of *Wigalois* and *Daniel* find the hero (or the hero's father: *Wigalois*) fighting knights of the Round Table at the outskirts of Arthur's court. These are also episodes of the second type, but without the optional beginning in society. Note that all type-two episodes that appear initially take place at King Arthur's.

The Childhood Sequence

Lanzelet, Meleranz, and *Wigamur* begin with stories of the heroes' childhoods, as do the main parts of *Parzival* and *Wigalois*. In every case the childhood sequence follows the same pattern. First we are told something of the hero's parentage: in *Parzival* and *Wigalois* this information turns into an extended narrative in its own right; in *Lanzelet* and *Wigamur* it forms a short episode; in *Meleranz* we get only a few facts. Second, we witness the hero as he grows up, always in some out-of-the-way place: Lanzelet and Gwigalois grow up in magical kingdoms; Parzival, in the woods; Wigamur, in a cave; Meleranz spends his first twelve years at the court of his father, the King of France, but he is far away from Arthur's. We learn something of the hero's character and education: he is always raised by his mother (or foster mother: *Lanzelet* and *Wigamur*; Wigamur is later abducted a second time and raised by a *merwunder*), even in the one case where his father is close at hand (*Meleranz*; see M:170). Third, even though knightly skills are invariably omitted from the young hero's education, he somehow does know about knighthood and is determined to know more; this causes him to want to leave his childhood home (except Wigamur, who is sent off on his own by the *merwunder*). In some cases reasons are advanced in addition to the hero's thirst for knightly glory: Lanzelet is supposed to kill Iwaret; Gwigalois wants to find his father. The hero's parents are distressed by his intention (except the foster parents in *Lanzelet* and *Wigamur*; in *Meleranz* the parents' distress is forecast for the moment when they will learn of their son's secret departure), but eventually they give in and impart good advice as he leaves.

The fourth position in the childhood scheme seems at first glance to contain whatever the author wishes: Lanzelet is struck by the dwarf at Pluris; Parzival attacks Jeschute, meets Sigune and the fisher, visits Arthur, and kills Ither; Gwigalois meets a messenger who directs him to Arthur's; Meleranz comes upon Tydomie in her forest clearing and dallies with her for one thousand lines; Wigamur witnesses the destruction of a castle, fights Glakotelesfloyr, and discovers Pioles. Yet in spite of this variety the fourth position always serves to demonstrate the hero's lack of knightly training: Lanzelet does not know how to react to the dwarf's insult; Parzival and Wigamur demonstrate their foolishness at every turn; Gwigalois does not know in what direction to proceed; Meleranz cannot stay with Tydomie simply because he has not yet proved himself as a knight. Whatever element is introduced in the fourth position invariably reappears later in the romance.

Finally, the young hero arrives at some centre of courtly culture where he is taken in hand by a model knight (Gawein, if he has reached Arthur's) and instructed in the skills and obligations of knighthood. The young hero's true identity is either not known to him (Lanzelet and Wigamur; Parzival learns his name at stage four) or is hidden from society (Gwigalois does not know that his father is Gawein – although he did know at line 1305; Meleranz keeps his parentage a secret). The hero's knightly education ends, for those educated at Arthur's (Gwigalois and Meleranz; also for Wigamur at Arthur's uncle's), with their knighting and, in every case, in a tourney at which the young knight displays his excellence at jousting. When an author decides to begin a romance with the story of the hero's childhood he commits himself to a traditional five-part scheme, of which only the fourth section allows him substantial room for variation.[8]

Ending a Romance

While the author of an Arthurian romance can choose one of three patterns to open his work, he is allowed considerably less latitude at its conclusion. The basic pattern seems to require a celebration with the heroine at King Arthur's (episode type three) and then a return to the hero's own kingdom. We recognize this sequence in *Erec*, with perfunctory return in *Gauriel*, and with elaborate return in *Tandareis* and *Garel*. In *Wigalois* both the reception at Arthur's and the return home appear in highly abbreviated form, but they are there as place-holders nevertheless. In *Lanzelet, Daniel,* and *Meleranz* the two stages of the conclusion are combined so that Arthur presides over a grand coronation celebration in the hero's own country. In *Lanzelet* two such episodes follow upon one another, one in each of Lanzelet's kingdoms. The orthodox ending for an Arthurian romance, then, employs four requisites to deactivate the hero: the heroine, a festival, Arthur's blessing, and the hero's own kingdom. The coincidence of these four unalterably reintegrates the hero into society and removes him from the forests of adventure.[9]

Note that the first part of *Erec* ends in practically the same way as its conclusion: hero and heroine are united; Arthur organizes a *hochzit*; there is a tournament; Erec and Enite return home. It almost seems as if this medial appearance of what was to become the traditional terminal sequence confused Erec and caused him to behave as if the romance had ended. This is after all the only instance where the terminal sequence appears medially, and Erec is the only hero who *sich verlit* before the end of the romance.

Four romances have endings that do not follow the regular formula. The conclusion of *Parzival* is like that of *Lanzelet*, except that the company at Munsalvaesche has replaced Arthur's court for the second celebration. Arthur is missing altogether from the end of *Wigamur*: after the last adventure the hero and heroine return home and organize a celebration on their own. This terminal festival might be considered merely the end of the preceding episode (type two, in which the hero finally wins the heroine! see note 1) were it not so clearly intended to signal the conclusion of the romance. *Diu Crone* ends with a rather cursory celebration at King Arthur's, but there is no heroine, and there is no return home. This is not altogether surprising, since Gawein takes no notice of his wife in the second half of the romance and since, traditionally, Arthur's court *is* his home. Perhaps this barren conclusion reflects the difficulty of dealing with a hero who must always represent the ideal member of Arthur's court. Of all the Arthurian romances, however, *Iwein* has the most unusual ending. There is no celebration either at King Arthur's or at the hero's home; that is, there is no episode of type three. Instead Iwein sets off for the magic fountain, just as he did at the beginning of the romance, and thus inaugurates another transformation encounter. Not only is it otherwise unknown to end a romance with an episode of the second type, but this particular example, in which the heroine is tricked into submission by her own maid (or does Lunete act as Iwein's auxiliary?) is unique among transformation encounters. There can be no question but that the unorthodox endings of *Parzival*, *Diu Crone*, and *Wigamur* are closely related to the orthodox formula; the anomalous conclusion to *Iwein*, on the other hand, stands by itself.[10]

Just as Arthur's court strives to guarantee its *vreude*, so an Arthurian romance, destined to conclude with the blessing of that court, strives towards a happy end. The initiate reader or auditor knows that the happy ending is assumed, that regardless of the obstacles that may be set in the hero's path his ultimate success is guaranteed by the rules of the genre itself. The beneficent teleology of Arthurian romance is one of the characteristics that distinguish it most clearly from the Tristan tradition, where the hero, as his very name foretells (GTr:1999), is doomed to a tragic end. The requisite happy end of an Arthurian romance distinguishes it as well from Middle High German heroic epics, which are allowed either successful or unsuccessful conclusions. Finally, we recognize the guaranteed success of an Arthurian hero as the syntagmatic equivalent to the strongly integrative tendency characteristic of the paradigmatic function S; that the happy ending and Arthur's court coincide at the conclusion of a romance reflects and emphasizes their common integrative tendency.[11]

That the last episodes of *Iwein*, *Parzival*, and *Wigalois* do *not* end at Arthur's court has led some scholars to detect 'implied criticism of Arthur.'[12] Actually only four romances do conclude with an episode that includes Arthur and his court (*Lanzelet*, *Diu Crone*, *Daniel*, *Gauriel*); are the other eight all implicitly critical of Arthur? I find that unlikely, especially considering the capacity of our authors to assert the conventions of their genre at the same moment they appear to be subverting them.[13] Even in those romances singled out by scholars there is evidence that clearly contradicts the supposedly critical attitude to Arthur. The beginning of *Iwein* is the *locus classicus* for 'Artusidealität.'[14] For about three thousand lines near the end of Parzival, Wolfram portrays 'Artus der wise hövesche man' (P:717,1) as active and undisputed head of courtly society, without a hint of criticism; and Parzival, near the end of his adventures, is eager to be readmitted to the Round Table (P:700,15–23). For Wirnt, Arthur is 'ane wandel gar' (W:1505); he is the 'aller tiursten man der künicriche ie gewan' (W:1441–2). By ending their works at Laudine's, Munsalvaesche, and Korntin the authors of Iwein, Parzival, and Wigalois may have wanted to stress some particular aspect of their work; they did not mean to criticize Arthur.

Structuring the Middle of a Romance

The Bracketed Series

We have seen the various ways an author can begin a romance as well as the manner in which it is usually brought to a conclusion. The perpetual scheme allows as well another type of choice, one by which an author can organize the episodes between the beginning and the end of a romance. The appearance of a type-one episode signals the start of a series of episodes. We know from experience that the unresolved challenge such an episode leaves ringing in the air must eventually be met by our hero, and this expectation causes us to group together all the episodes that fall between the challenge and its resolution: most of the episodes in Iwein fall between Lunete's denunciation of the hero and his final reconciliation with Laudine; the Pluris episode in Lanzelet is the answer to an insult delivered at the very outset of the hero's career; the larger part of Parzival is bracketed by Cundrie's accusations in book six and her gesture of submission in book fifteen, a smaller part by Kingrimursel's challenge and its resolution; much of Wigalois falls between Nereja's appearance at Arthur's and Gwigalois's arrival at Roimunt; most of the short episodes in Daniel and Garel are arranged between a challenge delivered by a giant and the battles that these challenges provoke.

Similarly, more than three-quarters of Tandareis is enclosed between the episode in which the hero is banished from Arthur's court and from Flordibel and the one in which they are reconciled and reunited; about half of Meleranz falls between the beginning of Meleranz's search for Tydomie and its conclusion. In Diu Crone we find three series of bracketed episodes: ten thousand lines elapse between the first news of Gasozein and the final resolution of his claims; within this span fall a series of episodes bounded by Gawein's resolution to aid King Flois and its accomplishment; more than one-third of the romance falls between the moment Gawein commits himself to seek the grail and the completion of his quest. In every case the episodes that separate a type-one episode from its resolution show the greatest variety and have, for the most part, nothing at all to do with the issue that embraces them; and yet, in spite of the heterogeneity of the episodes, they are marked as a group by the connection between the episode that precedes them and the one that follows them.

Strictly speaking, the second part of the bracket of which a type-one episode forms the first part functions as such only because the realization of its functional makeup coincides with that of the first part or because the causal explanation attached to the second part coincides with that attached to the first: we feel that Garel's battle with Ekunaver answers the initial challenge because the giant issued the challenge in Ekunaver's name; we connect the reconciliation of Erec and Enite at Limors with their departure from Karnant because both are explained in the same way (E:6781–2). Coincidences of realization and differentiation, however, belong not to the consideration of the skeleton but to that of how the skeleton acquires substance; they belong, that is, in the next section. Nevertheless the placement of an episode of type one does prepare for the eventual appearance of an episode that responds to the challenge; and this pair of episodes brackets and thus organizes the episodes that fall between. Episodes of type one in which O^- is a generalized abstraction (Gahmuret goes off in search of *any* adventure) cannot act as the first half of a bracket since there is no way to recognize which succeeding episode forms its pendant.

One might expect an independent challenge episode to appear at the outset of a romance and its resolution to coincide with the final celebration, but this is nowhere the case.[15] *Garel* comes closest to this pattern, for here the initial challenge is answered in a large battle and the only episodes to follow are a fight with Keie and the concluding sequence: a celebration at Arthur's and Garel's return home. *Gauriel* is the only other romance to open with a challenge episode, but this is resolved considerably before the end. We see then that the most telling means by which the perpetual formula can be articulated – a challenge episode and its resolution – are never engaged to structure an entire romance. Apparently the authors of German romance did not attach nearly so much importance to having the end of their works answer the beginning as did the canon in *Don Quixote*.[16]

The Major Independent Episode

In addition to the series of episodes initiated by a type-one episode, most romances include a major independent episode. With 'major independent episode' I do not mean to introduce a fourth basic type of episode; rather, I want to distinguish a variety of type-two episode that plays a decisive role in establishing the general shape of a romance. These are episodes of substantial length, usually longer than any of the episodes within the bracketed series (they average 15 per cent of the entire romance), that stand outside the brackets: Erec's combat at Tulmein (E:1–2221); Iwein's defeat of Ascalon and marriage with Laudine (I: 31–2445); Parzival at Pelrapeire (P:180,15–223,30); Gwigalois's campaign against Lion (W:9799–11284); the abduction of Arthur in *Daniel* (D:6900–7888); Gauriel's rescue of the daughter of Asterian (GM:3145–4161); Tandareis's flight from Arthur's court and Arthur's successful pursuit (T:264–3957). A romance will not usually have more than one major independent episode, or more than one bracketed series of episodes. The relative positions of the major independent episode and the bracketed series determine the basic contours of a romance.

Describing the Proportions of the Skeleton

Let us begin with *Iwein*. The events from the opening scene at Arthur's *hochzit* to the *hochzit* that celebrates Iwein's marriage with Laudine are part of a single elaborately differentiated episode. The marriage is followed by the fight with Keie at the well and the ensuing celebration: a second episode. Yet the crisis with Laudine has its beginnings in Gawein's speech at this celebration and is not resolved until the end of the romance; all the remaining episodes of *Iwein* fall within this bracket. Of what then does the celebrated bipartition of *Iwein* consist? The first part is composed of a major independent episode and the much shorter encounter with Keie; the second part, of the bracketed series. In many ways *Parzival* is similar to *Iwein*: the first part (after the childhood sequence) begins with the major independent episode (Pelrapeire) and ends with a skirmish with Keie (and others: multiplication of actor) leading to a celebration at Arthur's; the second part begins at that celebration, with Cundrie's attack on Parzival, and stretches to the end of the work.

We should note, however, that, while part one of *Iwein* is composed almost entirely of a single episode, part one of *Parzival* is much more heterogeneous. It is composed simply of all the episodes that precede the bracket: childhood sequence; major independent episode; the episode at Munsalvaesche; the fight with Orilus; the skirmishes with the Arthurian knights leading to the reunion with Arthur. The second part of *Parzival*, too, is much more elaborate than the second part of *Iwein*. Besides the bracketed series introduced by Cundrie it includes the adventures of Gawan: the bracketed series introduced by Kingrimursel in book six; Gawan's even less successful search for the grail; and his adventures in the company of Orgeluse. Although one can reduce the pattern of Parzival's adventures to something like that of Iwein's, one can hardly equate the structure of *Parzival* with the bipartition of *Iwein* without doing considerable violence to the organization of the larger work.

The orthodox analysis of *Erec* would put it, too, in the same category as *Iwein*: the first part includes the major independent episode in which Erec wins Enite – from the insult of the dwarf to their marriage at Arthur's – followed by the tournament and the return to Karnant; the second part begins with the crisis of *verligen* and ends with Erec's and Enite's final return home.[17] Yet the second part of *Erec* is not organized by a single bracket, as in *Iwein* and *Parzival*, for the crisis with Enite is resolved after the incident at Limors. Were the fight with Oringles followed by the closing sequence, then the second part of *Erec* would match the canonical pattern; instead, the end of the bracket is separated from the closing sequence by the accidental fight with Guivreiz and the 'joie de la curt.' You may protest, maintaining that our anticipation of the final return to Karnant unifies the second part of *Erec* so strongly that the bracketed series is barely noticed; but if geography is your only criterion you will have to make a bracket out of all of *Parzival* from the first visit to Munsalvaesche to the second, or you will have to break off the second part in book fifteen, when Parzival returns to the site (Arthur's court) at which the most obvious bracket began. If on the other hand we follow the bracket in *Erec* only to the resolution of the crisis that opens it, then the 'joie de la curt' begins to look like a second major independent episode: it is nearly as long as the opening episode, in which Erec wins Enite, and it has no intrinsic relation to the episodes of the bracketed series.

In the case of *Iwein*, the bipartite construction is quite clear: part one is a large major independent episode (30 per cent of the work) plus a small type-two episode; part two, a bracketed series (62 per cent). In the case of *Parzival* roughly the same proportions obtain (27 per cent; 60 per cent), but only if one is willing to accept as the first part a proportionally small major independent episode (5 per cent) along with everything else that falls outside the bracketed series and as a second part a major bracketed series that includes several shorter series. In the case of *Erec* a substantial independent episode (22 per cent) and a small type-two episode form the first part; this is followed by a bracketed series (38 per cent), a small type-two episode, and a second major independent episode (20 per cent). To consider this latter group – from the crisis of *verligen* to the end – as the second part of *Erec* is to make an interpretative decision. It is coherent not by virtue of a causal bracket but only by the decision that, in this case, the series of episodes ends *not* with the resolution of the crisis that motivated it but with the return to the location at which it began. We see then that, even with regard to the canonical works, the 'two-part structure of Arthurian romance'[18] rests in each case on different standards.

If we consider as well the lesser works, the so-called 'niedere Artus-epik,' we will have even more difficulty accepting bipartition as the norm for our genre. At first glance there seems to be a group of works that reverses the canonical pattern. *Daniel* (after the opening episode: skirmishes with Arthurian knights leading to admission into the Round Table), *Wigalois* (after the lengthy childhood sequence), and *Gauriel* all begin with episodes of the first type that introduce a bracketed series. In every case the end of the series (victory in Cluse; victory in Korntin; regaining favour of one's lady) is followed by a long episode essentially unrelated to the series (abduction of Arthur; campaign against Lion; abduction of the daughter of Asterian), and these episodes lead directly into the closing sequence. These three romances seem to be built on a two-part pattern in which the bracketed series comes first and the major independent episode second. But whereas in *Iwein* independent episode and bracketed series stand in a relationship of 30 per cent to 62 per cent, here the equivalent parts stand in the relationship of 13 per cent to 76 per cent (*Daniel*), 13 per cent to 67 per cent (*Wigalois*), and 15 per cent to 74 per cent (*Gauriel*). Are we really justified in talking of bipartition when the two parts are so unevenly balanced? The situation in *Wigalois* is complicated by the presence of an initial childhood sequence the same length as the final campaign against Lion: the bracketed series falls precisely in the middle of the work.

Tandareis and *Meleranz* seem to follow the *Iwein* pattern more closely than any of the other less familiar romances: a major independent episode is followed by a bracketed series. But in the case of *Tandareis* the proportions are different. Rather than standing in the ratio of one to two as they do in *Iwein*, the two parts of *Tandareis* stand in the ratio of one to four; and in the case of *Meleranz* the first third is not an episode in the ordinary sense but rather an elaborate childhood sequence.

Finally, there are romances like *Lanzelet* and *Garel* where an initial bracketed series is followed by an assortment of episodes, none sizable enough to figure as a major independent episode. In most of the non-canonical works one can establish a bipartite structure if one is determined enough to find it; but in talking of a bipartite structure, it seems to me, one implies two coherent parts that stand in some reasonable proportion to one another, and this is not the case in a single one of the 'niedere Artusepen' (except *Meleranz*, with its long childhood sequence, and perhaps *Tandareis*). Does this then distinguish them from the canonical works? No, it distinguishes them only from *Iwein*.

In describing the structural outline of an Arthurian romance I think we would do well to overcome the critical prejudice in favour of bipartition. Instead we might content ourselves by noting whether the major independent episode comes at the beginning of a work (*Iwein, Erec, Tandareis*) or at the end (*Daniel, Wigalois, Gauriel*) and whether the bracketed series falls at the end (*Iwein, Parzival, Meleranz, Tandareis, Erec* – according to the orthodox interpretation), at the beginning (*Lanzelet, Daniel, Gauriel, Garel*), or in the middle (*Erec, Wigalois*); this distribution will establish the basic shape of a romance. The pattern of the canonical romances, it turns out, is only one of the possible arrangements of major independent episode and bracketed series – it is not even the most popular arrangement. I think that the skeletal structure of *Erec* would be more accurately described if, instead of insisting on 'Zweiteilung,' we listed its largest independent components: major independent episode + type-two episode (tournament) + bracketed series + type-two episode (Guivreiz) + major independent episode + concluding sequence.

In investigating the substance of *Erec* we will consider features that establish patterns among the episodes of the work quite different from those I have just isolated (the several appearances of Guivreiz or Arthur, for instance, connect episodes within the bracketed series with those outside of it), and the sensitive interpreter of *Erec* will discover other relationships as well (between the 'joie de la curt,' for instance, and the bracketed series). That these patterns coincide neither with each other nor with that of the skeletal structure does not necessarily mean that someone has gone astray; it testifies rather to the relative independence of the various levels of Arthurian romance. In describing the poetics of romance we need only note the existence of this incongruence; the interpreter of romance, however, must find either a way of reconciling the various levels or reasons for ignoring some of them.

We began in agreement with Northrop Frye and the canon from *Don Quixote*: essentially an Arthurian romance is nothing but a potentially endless series of episodes. We have seen now how an author can articulate this series at the most basic level: how he will set the series in motion; what kind of conclusion he must use; the ways in which the middle of a romance can be shaped. We have determined, that is, the larger patterns of skeletal organization. Yet we are still in agreement with Frye and the canon. We have merely substituted somewhat larger patterns for the string of individual episodes: Arthurian romance, we have established, is a potentially endless series of episodes some of which may be collected into larger groups. Even with this modification the essential parataxis of Arthurian romance remains clear.

The paratactic, episodic skeletal structure of Arthurian romance distinguishes the works in our genre from most of the rest of the Middle High German corpus. The *Nibelungenlied, Kudrun*, the so-called *Spielmannsepen*, the Tristan romances: all are constructed on the established model of the courtship pattern, the *Brautwerbungsschema*. This skeletal pattern differs from that of Arthurian romance in two ways. First, it cannot be expanded indefinitely; authors of works based on the courtship pattern, if they want more material, have to repeat the entire pattern (*Salman und Morolf, König Rother, Nibelungenlied*). Second, the constituent elements of the courtship pattern are not essentially equivalent, as are the episodes of Arthurian romance, but stand in necessary relations of subordination to one another (the raven is dispatched *so that* Oswald can establish contact with his bride). The skeletal pattern of these works implies hypotactic relations; that of Arthurian romance, paratactic ones.

Of the works based on the courtship pattern, the Tristan romances approach Arthurian romance more nearly than any of the others. Clearly the core of the Tristan story is the wooing of Isolt for Marke, and this takes place according to the courtship pattern. Yet after Isolt has arrived at Cornwall the structure becomes looser and more episodic: Gottfried, following Thomas (assuming one can judge from Brother Robert), includes the Gilan adventure, which Eilhart does not; the near execution of Isalde followed by the lovers' flight into the woods is absent in Gottfried's version, although we find it in those of Eilhart and Beroul. This freedom to treat episodes like interchangeable parts reminds us of Arthurian romance (who would notice one episode more or less in *Diu Crone*?). Closest of all, of course, is the last half of Eilhart's work. The internal structure of the episodes in which Tristrant returns to Cornwall differs considerably from that of an Arthurian episode; yet as a series of episodes, parallel in structure yet almost completely independent of each other, they strongly resemble the paratactic, episodic structure of Arthurian romance. Eilhart alerts us to this kinship by setting the first episode of his series at the court of King Arthur.

SUBSTANCE: THE FABRICATION OF COHERENCE

In realizing the abstract functions of the skeletal romance and in applying the techniques of differentiation an author creates the distinctive features by which we recognize his work. These distinctive features, however, coincide and differ in ways that obscure the fundamental paratactic structure of the romance skeleton. At the skeletal level the two episodes in which Guivreiz fights Erec are no more closely related to one another than they are to Erec's fight with Keie or to the 'joie de la curt,' yet the identical realization of O⁻ in both episodes creates an undeniable connection between them. The patterns that an author establishes in the realization of functions and in his handling of the various techniques of differentiation provide the most effective means for articulating the series of romance episodes and for establishing meaningful relations between disjunct episodes. These are the best means by which he can counter the fundamental parataxis of Arthurian romance and arrange the episodes of his work according to an 'ingenious disposition.'

Static Differentiation

To a large extent the overall disposition of an Arthurian romance depends on casting decisions: what actors fill which roles in which episodes. First of all names must be assigned: the character who fills the role of hero will be called Lanzelet in every episode; somewhere near the middle of the romance will be an episode where O⁻ is called Mabuz. Various kinds of straightforward description will be attached to a given name: Lanzelet will repeatedly be called 'der beste'; Mabuz is 'der bloede.' Then the material props that differentiate the characters must be established along with the episodes in which they appear: after Lanzelet wins Iblis he is given a jewel-studded, magical tent. At the same time the specific realizations of W and S will be assigned: at one point W will produce Schatel le Mort, at another the Genibeleter Se; S will appear as Arthur's court or the society of Dodone. More important than any of these individual determinations, however, is the way these casting decisions are integrated and apportioned throughout the romance. Certain characters will be connected with certain material props and will be set in particular settings: Lanzelet grows up in a magical kingdom where a special crystal rock guarantees everyone's happiness; Mabuz presides over Schatel le Mort, which paralyses all brave knights who enter. The characters and settings enter into that relationship of reciprocal definition by contiguity that I have called static differentiation.

We recognize episodes by alternations in the realization of functions: Mabuz and Schatel le Mort are replaced by Iwaret and his magical spring. This pattern of changing associations is essential to the progressive differentiation of the hero. Gwigalois kills the knight who might have fed him; he liberates the maiden from the giants; he defends his seizure of the dog; he retakes the stolen horse in trial by combat with Hojir; finally he defeats Schaffilun, the knight who also wanted to liberate Korntin. By this sequence of combats, each characterized by a special combination of opponent and setting, Gwigalois wins the favour of the suspicious Nereja and at the same time impresses us with his prowess. The distribution of static differentiation combinations throughout a romance is one of the chief ways an author gives the skeletal romance its distinctive shape.

The distinctive shape of a romance, however, is determined not only by the overall pattern generated by the author's casting decisions, but also by the connections that these decisions establish between episodes with identical casts or locations. On the one hand the uniform realization of the function I in virtually every episode of a romance helps hold a romance together: 'Usually,' writes William Ryding, 'a single hero serves to provide the elementary principle of unity in this sort of narrative.'[19] On the other hand coincidences in the realization of functions in disjunct episodes articulate this uniform series and generate subsidiary patterns within it. Every romance, for instance, will include more than one episode in which S is realized as Arthur's court. We quite naturally assume a stronger relation among such episodes than between one of them and, say, the Harpin adventure in *Iwein*, where S has a unique realization.

The same is true of characters. When Iwein finally regains Laudine at the end of the romance, we remember the episode in which he won her, the episode in which he left her, and the episode in which he met her after rescuing Lunete. As a result we attach more importance to the final

scene in which Iwein wins Laudine than we do to the episode in which
he in effect wins the besieged Vrouwe von Narison. According to the
perpetual scheme an Arthurian romance could well be a series of Narison episodes, a string of adventures joined only by their common hero:
Lanzelet most closely approaches this extreme, although even here Pluris,
Dodone, Genewis, and Arthur's court all make more than one appearance. *Iwein* is at the other extreme: here the alternating recurrence of
Arthur episodes and Laudine episodes gives the romance an unusual
coherence.

And how do we recognize Laudine? By her name and by her magic
well, which Iwein passes every time he approaches his wife. Thus the
Laudine episodes are marked by the repeated coincidence of name and
setting, that is by the repeated occurrence of an identical static differentiation combination. The pattern created by this recurring combination gives *Iwein* its particular contours.

In the preceding section we considered the technique by which a large
group of unrelated episodes is bracketed by a type-one episode and its
resolution. Our perception of the connection between the two bracketing
episodes depends on the identical realization of O and I in both episodes:
Iwein leaves Laudine; Iwein returns to Laudine. But not all type-one
episodes introduce brackets. Thus in *Diu Crone* news of the tournament
at Jaschune serves as a type-one episode separating Gawein from court,
but the potential bracket is not realized, for Gawein never reaches Jaschune. The potential opponents do not materialize. Gawein does not
reach Jaschune because he is requested to aid King Flois against the giant
Assiles. This request (type-one episode) is matched, after a series of
unrelated episodes, by Gawein's defeat of the giant: here the promised
opponent does appear and the potential bracket is realized.

While bracketing can help organize large stretches of a romance, a
reduced version of the same technique adds coherence to shorter passages. When Iwein comes upon the imprisoned Lunete he undertakes to
defend her the next day (type-one episode); he then rides off and stumbles on the fight with Harpin (type-two episode) before returning to
rescue Lunete (type-two episode with the same realization of $S/O^-/I$ as
the most recent type-one episode). The initial meeting with Lunete might
have led to a long bracketed series, but it does not; it is separated from its
resolution only by the Harpin episode. It is more reasonable, I think, to
regard the two appearances of Lunete as an extended type-two episode
in which the Harpin adventure is embedded. In the same way the 'pesme
aventure' is embedded in the episode of Iwein's defence of the daughter

of the Grave von dem Swarzen Dorne; the 'Becherprobe' is embedded in the episode of Lanzelet's captivity at Pluris; and Gawein's fight with the knight brought by Mancipicelle is embedded between news of the adventures at Salie and Gawein's arrival there.

A slightly more elaborate form of embedding occurs when what appears to be an embedded episode is not concluded until after the end of the episode in which its beginning is embedded. In *Lanzelet*, Ginover is abducted by Valerin (A^1) and Malduc's aid in rescuing her is secured by delivering Erec and Walwein to him (B^1); then Ginover is liberated (A^2) and the captives rescued (B^2). Similarly Daniel's initial contact with the Herre von der Grüenen Ouwe (A^1) is followed by the first day of the battle at Cluse (B^1); then Daniel returns to rescue the lord and his land (A^2) after which the battle of Cluse continues (B^2). Bracketing and embedding require that O, I, and often W or S be realized identically in disjunct episodes or, in the case of embedding, in what might have been disjunct episodes. The realization of these functions, assigning them names and other static properties, is the result of what I have called static differentiation. It is one of the most effective ways in which an Arthurian author can articulate and organize the episodes of his romance.

Active Differentiation

In one sense, active differentiation functions throughout an entire romance very much like static differentiation: disparities among the various instances of differentiation generate variety; coincidences between disjunct instances of differentiation foster coherence. Thus the mere appearance of Sigune in four scenes in *Parzival*, along with Schianatulander's body or at his grave, automatically establishes a connection among these scenes; coincidence of casting and prop (static differentiation) fosters coherence. Yet the different patterns of active differentiation divide Sigune's four appearances into two pairs: twice Parzival hears her lament as he approaches (P:138,13, 249,12); twice he comes upon her as she prays (P:437,21, 804,23). The differences (lament, prayer) distinguish the two pairs, while a similarity (lament *or* prayer) unites each pair.

In the case of Sigune connections are established because a single action used to differentiate a character appears more than once; the same is true of the several episodes in which Enite warns Erec of approaching danger or the series of episodes in which Nereja shows her contempt for Gwigalois. In other cases, however, a *series* of actions can appear more than once and thus establish a connection between two parts of a work. After Iwein recovers from his fight with Gawein he sneaks away from court, rides off to Laudine's magic well, and pours water on the stone; this is exactly what he did after he heard Kalogrenant's story. Although most of the other actions of the two episodes are different, the author in recalling the earlier pattern surely means to signal the connection between these two episodes, the two episodes in which Iwein wins Laudine. The author of *Garel* exploits a similar technique at the end of that work. There the hero travels from Arthur's court to Anferre, revisiting in the original order the scenes of his previous adventures. In *Garel*, however, the identity of the sequence draws our attention to differences of content: the first time around Garel must fight his way through eight thousand lines; the second time he makes the trip in five hundred lines, stopping at the site of each earlier combat only long enough to marry off one of his lieutenants.

Although active differentiation, like static differentiation, can establish connections between distant parts of a work, it differs from static differentiation in its susceptibility to analogical interpretation. Daniel wins his battle with the dwarf Juran by convincing him not to fight with his magic sword; he kills the *buchloser valant* by borrowing a trick from Perseus; he wins the battle with the forces of Matur by figuring out how to make use of a mechanical beast with a deafening roar. Although the action patterns in these episodes do not reveal any striking parallelism we can easily deduce a common feature: in every case Daniel triumphs not so much by brute strength as by the exercise of his wits. A speech of the narrator in which he points out the great utility of 'rehte guote liste' (D:7506) strengthens our suspicion that the repeated demonstration of Daniel's cleverness is more than coincidental.[20] We must recognize, however, that the analogy we have posited results not from a direct correspondence but from a uniform interpretation we – and the narrator – have given these episodes.[21]

Differentiation by Multiplication

Actor

There are two ways an author can manipulate multiplication of actor to further the coherence of an entire romance. The first is merely the extension of the principle advanced above, that the appearance of a single character in several episodes establishes a connection among those episodes. Coincidence of auxiliary characters among several episodes has the same effect. Thus the correspondence between the various Laudine episodes in *Iwein* is increased by the regular presence of the auxiliary character Lunete; in the same way the repeated presence of Iwein's lion helps tie together the otherwise disparate episodes in which he figures.

The other way in which multiplication of actor can further coherence is somewhat more involved. When a giant appears at Arthur's court near the beginning of *Daniel* and delivers the challenge of King Matur, the giant functions as the concrete realization of O^-: his is the particular action that separates Daniel from society and inaugurates the series of bracketed adventures. Yet the giant states quite clearly that he is merely the messenger of Matur; he is, in other words, merely the auxiliary of an as yet unseen opponent. The relation of auxiliary to principal (multiplication of actor) thus establishes a clear relationship of subordination between the episode of the challenge and the battle, where Matur finally makes his appearance. Similarly the appearances at Arthur's court of Lunete, Cundrie, Nereja, and the 'Ritter mit dem boc' (*Diu Crone*) are all integrated into the larger plan of the whole romance by the subordination of these characters as auxiliaries of more important characters. In the same way the episode in which Iwein defends Lunete is important not because Laudine herself appears – her encounter with the hero brings them no closer together – but because Iwein wins Laudine's auxiliary and in that way moves closer to reunion with his wife. (We note again the fundamentally a-psychological, external mechanisms of Arthurian romance.)

In most of the instances in which multiplication of actor establishes relations between disjunct episodes this is accomplished by the multiplication of the function O; but this is not always the case. In *Parzival* the title hero is absent from long stretches of the romance. While he is absent the function of I is filled by Gahmuret or Gawan. One would have supposed the continuous presence of a single hero to be the one essential of a coherent romance. How then can *Parzival* support three realizations of I without breaking up into three works? The breakup is prevented by the careful subordination of the auxiliary heroes to the principal hero. When Gahmuret dies and Parzival is born (the heroes replace each other with wonderful economy), Wolfram tells us clearly that we have just witnessed the appearance of 'dises maeres sachewalde' (P:112,17) and that 'sins vater vreude und des not, beidiu sin leben und sin tot' (P:112, 13–14) were merely introductory. Gawan too is carefully subordinated to Parzival. Like Parzival he is in search of the grail, but he does not reach it; he struggles to win Orgeluse, but she offers her love to Parzival unbidden (P:619,1–3); Gawan and Parzival are both related to Arthur, but Parzival is Anfortas's nephew as well; Parzival would have defeated Gawan in combat had their fight not been broken off (P:688,11–13): in every case Gawan is shown to be slightly less than Parzival. That Gawan is subordinated to Parzival in these very concrete ways guarantees the structural coherence of *Parzival*; it does not mean that Gawan is less important in the overall conception of the romance.

The interweaving of episodes devoted to one hero and those devoted to another, which generates two more or less independent but carefully intertwined narrative strands, is the origin of *entrelacement*. This technique, the structural basis of the French prose cycle, is not particularly popular in Germany: besides *Parzival*, it plays a role only in *Diu Crône*, where Arthur's conflict with Gasozein is interwoven with Gawein's early adventures and where Keie's search for the grail almost develops into a separate narrative thread. While in fully developed instances of *entrelacement* the several heroes are nearly equal in importance, in the Middle High German romances the principal hero never relinquishes his pre-eminence.

Sometimes multiplication of actor of a very literal sort will establish connections between one part of a romance and another. The giant who challenges Arthur in *Daniel* tells the court that he has a giant brother and that their father is uncommonly fast and strong (D:761–94). Daniel kills the brother before he enters the land of Cluse and defeats the messenger giant during the first day of battle. When an old man appears and carries off King Arthur from the post-bellum feast we are at first quite surprised, but then we find out that he is the father of the dead giants (D:6986–7). Thus biological multiplication serves to connect four disparate episodes in *Daniel*. Romance authors frequently use family ties to establish some kind of hypotactic order among the episodes of their works: Joram and Gawein, whose combat opens *Wigalois*, turn out to be respectively the uncle and father of Gwigalois; Gwigalois undertakes the campaign against Namur because Lion has killed Amire, the husband of Gwigalois's wife's second cousin (W:9869–82); Dulceflor, whom Meleranz rescues in his penultimate combat, turns out to be the daughter of the great-uncle of Tydomie, Meleranz's beloved (M:7663–82); the ties of consanguinity are so extensive in *Parzival* that one can safely say there is hardly a character, no matter how slight his or her importance, who is not somehow related to most of the other characters in the work. Like proxies and their principals, relatives are bound to be on the same side of any issue: the fight between Gawan and Kingrimursel is finally called off, after hanging in the air for over five thousand lines, because the two turn out to be distant relatives (P:503,14–15).

One of the most common family ties in Arthurian romance is the one that relates the hero of a particular romance to King Arthur: Lanzelet is Arthur's nephew, as is Gawein; Gwigalois is the son of Gawein; Parzival is also related to Arthur, although the relation is quite distant. These relations cannot be considered multiplication of actor, however, for the hero and Arthur each have their own functional identities; neither can be regarded as an auxiliary of the other. The hero's kinship with Arthur does not serve the coherence of an individual romance so much as it does the coherence of the entire genre: through Arthur the hero is related to *all* the romances. The tendency to extend family ties between romances is most evident in the works of der Pleier. Garel's mother is the sister of Gahmuret, his father is Meleranz; Meleranz's mother is a sister of Arthur; Tandareis's mother is Anticonie, from *Parzival* book eight, his father is Ginover's uncle. These relationships, like the appearance of the earlier heroes in the later romances, seem to reflect the thirteenth-century tendency to collect and systematize related material. They are not multiplication of actor, however; they are rather an expression of the hero's essential tie to S.

Often a narrator will use his control over the disclosure of information to hide the relation of a character by proxy to his or her principal. We learn at Sigune's first appearance that she is Parzival's cousin (P:140,22) and realize at her second appearance that she is well informed about affairs at Munsalvaesche, but it is not until Parzival reaches Trevrizent that we learn that Sigune is Anfortas's niece (P:477,1–8). That is, we must wait until halfway through the romance before the mysterious relationship of Sigune to the grail world is clarified. Only then do we realize that, from the perspective of the whole romance, Sigune is an auxiliary of Anfortas – like him, she suffers for mistakes in love – and that her reaction to Parzival reflects the state of his relations with Munsalvaesche. A mystery is introduced which, after titillating us for ten thousand lines, is finally clarified by the revelation that one character is the consanguineous multiple of another. 'Such an explanation,' says Northrop Frye, 'transforms a story into a kind of game.'[22]

Although *Parzival* combines multiplication of actor with the resolution of mystery more often than other romances, the combination does appear elsewhere. In *Daniel* the mysterious disappearance of the Grave von dem Liehten Brunnen with a silent knight (D:2444–545) is finally resolved two thousand lines later, when we learn that this knight is an unwilling auxiliary of the monster that bathes in blood (D:4244–518). Similarly the blow that the dwarf at Pluris administers the young Lanzelet (L:420–51) remains incomprehensible until we learn, five thousand lines later, that the dwarf is the auxiliary of the Künegin von Pluris (L:5468–71). In every case we see that an author employs multiplication of actor to subordinate one character of his romance to another and thus to establish hypotactic relations between otherwise unrelated episodes.

Perspective

Often a romance character will view several episodes from the same perspective; thus multiplication of perspective (the character's own evaluation of an episode) will foster coherence (several episodes will receive the same evaluation). Just after Gwigalois and Nereja arrive at Roimunt, Wirnt exclaims:

> owi, waz da wart gesaget
> maere von ir reise!
> si zalte mange vreise
> die si von vorhten leit
> als ir geselle streit.   (W:4023–7)

Wirnt brings all of Gwigalois's previous adventures together under the heading *reise*, rather as we might: they all occurred on the journey between Arthur's court and Larie's castle. But Nereja tells of the many frights that she suffered: for her the adventures form a group not because of the geographical framework in which they took place, but because of the fear they inspired in her. Thus, although Wirnt classifies the group of episodes from his perspective as narrator and Nereja from her reaction as onlooker, both perceive the same group of adventures as a unit. That they agree on the same grouping from their different perspectives strengthens our own sense of the coherence of the group.

Not surprisingly the narrator is the most frequent figure to view parts of a romance from a single, unifying perspective. Just as Erec and Enite are reconciled, after the episode at Limors, Hartman groups together all the adventures 'sit er mit ir von huse reit' (E:6777). A bit later he reintroduces Guivreiz and reminds us, 'ich han iu e von im gesaget' (E:6821). Hartman's perspective as narrator enables him to make these connections and to recognize these groups. When Wirnt addresses his audience he usually berates them for the sorry state of their social virtue; his uniform perspective on the condition of his listeners unites his scattered complaints.

But other romance characters can also perceive similarities between episodes. Adan groups together Gwigalois's victories over Garel, Karrioz, and Marrien (W:8625–9); and Gwigalois himself, in addressing Larie, considers his entire undertaking in Korntin as a single project (W:8768–71). Remarks like these strengthen our own perceptions of which episodes form coherent groups.

Perhaps the most interesting case in which multiple perspective unifies the episodes of a romance occurs in *Daniel*. Shortly after Daniel leaves Arthur's he comes upon the giant who guards the passage into Cluse. If this were Garel he would adjust his armour and attack the giant at once, but not Daniel. No sooner does he spot his opponent than he starts thinking. He remembers that the giant's skin cannot be cut and wonders if it might not be better to pass up a hopeless fight when no one is watching than to attack, as the knightly code demands (D:1056–74). Of course he decides to fight, but even after the decision he considers the two possible outcomes: victory or defeat (D:1075–110).

The habit of mind by which Daniel first considers a wrong reaction to a situation and then settles on the right one appears repeatedly: he wonders whether he should not fight the giant before listening to the Frouwe von dem Trüeben Berge (D:1144–74); he considers whether he should pursue his original goal or listen to the Frouwe von dem Liehten Brunnen (D:1843–73); he contemplates keeping the Gorgon head for his own use but then throws it into the sea (D:2167–203); he is undecided whether he should wait for his companion at the tent filled with food or whether he should set off again for Cluse (D:2688–93). In every case Daniel sees a single situation from two points of view; a double perspective is attributed to a single character. Daniel does not group several episodes together by considering them from a single perspective, like Wirnt and Nereja; rather the identical structure of his perception of several episodes, his double perspective, establishes a connection between them.[23]

When considering multiplication of perspective, as when we consider multiplication of actor or cause, we should not let our eagerness to detect coherence blind us to the irregularity with which these devices are employed in the interests of romance coherence. I have, for instance, not been able to find any passage in *Iwein* where any character, including the narrator, groups several episodes together. Still there is a sense in which a single perspective, that of the narrator, does unify an Arthurian romance. Even in *Iwein*, where we never find tangible evidence of the narrator's encompassing perspective, we sense an element of coherence in Hartman's apparent omniscience: he knows what Iwein thinks when he first espies Laudine (I:1331–54) as well as what Laudine thinks after she has dismissed Lunete (I:2009–50); and he can tell us about the daughters of the Grave von dem Swarzen Dorne long before Iwein knows anything about them. The narrator's omniscience, along with his uninterrupted presence, contributes greatly to the coherence of a romance.

Yet there are moments when the narrator relinquishes his omniscience and presents events from the hero's perspective: when Iwein is within the castle of the 'pesme aventure' we learn what is going on only as things become clear to Iwein; when Lanzelet remains unimpressed by the gifts of the Künegin von Pluris, Uolrich takes the same position: 'da von wil ich lützel sagen, wan erz niht so hohe wac' (L:6502–3); the first time at Munsalvaesche Wolfram explicitly refuses to tell us any more than Parzival himself might deduce.[24] This is not to say that the author of *Parzival* is a precursor of Henry James; no, Arthurian narrators are clearly omniscient and modify their stance only occasionally. Yet should a narrator wish to relinquish that omniscience, he will do so by adopting the perspective of the hero. There are then two coherent points of view in romance from which an author can present his tale: that of the narrator and that of the hero; that of the hero of the narration and that of the hero of the story.[25]

Gérard Genette compares the traditional narrative to tonal music: even though local changes of tonality are allowed – temporary shifts of point of view to one character or another – the presence of an omniscient narrator firmly establishes the principal key.[26] Essentially I would say the same of Arthurian romance: the single narrator firmly establishes the tonic, even though local shifts of perspective add accidental interest. Yet I would add that the shift of perspective to the hero's point of view is so important that it acts like the dominant in tonal music: it forms a well-established contrast to the tonic.

Cause

The real reason why things happen in Arthurian romance is rooted in the functional dynamics of the perpetual scheme. But these happenings, as we have already seen, are often assigned various ostensible causes that explain them in ways credible to our everyday logic. The author has jurisdiction over the distribution of these ostensible causes and, by engineering coincidences of cause, can organize the various episodes of a romance into larger patterns, just as he could by organizing correspondences of actor. But there is a difference. A given function tends to have the same realization in disjunct episodes, while a single ostensible cause tends to embrace several adjacent episodes; thus coincidence of actor tends to organize the narrative by marking boundaries between various groups of episodes, and coincidence of cause by joining episodes into continuous segments. In *Wigalois,* for example, Arthur's court provides the realization of S on four separate occasions: it marks the beginning of the work (W:145–522), the end of the introductory Gawein section (W:1133–89), the end of Gwigalois's childhood and the beginning of his adventures (W:1475–883), and the end of the work (W:11393–517). A single motivation, on the other hand, Gwigalois's determination to answer the challenge delivered by Nereja, unites a long series of episodes encompassing nearly two-thirds of the entire romance (W:1884–9798).

These two-thirds of *Wigalois* fall into two parts that illustrate different ways in which a single motivation can unite a series of episodes. The first part is bounded by Nereja's announcement of the *aventiure* at Korntin (W:1750–68) and Gwigalois's entry into that land (W:4533). The six episodes that fall between these boundaries, only the last two of which have any inherent relation to Korntin, are united only because they happen along Gwigalois's route to a previously announced goal. There is a geographical space between $S/O^-/I$ and $W/O^-/I \rightarrow W/O^+/I$, and whatever episodes must be accomplished while traversing that space are necessary means to that end. A second series, of seven episodes, begins once Gwigalois enters Korntin; these are components of a single *aventiure,* preordained stages in the reconquest of Korntin.

In discussing multiplication of cause we distinguished two types of ostensible cause: that in which an action is assigned an external cause (breaking flowers in a garden) and that in which it is given an internal motivation ('durch sinen spot'). The same division holds as well for series of episodes: the second series from *Wigalois* is united by a single external cause (components of one *aventiure*), and the first series by a single motivation (Gwigalois's resolve to accept a distant challenge). Attribution to a single cause unites those episodes in *Parzival* that Gawan undertakes to satisfy Orgeluse (P:508,14–552,30, 583,1–612,20) and those episodes in *Diu Crone* generated directly or indirectly by Lohenis (C:19346–20561, 21095–21740). Subordinate to a single motivation are those episodes from Daniel's departure from King Arthur's to King

Arthur's arrival at Cluse (D:987–2844) and that part of *Meleranz* between the hero's departure from King Arthur's and his reunion with Tydomie (M:4218–9174).

When Parzival is offstage fighting his way back to Munsalvaesche he is motivated only by a desperate hope; when Daniel is engaged in outsmarting assorted monsters he never forgets the reason he set out – but here too his motivation is only the memory of a challenge and the anticipation of success; when Gawan is struggling to win Orgeluse, however, there she is right next to him, making nasty remarks all the while. She, like the giant's challenge in *Daniel*, is the ostensible cause for a series of adventures; yet she motivates Gawan not as a remembered obligation but as an undeniable presence. She accompanies him, an incarnate cause, throughout the entire series. This is a special ability of Arthurian women. A male opponent when he appears must either be fought at once or abstracted into a distant challenge; he cannot, in person, motivate the hero for any length of time. A woman, however, can accompany a hero for long stretches, inspiring him to undertake one adventure after another.

Authors of romances exploit this ability of Arthurian women in order to generate coherence. The presence of Orgeluse at Gawan's fight with Lischois, at his fight with Florant, and at his encounter with Gramoflanz unites these episodes. Similarly the hostile presence of Nereja accompanies Gwigalois from Arthur's to Roimunt and helps unify this journey, just as the constant presence of Enite for the second part of *Erec* increases the coherence of this section. Notice that, although each of these relationships of a hero and a woman involves a high degree of hostility, they differ considerably in other respects: Orgeluse has a specific goal in mind, getting Gawan to fight Gramoflanz, and abandons her resistance as soon as her object is achieved; Nereja is a messenger who withholds the bulk of her message until she is satisfied with Gwigalois, only then to disappear entirely – to be replaced by her principal, Larie, Gwigalois's love; Enite must wait until Erec has overcome his hostility to her, after which she herself ceases to provoke adventures.[27] In every case, however, the extended presence of a woman acts as ostensible cause for a series of episodes and thus organizes them into a coherent group.

Often the hero and the accompanying woman are in love; then her presence, as multiplication of cause, gives the author the opportunity to develop one of his favorite themes: *minne*. Thus in *Parzival* the love of Gawan for Orgeluse is developed and analysed over thousands of lines. Parzival's love for Condwiramurs, on the other hand, is a static quantity: occasionally he remembers her (P:282,24–283,23, 732,1–733,20); more often she is abstracted, along with the grail, into an unchanging formula (P:740,19–20, 743,13). We cannot deny that love of Condwiramurs motivates Parzival; and yet when Parzival is separated from his wife the author has little opportunity to elaborate on that love. For the same reasons we find much more explicit evidence of the author's attitude to love after the crisis in *Erec*, where Enite is almost always present, than after the crisis in *Iwein*, where Laudine makes only sporadic appearances. To be sure, Iwein often demonstrates his love of Laudine, as any interpretation of *Iwein* will certainly show; but in the absence of Laudine this love is articulated on only a few occasions.

Of all the ways in which a series of Arthurian episodes can be given added coherence, we in the twentieth century are most receptive to consolidation of cause. We acquired, in the eighteenth century I suppose, a great appetite for consistent explanations – Laws of Nature – and are always gratified when we think we can detect them. Faced with a work of literature we automatically start rummaging about, looking for the one principle that will explain everything. Why was Faust saved? we ask ourselves and assume that we have gotten to the heart of the matter by pointing to lines 11936–7 and answering, because he was always striving. Faust was a man of consistent purpose, a man of principle; no wonder he was saved. We are gratified to think we have discovered at the same time the essence of Faust's being and the causal mainspring of the entire work. Leaving aside the question whether this kind of inquiry does justice to the literature of any century, where will it lead us when applied to Arthurian romance? We will, I believe, either be forced to abandon it entirely for lack of results or, if we stick to it, will distort the works we seek to understand. In our romances consistent explanation is a local phenomenon, a technique used to add greater coherence to a series of episodes; if we seek the law according to which a whole romance is organized at the level of some character's conscious intention we will only distort the work.

The author of *Erec* apparently did not regard a uniform causality as an essential ingredient of his romance. When Erec imposes silence upon Enite and they leave Karnant, we have no idea what he has in mind. Only when the two are reconciled again, after the episode at Limors, are we told: 'ez was durch versuochen getan ob si im waere ein rehtez wip' (E:6781–2). This not entirely satisfying explanation links together all the episodes since line 3106. And what of those that follow? The fight with Guivreiz is a mistake from everybody's point of view, and the 'joie de la curt,' considered the crowning episode of the entire work, is undertaken by Erec merely because he happens to stumble upon it. There is no consistent causal explanation for the episodes after line 6814 other than that the author has chosen to let the perpetual scheme run a little longer before allowing Erec to reach home. While it might be argued that the author included the extra episodes in the interest of the overall architecture of his work, it is quite clear that he did not feel the need to integrate them into any inclusive causal scheme.[28]

What Propp says of the Russian fairy tale applies just as well to German Arthurian romance: 'Motivations often add to a tale a completely distinctive, vivid coloring, but nevertheless motivations belong to the most inconstant and unstable elements of the tale.'[29] Our interpretations of Arthurian romance will often depend on our analysis of the 'distinctive, vivid coloring' added by ostensible motivations to an episode or series of episodes; yet we must not blind ourselves, when considering an entire romance, to the inconsistency and instability of these same motivations.

Nowhere is the instability of Arthurian motivation more striking than in *Diu Crone*. After the introductory 'Becherprobe,' the first combats in the romance are Gasozein's victories over King Arthur's knights followed by his inconclusive battle with the king himself. Nearly five thousand lines later this fight is taken up again, this time before the court; after the fight is frustrated Ginover is abducted by her brother, rescued by Gasozein, who then assaults her, and delivered finally by Gawein, who fights Gasozein until both are exhausted. The ostensible reason for Gasozein's aggressiveness is his claim that Ginover should be his and not Arthur's (C:4832–69); Ginover's own behaviour fosters our suspicion that there is in fact some sort of illicit liaison between them (C:3373–427, 10965–80, 11003–8). Yet just before Gasozein is to fight Gawein again, he admits that all he has said about the queen is false (C:12549–83); Arthur and Ginover (!) forgive him at once, and somewhat later Gasozein is married to Gawein's sister-in-law. Gasozein's desire for Ginover provides the ostensible motivation for half a dozen fights spanning nearly ten thousand lines; then all at once this motivation is declared no longer valid. Arthur's court accepts the retraction without a moment's thought and proceeds to behave as if the episodes that this motivation had seemed to generate were suddenly declared invalid as well. The court, that is, accepts the contingency of romance motivation as perfectly natural.

The ad hoc nature of Arthurian causality helps explain the embarrassment we sometimes sense at the end of a romance. Iwein is captivated by

Laudine from the moment he sets eyes on her (I:1331) and goes mad when he loses her; one would expect their final reunion to be the high point of the work. Not at all. It is accomplished by a cheap trick of Lunete, who used to be so sensitive and resourceful, and is only barely credible. We have the feeling that the all-encompassing motivation is merely an excuse, that it exists only as a surface technique for uniting a series of adventures. When the goal is achieved it turns out to be considerably less important than we had thought.

We have the same feeling in *Wigalois* and *Daniel*. The first three-quarters of both works are organized in an entirely credible causal frame; when the latter end of this frame is reached – Korntin is won back; King Matur is defeated – the entire cast joins in a large and, for our taste, very satisfying party. Then all of a sudden there's another episode: we are deprived of our little esthetic satisfaction for the battle at Namur – led, of all things, not by Gwigalois but by Gawein! – and the rescue of King Arthur, who in strange disregard of Arthurian probability has been carried off by a bitter old man! There is little to be said but that the authors of these romances were, for one reason or another, more eager to present an additional adventure than to satisfy our sense of proportion or our hunger for consistent cause.

When we rummage about in Arthurian romances and come up with consistent motivations we distort the works, burdening them with consistency at a level on which none was meant to exist. A romance is predictable only as a series of discrete episodes; coincidence of cause, like that of actor and perspective, can be manipulated to organize segments of this series, but it is never applied rigorously to unify an entire romance. As Walter Haug remarks: 'The desire to establish causal connections throughout is not compatible with the episodic structure of Arthurian romance.'[30]

SURFACE: TRANSMITTING THE WHOLE ROMANCE

By his decisions at the skeletal level the author establishes the essential proportions of his romance; by the way in which the elements of the skeleton acquire substance he determines the apparent relations and proportions of the work; by his portrayal of the act of transmission, which constitutes the surface of the romance, the author betrays the nature of the entire undertaking. In investigating the surface of the individual episode we found that the boundaries between episodes tend to disappear when we focus our attention on the role of the narrator. We borrowed Michael Curschmann's term, 'the adventure of narrating,' to distinguish the series of discrete adventures of the hero, which constitute the story, from the single adventure of the narrator, which comprises the entire romance. Let us turn now to that single adventure and consider how the narrator's transmission of his story affects our perception of that story, our estimation of the narrator's role, and, ultimately, our understanding of romance itself.

Articulating the Surface

While the basic unit of heroic activity is the episode, the basic unit of the narrator's activity is the four-stress rhymed couplet. These two kinds of basic unit do not show an equal tendency to cohere: the single episode, realized differently from its neighbour, tends to isolate itself; the much smaller unit of the individual couplet, looking very much like its neighbours, tends to get lost in a uniform series.[31] Thus the author must approach the essential structure of the story differently from the way in which he approaches the essential structure of the narration. The substance of the story is a series of discrete episodes that he must somehow contrive to connect; the surface of the narration is a series of monotonous rhymed couplets that he must somehow manage to articulate.

The most significant point of articulation in Arthurian romance is its beginning, for here the author provides two obligatory 'specific signals' that distinguish his work from the world around it.[32] First, the beginning of a romance marks the commencement of speech in four-stress rhymed couplets, a variety of Middle High German that is systematically distinct from the everyday sort. Its grammar requires a regularity of rhythmic and phonic organization that ordinary speech does not; at the same time it allows greater freedom in syntax and lexical juncture. By choosing recognizably poetic language the author establishes a clear boundary between the romance and the non-literary world around it.

The significance of this initial, linguistic boundary is increased by a second even more specific signal, the romance prologue. Nowadays we have title pages; medieval scribes composed superscriptions on their own; but the romance author relied on the prologue to set off his work both from the non-poetic world and from other kinds of poetic work. It articulates what follows from what precedes it: conversation (in performance); another text (in a manuscript). To serve this function of course an Arthurian prologue has to be recognizable as such; and indeed they all betray a strong family resemblance.

The Prologue

An Arthurian prologue falls into two parts.[33] The first part establishes the relation between narrator and audience in a general way; it often begins with a proverb or an example. The second part introduces the particular matter at hand; often it names the hero or the author or offers a preview of what is to come. At this level of generalization the two-part pattern can apply to many Middle High German prologues.[34] Within this group, however, the authors of Arthurian romances developed their own characteristic traditions for realizing the orthodox pattern.

All but two of the Arthurian romances begin by stating some general principle (*sententia*), in most cases introduced by *swer* (L:1–4; I:1–3; W:20–32; D:1–6; T:1–5) but not always (P:1,1–1,2; C:1–8; but cf. C:6, 22, 29). Those works that do not begin with a proverb open with an invocation of the glories of the past (GM:1–4; M:1–22). These openings include or imply an opposition, the discussion of which follows: *die frumen* and *die zagen*, *hübsche liute* and *die boesen nidaere* (L:7–19); *tumbe liute* and *der wise man*, good and bad men and women (P:1,15–4,8); *ein wise man* and *ein tore* (C:1–39); *guote liute* and those who do not listen (D:1–6); lovers with *staeter* and *unstaeter muot* (T:6–102). Those works that begin with a *laudatio temporis acti* continue by comparing the glorious past to the miserable present (GM:5–18; M:23–37). In many cases the opposition leads the narrator to distinguish two camps in his audience: those favourably disposed to his work or capable of understanding it, and those not (L:14–23; P:1,15–2,16; W:43–5, 82–123; C:64–88; D:23–32). Of all the Arthurian romances only Iwein includes an *exemplum* in the first part of its prologue – 'des git gewisse lere künec Artus der guote' (I:4–5) – and it is the only romance not to develop an opposition.

In addition to the general principle and the opposition, the first part of an Arthurian prologue (occasionally the second part) may include a number of common but optional features. Many of them have to do with the reception of the work: Uolrich, Wirnt, and Heinrich care only how the better part of their audience judges their works (L:14–17; W:40–5; C:108–39); Wolfram and Heinrich counsel their hearers to look beneath the surface of their works (P:1,15–2,16; C:89–114); Wirnt and der Strikkaere request quiet (W:82–4; D:19–22). Some narrators will protest their inadequacy (W:33–9; C:40–72, 140–8; M:106–11) or hold forth shamelessly on the proper use of wealth (W:54–81; M:36–93). Frequently, mention will be made of the use of such works: *lere* (I:4; P:2,8; W:86–9); *kurzwile* (C:226–9; D:12); *wibes gruoz* (C:231–45; T:103–71). The first part of a prologue, then, moves from a general principle through the consideration of an abstract opposition to a discussion of the relations between a narrator and his audience, a narrator and his patron, a work and its public.

The second part of the prologue is usually heralded by a phrase like 'nu hoert ein fremdez maere' (G:31; M:101; cf. L:11; P:3,23) or 'nu wil ich iu ein maere sagen' (W:131–2; cf. T:161–3). These formulas, however, do not in fact begin the tale itself; instead, they signal the shift from the consideration of general topics to that of the particular romance at hand. In *Iwein* (I:21), *Daniel* (D:7), *Diu Crone* (C:140), and *Gauriel* (GM:19) the start of the second part of the prologue is not marked by an explicit call for attention – although *Daniel* (D:15) and *Diu Crone* (C:217) do incorporate such lines slightly later on. The second part of the prologue will include either the name of the author (I:21–30; W:136–44; C:246–9; D:16–17; M:101–5) or a general introduction to the as yet nameless hero (L:25–40; P:4,14–26; GM:33–51; T:172–93); curiously, the hero of the story and the hero of its narration never appear together in a single prologue.

Often, especially in the later works, the second part of the prologue will include some reference to the literary tradition to which the work belongs: Hartman (I:22) and Wirnt (W:132) refer vaguely to a source; Heinrich, der Strickaere, and der Pleiaere explicitly mention having translated a French original (C:217–30; D:7–11; M:101–5). Der Pleiaere names Hartmann (G:32) or Hartmann and Wolfram (M:106–11); Cuonrat even adds Gottfried to the list (GM:29–30); *Garel* and *Meleranz* include quotations from the beginning of *Iwein* (G:39–41 = I:35–7; M:114–16 = I:8–10). Note that some of the works that do *not* refer to literary tradition display their literariness in the *first* section with bravura displays of technique: Wolfram opens with his *vliegendez bispel* (P:1,1–1,15); before *Wigalois* reaches its general principle the book addresses the soul who has opened it (W:1–19); Heinrich incorporates a complete sentence, including his name, into an acrostic (C:182–216); der Pleiaere works a *Minnelied* of six strophes into the beginning of *Tandareis* (T:103–38).

King Arthur appears in every romance prologue save those to *Lanzelet* and *Parzival*. Except in the case of *Iwein*, where he serves as *exemplum* in part one, Arthur always figures in the second part of the prologue; he belongs, that is, not to the general introductory remarks but to those relevant to the particular work at hand. One is usually content to call mention of Arthur a 'citation of genre,'[35] as indeed it probably is, but closer investigation reveals three distinct attitudes with regard to Arthur's function in a romance prologue. If the prologue to the French *Erec* is any indication – which it may not be; the epilogues have nothing in common – then its German adaptation did not include any mention of Arthur. If we recall that neither the prologue to *Lanzelet* nor that to *Parzival* includes Arthur, and if we assume that he was absent from *Erec*, then his presence can hardly be called obligatory in romance prologues before *Wigalois*. Arthur's exemplary appearance in *Iwein* is, again, a special case.

Of the three romances that follow *Parzival*, one – *Diu Crone* – mentions Arthur briefly in the second part of the prologue, while two – *Wigalois* and *Daniel* – do not include him at all. All three works, however, append to the prologue a rather lengthy section in which they praise Arthur and describe his childhood (C:249–465) or his court and its customs (W: 145–246; D:33–142); the first episode develops almost unnoticed out of these descriptions.[36] Brief mention of Arthur in *Gauriel*, *Tandareis*, and *Meleranz* is incorporated into the second part of the prologue proper, where it serves as a simple announcement of genre, rather like the mention of Hartmann and Wolfram (GM:19–25; T:178–81; M:113–26). The German romances thus fall into three diachronic groups with regard to their introduction of Arthur: the first group is content to ignore him until his first appearance in the story; the second is concerned to consolidate and glorify his legend, building at the same time a bridge between prologue and first episode; the third treats him as a self-explanatory signal of genre. Note that the changing fashions with regard to Arthur parallel the growing tendency to claim a specific French source and to salute the classical masters.

The archetypical prologue to an Arthurian romance consists, then, of two sections. The first establishes a generalized space for the reception of a literary work: it clears the air with the proclamation of a general principle; it demonstrates its seriousness by working out some opposition; often it includes more particular remarks calculated to foster a favourable reception. The second section introduces the particular matter at hand: usually it is articulated by a specific call for attention, inconceivable at the outset of part one; it will either introduce its author by name or paint a generalized picture of its hero; the later authors will include mention of King Arthur, presiding genius of the genre, and often more specific information on the literary pedigree of their works.

The Epilogue

The romance prologue is balanced by an epilogue, but, as is so often the case with our genre, its ends are less impressive than its beginnings. In general one can say that an Arthurian epilogue consists of at least three elements: information about the hero's future (except in *Diu Crone* and *Gauriel*); specific notice that the tale is over (except in *Iwein* and *Gauriel*); and a prayer for our salvation (except in *Parzival* and, very nearly, *Iwein*). Ordinarily the hero and heroine will have returned home, and, if there was a celebration, the guests will have left; this signals the end of the last episode. The narrator will sketch the rest of the hero's life, either in general terms (E:10097–129; L:9350–425; W:11605–28; M:12786–827; Wm:6095–102; but cf. I:8159–65!) or incorporating some specific feature of the work: Erec never again *verlit sich* (E:10119–23); Lunete was rewarded (I:8149–58); Feirefiz and Loherangrin carry on the international work of the grail (P:822,28–823,1, 823,27–826,30); Daniel and Arthur continue to see one another often (D:8450–8); Garel and Ekunaver endow a monastery at the site of their battle (G:21067–253); Tandareis is admired forever after for his victory over the giant at Mermin (T:18248–68). Those romances that began with childhood sequences include in their epilogues mention of the hero's children (L:9379–85; P:823,27–826,30; W:11626–74; M:12800–16; Wm:6096–102). Yet even those epilogues that incorporate echoes of the particular work portray the hero's future only in the vaguest terms. The first part of the epilogue, then, mirrors the generalized praise that often appears near the end of a romance prologue; and, just as the second part of the prologue is introduced with a *nu hoeret* line, so in most cases the sketch of the hero's future will conclude with an explicit marker: 'alsus endet sich daz liet' (L:9432); 'hie hat daz buoch ein ende' (G:21286).

This marker, however, is not the signal for the end of the work but merely for the end of the story; ordinarily material specific to the narration will follow. Sometimes the author's name will be given (L:9344; P:827,13; C:30011; G:21303; T:18305; M:12766) or a general moral drawn for the audience (P:827,19–24; M:12828–33). The narrator may ask for the favour of his listeners (L:9440–1; G:21287–304) or of his patron (L:9434–41; M:12766–85) or of women (P:827,25–30; C:29989–30000); or he may more or less openly ask for money (L:9434–9; W:11676–85; D:8444–9; T:18269–76, 18297–302; M:12779). In two cases parts of the epilogue recall specific elements of the prologue: the 'saelde und ere' that conclude Iwein (I:8166) mirror those that opened the work (I:3); 'diu krone' with which Heinrich ends his work (C:29966–90) recalls 'des riches krone' (C:54) as well as the lapidary and metallurgical metaphors with which he ornamented his prologue (C:49–72, 94–107). Finally, the general precept that opens an Arthurian romance finds its counterpart in the prayer with which it closes; both precept and prayer are expressions to which all readily subscribe but which are only loosely related to the work itself.

On the one hand my analysis of romance epilogues suggests a uniformity that does not exist: in *Iwein* and *Gauriel*, and to a lesser extent in *Erec*, the pattern appears in such abbreviated form that it can only be detected with the aid of other works; in *Lanzelet* and *Meleranz* sizable considerations of source and patronage are inserted into the depiction of the final celebration (L:9309–49; M:12766–85), not, as I would have them, in the second part of the epilogue; in *Parzival* and *Wigalois* material that bears only on the transmission or reception of the tale appears before the line that marks the end of the story. On the other hand we can note in most cases a clearly articulated progression out of the story: from the last episode, through the general portrayal of the hero's future, across a line marking the end of the story, followed by various concerns of the narration itself, to the concluding prayer for the salvation of all.

We see then that, while the prologue moves from a general principle through concerns of the narration into the story itself, the epilogue reverses this progression, leading us out of the story and out of the narration back into the world of general principles and inevitable death. As we have already seen, the story has its own traditional opening scenes (type-one episode; type-two episode at Arthur's court; childhood sequence) and a standard closing sequence (a celebration at Arthur's and a journey home). The narrator sets his prologue and epilogue before and after these marked sequences so that the beginning and ending of the narration frame the start and finish of the story that this narration relates. The exterior limits of this frame mark a vertical boundary, between the romance and the non-literary world surrounding it; the interior limits of the frame mark a horizontal boundary within the work, between the level of the narrator, the narration, and that of the hero, the story.[37]

The Consciousness of the Whole

Within the body of a romance articulation is possible both at the level of the narration and at that of the story. The most obvious divisions, of course, are those generated by the transition from one episode to another in the story. Sometimes the narrator will draw our attention to these natural divisions by accompanying them with a break in the quality of the narration. Shortly after Gahmuret disappears from *Parzival*, Wolfram pauses to address the audience in his own right (P:114,5–116,4), as he does also after the type-one episode at Arthur's court (P:337,1–30). Hartmann marks the end of the first part of *Iwein* by his dialogue with Vrou Minne (I:2971–3028) and Heinrich concludes the first third of *Diu Crone* by delivering a speech on women (C:13888–920). Der Pleiaere gives the second part of *Tandareis* its own regulation prologue (T:4057–91). In all of these cases the narrator emphasizes a major division of his story by breaking off the narration altogether, turning to the audience with a speech of his own and thus drawing attention to himself as the hero of the narration.

The narrator may articulate his narration not only at its major divisions but also between individual episodes. Wirnt separates two episodes by a lament on his own time (W:2319–48, 2358–95). The narrator of *Tandareis* likes to begin an episode with a formula like 'die rede lat sin unt hoeret hie' (T:13496; cf. T:264–8, 8301–3, 10715–16). Wirnt and Heinrich will mark the ends of episodes by rhyming three lines instead of two. By far the least dramatic but at the same time the most common way in which a narrator can signal the commencement of a new episode of his story is to begin with the adverbs *nu* or *do*. At the start of the Cadoc episode in *Erec*, Hartmann tells us, 'nu reit der ritter Erec als in bewiste der wec' (E:5288–9); the following episode begins, 'nu hate er sich ervohten' (E:5716); and the next starts off, 'do diz wunder ergie uf Limors, nu sehet hie wa ein garzun entran' (E:6814–16).

The evidence appears unambiguous: divisions of the narration coincide with divisions of the story. Yet the evidence is deceptive. The first line of the Cadoc episode begins with *nu*, but so does the sixth (E:5293); and the ninth starts with *do* (E:5296). Clearly these can only relfect very minor divisions of the narrative. A few lines later Hartmann introduces a generalizing observation of his own in the same way: 'do was doch sin manheit schin' (E:5305). In *Wigalois* the segments marked by triple rhymes range from 9 to 123 lines;[38] the divisions can fall within the speech of a single character (W:4706–7, 9843–4) or between the introduction to direct speech and its commencement (W:4902–3, 5246–7). The triple rhymes in *Diu Crone* seldom mark sections longer than thirty lines; like those in *Wigalois*, they do not necessarily coincide with the narrative divisions (Keie's lament on the supposed death of Gawein begins without the articulation of a triple rhyme, although rhymes occur five times within the speech and at its conclusion [C:16953–17091]); occasionally Heinrich will bridge the division by enjambment (C:6449–50, 25993–4).

Even the more dramatic kinds of intrusion by the narrator do not necessarily coincide with the divisions of the story: Hartman inserts a meditation on *minne* into the episode with Enite's would-be abductor (E:3694–716); Wolfram addresses a personal complaint to Vrou Minne while Keie rides out to fight Parzival (P:291,1–293,17); Wirnt speaks on the inspiration of womanly beauty midway through Gwigalois's fight with Roaz (W:7562–80); der Strickaere praises *list*, Daniel's distinguishing virtue, just as Daniel figures out how to rescue King Arthur (D:7487–548); the very clear markers in *Tandareis* are more likely to signal a change of focus within an episode than the beginning of a new episode (T:12800–4, 13223–4, 13263, 13976–8).[39] It seems then that, while the articulation of the narration may coincide with that of the story, this coincidence is accidental – or at least optional. And this is not surprising, for the means of articulation at the narrator's disposal – whether long speeches or the single word *nu* – have no intrinsic relation to the divisions of the story: the means of the narration are words; those of the story are actions. By the employment of techniques available only to him in his function as mediator and demonstrably independent of the substance of his tale, the narrator constantly draws our attention to the horizontal boundary between him and the hero that was established in the prologue.[40]

More clearly dependent on the unique perspective of the narrator are those moments when he looks ahead and predicts the future course of his story. When Lanzelet approaches Schatel le Mort, Uolrich tells us that in a future episode Iwaret will be killed (L:3596–9), 'doch ensin wir dar noch niht komen' (L:3600); after Valerin is defeated the first time Uolrich warns us that we can expect more trouble from the same source in the future (L:5353–7), but it does not materialize for another fourteen hundred lines. Before Erec's first fight with Guivreiz, Hartman tells us that whatever hardships Erec has endured in the past are mere child's play in comparison with what is in store (E:4268–72). Wolfram insists that he will explain the goings-on at Munsalvaesche at the proper moment (P:241,1–30); he compares Gawan's suffering in love to his ordeal at Li Gweiz Preljus, an adventure that is still in the future (P: 583,25); and, as we have already noted, he gives away the end of the romance before narrating Parzival's fight with Feirefiz (P:734,1–15). These remarks – and they represent a vast number of similar ones – can serve a variety of functions: some increase suspense; some decrease suspense; some articulate one episode from another.[41] Yet regardless of their function they all depend on the narrator's knowledge, at any one moment, of the entire story. By reminding us of his encompassing knowledge the narrator reminds us at the same time that for him the romance is a single unit, that his is a single adventure.

The Act of Transmission

The single adventure of the narrator is, as we have remarked a number of times, the transmission of the story. Often the narrator will draw our attention explicitly to the act of transmission in which he is engaged. Directly after relating Iblis's dream, for instance, Uolrich proceeds:

> sit manz an den buochen las,
> so si ez iu für war gesaget,
> vor liebe wachet diu maget. (L:4238–40)

The information conveyed – Iblis was so much in love that she couldn't get back to sleep – fills only one line in three. The other two define the nature of the transmission itself: one has read the fact in books, therefore it is true, therefore I will tell you. Such devices, extremely common in Arthurian romance, fall into two categories. The first includes those figures in which the narrator is recipient: 'von dem ich die rede han' (E:7488); 'als ich an sinem buoche las' (E:7491); 'ich horte sagen' (L: 4180). Often he stands explicitly with the recipients: 'fürbaz kündet uns daz liet' (L:3808); 'sie sagent uns' (D:3582). The second category comprises those figures in which the audience is recipient: 'als ich iu gesaget han' (W:8324); 'nu hoeret ein spaehez maere' (D:5161); 'mine friunt ich niht verhil' (L:3475). In all these cases, and they are but a few of many variations, the narrator portrays the act of communication itself.

Tampering with the Story

This consciousness of the act of communication had remarkable consequences. What appears in the above examples to be an assortment of formulaic devices appears in other instances as a self-consciousness bordering on romantic irony. Since the recipient is included in the text it is not surprising that one of the audience occasionally poses questions: when Erec and Enite sleep out of doors there is an inquiry concerning their bedclothes (E:7106); when Erec and Mabonagrin fight, someone wants to know where they get their strength (E:9169–70). More surprising is the self-assurance – Hartman calls it 'kintlicher wan' (E:7524) – of a listener who pretends to know more than the storyteller: one of Hartman's audience attempts the description of Enite's horse's saddle (E: 7493–525); in *Iwein* someone questions Hartman's *bispel* about love and hatred in one container (I:7027–40). In both cases Hartman knows better. By the time of *Tandareis* the lesson has been learned, and the narrator feels free to taunt the audience for its earlier mistakes: in describing the colour of Flordibel's horse (virtually the same situation as in *Erec*) der Pleiaere turns to his listeners with the aside, 'ich waene daz gevriescht ir nie!' (T:402).

Although Arthurian narrators are quick to rebuke their audience should any of its number be so deluded as to try to meddle with the story, the narrators acknowledge no such restriction for themselves. Sometimes their apparent meddling takes a relatively innocent form: after Lanzelet has outshone all the others at a *vesperie* Uolrich says, 'nu sul wir in lazen riten ze herberge unz morgen fruo' (L:3072–3); when Gawan goes to bed Wolfram wishes him good night (P:552,30); Heinrich does the same (C:6253–4); as der Pleiaere turns from the dignitaries arriving for Arthur's tournament to the activities of his hero he remarks, 'die künege laz wir ligen hie' (T:12801). In these cases it is quite clear that the narrators do not mean to affect the tale; they are merely providing narrative markers.

But similar expressions in other situations can be much bolder. When Erec at his first tourney outshines Gawein, Hartman claims personal responsibility for the anomaly: 'den laze ich vor den einen tac (vürbaz engetar ich)' (E:2757–8). Wolfram marvels at how nicely *he* has set Utepandragun down upon the grass at Kanvoleis (P:74,10–15) and claims that he could avenge Gawan on Orgeluse – although he won't (P:516,9–14). Wirnt defends the clothes that he, 'mit worten,' has given Florie (W:856–62). Heinrich wonders what difference it would make if he, 'von spaehen worten mit sage,' should make one of two contestants stronger or weaker (C:16655–8); and after Keie has assembled an army for the trip to Salie, Heinrich decides, 'ich sol sie schiere riten lan, sit ichs ze hove braht han' (C:22188–9). In these cases the narrator claims direct responsibility for an event in the story, sometimes by virtue of his legitimate control over words, other times absolutely. The implication of these claims, that the narrator can in any way affect the material being transmitted, drastically undermines the notion – advanced with much greater frequency – that the narrator is conscientiously purveying a true account of an already fixed tale.

In other related cases the narrator may turn to the audience and ask their advice about the hero's next move, thus implying that they in fact might have some influence over the story after all. When Lanzelet has defeated Iwaret, Uolrich asks, 'nu waz welt irs mere wan der imz houbet abe sluoc?' (L:4556–7); while the mad Iwein is wandering about the woods Hartman asks, 'waz welt ir daz der tore tuo?' (I:3309; cf. E:6902, 9263). After a page informs Gawan of the situation at Bearosche, Wolfram asks, 'waz welt ir, daz Gawan nu tuo, er enbesehe waz disiu maere sin?' (P:349,28–9). When Gawein and Amurfina sit down to dinner, Heinrich invites us to choose the number of courses they eat (C:8405–9). When the narrator turns to the audience and asks them to determine the next events in the story, he violates that distinction – otherwise so scrupulously maintained and often defended by the narrator himself – between the French story and its German recipients. While it seemed presumptuous of the narrator to claim to be able to affect the course of his true story, it seems preposterous that his audience should possess that same ability. We begin to see how, in transmitting his story, the narrator allows himself a surprising freedom with the conventions of the genre.

Exposing the Conventions

The narrator practises his subversion in other ways as well. Not infrequently he implies that his source might not be altogether trustworthy. Hartman claims to give a true description of the site of the 'joie de la curt,' 'ob uns daz buoch niht liuget' (E:8698). Similar conditions are repeated throughout the corpus: 'ob uns daz liet niht liuget' (L:3264); 'ob Kiot die warheit sprach' (P:776,10); 'louc er mir, so liug ouch ich' (D:14). Still, it is clear that most of these are rhetorical formulas, variations on the familiar assertions of veracity, and that we are not to lose faith. More subversive are cases in which the narrator deliberately refuses to vouch for the truth of his narrative: in describing the sword that hangs over Amurfina's bed Heinrich warns us, 'ouch nim ichz uf die triuwe min niht, daz ez war si' (C:8515–16); on two occasions der Pleiaere wonders if his source hasn't erred in reporting a length of time (M:7078–87, 9238–43); Hartman calls down God's blessing on anyone who believes that fire sprang from Erec's helmet, 'wan ich niht drumbe geswern enmac' (E:9210).

This last example, in which Hartman questions literary convention, is noteworthy. Fire springing from fighters' helmets is a common topos meant to reflect the valour of the combatants: we find it in *Lanzelet*

(L:2588–93, 4494–7, 5316–19), *Iwein* (I:3353), and *Parzival* (P:211,25–6, 742,12, 743,28). Indeed, Hartman himself did not disdain the conventional formula in describing Erec's fight with Iders (E:836). But suddenly, during the fight with Mabonagrin, he finds it improbable! The author Hartmann has the same ambivalent reaction to another topos, the exchange of hearts between two lovers. When Erec rides off to his first tourney the narrator explains quite simply that Erec left his heart with Enite and took hers with him (E:2358–67); yet when another story requires the same exchange between Iwein and Laudine the narrator pretends to find it completely incomprehensible, in spite of detailed instruction from Vrou Minne (I:2971–3028).[42] By himself doubting the credibility of these conventions the narrator draws our attention to their artificiality; that he has employed them elsewhere himself without reservations only heightens the effect.

Narrators draw our attention to the artificiality of the romance world in other ways as well. Wolfram maintains that he wouldn't have taken his wife to Arthur's under any condition (P:216,26–217,6); Wirnt doesn't think he would have lasted very long in Gwigalois's army (W:10682–6); Heinrich couldn't have afforded to outfit Amurfina's maid (C:7712–13); had der Pleiaere wanted flowers he would have picked them in the woods rather than invite a fight by entering Eskilabon's garden (G:3656–65). Statements like these juxtapose the sensible, everyday reactions of the narrator to the exalted behaviour we automatically expect of romance characters: who wouldn't want to go to Arthur's? what hero would avoid a fight? Like Hartman's difficulties with the exchange of hearts, these juxtapositions make the conventions of Arthurian romance seem absurdly artificial.[43]

Just as threatening to the integrity of the romance world are those cases in which the narrator is suddenly ignorant: Hartman tells us what mantle the 'joie de la curt' lady had on, but cannot tell us about her dress: 'ich gesach in weizgot nie, wan ich niht dicke vür sie gie' (E: 8948–9); after Lanzelet's coronation King Arthur stays around for three months of partying, then he leaves 'wan im von heime ein bote kam, der seit im des ich niht vernam' (L:9275–6); Gawan leaves Arthur's, but Wolfram doesn't know how long it takes him to reach Bearosche (P:339,12 –14); Wirnt reports that Gwigalois returned to Korntin with Gawein 'und manic ander werder man, der ich niht genennen kan' (W:11516– 17); Heinrich knows that Amurfina's messenger returned to Gawein, but 'war sie kam, des weiz ich nieht' (C:7890); der Pleiaere doesn't know how long it took Tandareis and his companions to reach Arthur's (T:

12740–2). For eight thousand lines Hartman could describe everybody's attire; suddenly he's missing a detail. For nine thousand Uolrich has known the message of every courier; suddenly he can't hear. These sudden twists subvert the entire narration: if he cannot tell us now, how did he know before? In general the Arthurian narrator appears altogether trustworthy – indeed, he is quick to defend his authority and his accuracy – but occasionally he turns around and implies that he is making it all up. When he does so he undermines the relation between narrator and recipient and subverts the trust on which the act of communication depends; the whole romance edifice, subject as it is to his caprice, seems on the verge of collapse.

The phenomena assembled above are scattered throughout the Arthurian corpus. Because of their isolation an individual occurrence often seems little more than a local trick of the narrator, a pose that he assumes for a moment and then abandons. Yet, having assembled these isolated phenomena in one place, we find that the narrator's poses can be classified according to type; more surprising, we find that the various types contradict each other. One moment the narrator silences his audience; the next he asks them to determine the course of his story. One moment the narrator defends the truth of his tale; the next he suggests his source might have lied. One moment the narrator introduces a conventional topos; the next he finds it absurd. One moment the narrator claims direct responsibility for the fate of his characters; the next he protests his ignorance. The common thread running through all these apparent contradictions is the narrator's tendency to balk at romance convention. Of course he is working in a highly structured genre and has no choice, in general, but to abide by its conventions. Yet from time to time the narrator appears to resist the generic restraints and by this means actually draws our attention to them. He is doing what the Russian formalists call 'laying bare a device.' He thus forestalls our realization that the conventional devices of the genre are absurd and turns their artificiality to his advantage. Such behaviour, says Tomashevsky, is 'an indication of the literariness of a literary work.'[44]

The Sovereignty of the Author

To understand fully the significance of the narrator's apparently quixotic behaviour we must remember that his role parallels that of the author: the opposition of the narrator and the internal audience, as we have already seen, mirrors that of the author and his real public. This structural analogy reinforces our intuition that the narrator is the author's representative within the closed literary world he has created; the narrator is the author's deputy. Thus when the narrator asserts his control over the tale he tells, we are justified in interpreting this as a displaced assertion by the author of his own authority. When the narrator interrupts with 'ich wil iu sagen' he draws our attention away from the tale to his own presence; yet at the same time he reflects the author's extra-literary presence. When the narrator refers to 'daz buoch' he reminds us of our dependence on his transmission – and ultimately on the communicative intent of the author. When the narrator questions a romance convention that he had seemed to accept he implies that we are completely at his mercy – thus proclaiming, on behalf of the author, the author's sovereign control over his romance.

And yet the author does not always depend on his deputy to speak on his behalf. Quite the contrary. The boldest assertions of authorial control occur at those moments in which the author deliberately undermines the authority of his deputy, in which the narrator, whose authority seems so considerable, is himself revealed to be a mere plaything of the author. If we remain within the system of the work we will interpret the narrator's contradictory behaviour, as we have just done, as a display of authority for the benefit of his audience: one moment I assert the convention of the exchange of hearts, the next I pretend not to understand it; look, I, the narrator, can do whatever I please. Yet from without the work this game that the narrator plays with his audience turns into a game that the author plays at the expense of his narrator: at one moment my narrator claims complete control over the story, the next he must confess that he is missing a detail; I can make him contradictory, I can make him unreliable; I, the author, can make him whatever I please.

Just as the narrator, ostensibly responsible for the transmission of the tale to his audience, plays games with the audience and draws attention both to the artificial conventions of his material and to his own authority, so too the author, responsible for the creation of this narrator and the poses this narrator assumes, undermines the conventional role of the reliable narrator and draws attention to his own much greater authority. As Rainer Warning observes, the 'auctoritas' of the narrator is a created authority and remains dependent on its creator-subject, the author. 'As such, however, it itself can become the object of the author's play; the stance according to which the narrator poses as the guarantor of the story can always be upset and turned into a thematization of its artificiality, its createdness.'[45] Thus the narrator is made the plaything of the author and the authority of the deputy is undermined to reveal the greater authority of the creator.

Usually the author is no more eager to undermine the authority of the narrator than the narrator is to undermine the credibility of his tale. Both are eager to uphold the conventions of Arthurian romance, for it is on these conventions that the integrity of their work depends. We too, schooled as we are in the conventions of Arthurian romance, tend during the course of a work to accept these conventions as self-evident. This the romance author tries to prevent. He reminds us from time to time that the conventions are absurd. He reminds us that even though he has accepted these conventions he does not accord them undue importance; therefore he can play with them. He reminds us that his work is an artificial system over which he has ultimate control, that the tale to which we so eagerly devote our attention depends on his act of creation. He claims in effect that he is sovereign in the world of Arthurian romance, not King Arthur.

CONCLUSION

Contradiction and Meaning:
The Intersecting Systems
of Arthurian Romance

Nearly one hundred years ago Max Jellinek and Carl Kraus published an article on contradiction in literary works.[1] By far the largest part of the article is devoted to an annotated list, thirty-two pages long, of contradictions that the authors had collected from a considerable number of Middle High German epics. On the first page of their list we find an example from *Parzival*, and on the last page, one from *Meleranz*. That Arthurian romance is well represented on the intervening pages as well should not surprise anyone who is at all familiar with the genre. Even the casual reader of Arthurian romance is bound to be struck by the frequency with which its authors seem to contradict themselves.

To judge by all but the most recent critical literature, there are only three possible reactions to the contradictions of Arthurian romance. One can take the romance authors to task for their carelessness and inconsistency: this is the treatment traditionally accorded the less celebrated writers. One can ignore the contradictions, the approach favoured by those who treat the canonical works as well as by those seeking to rehabilitate the rest. Or finally one can isolate a particular class of contradictions and attempt to reconcile them, an elaborate and often enlightening undertaking that nevertheless, by deactivating the set of contradictions under consideration and ignoring the rest, once again causes them all to disappear. Yet the inconsistencies we recognize in Arthurian romance cannot be ignored, nor should they be rendered harmless, for they constitute an obvious and characteristic feature of the genre. In a structural analysis such as ours we must attempt to account not only for the regular patterns of Arthurian romance but also for its typical irregularities. How can the inconsistencies we recognize be reconciled with the systems we have isolated?

After Lanzelet kills Iwaret we are told of the intense reciprocal love between our hero and Iblis, daughter of the slain Iwaret (L:4616–21). This love, however, which seems so important in the episode of the magic tent, is forgotten while Lanzelet fights Valerin and violated, one would think, during Lanzelet's one-year stay with the Künegin von Pluris. We hear that Iblis pines away back at Arthur's (L:5625–40) but of Lanzelet, we learn only that he was 'wilent truric, wilent fro' (L:5645) and that he would rather like to see Iblis again 'swenn ez mit fuoge möhte sin' (L:5650). On his way back from Pluris Lanzelet meets 'der stumme Gilimar' who, in obedience to the command of his lady, will not speak a word; Lanzelet, we are told, approves such behaviour (L:6671–2). And yet twelve hundred lines later, when Iblis asks him not to kiss the dragon Elidia, Lanzelet has no use for such devotion and violates his lady's request at once (L:7864–87). Lanzelet's behaviour towards women, and particularly towards Iblis, seems highly contradictory.

The behaviour of Iwein is not all that different. We know that he loves Laudine from the moment he sees her (I:1331–8), and Hartman assures us that Minne 'erwelte hie nu einen wirt deiswar von dem si niemer wirt geswachet noch guneret' (I:1587–9). When Iwein must leave his wife he is distraught (I:2962–8), and Hartman takes advantage of the occasion to carry on about the exchange of hearts (I:2971–3028). Yet no sooner is he gone than Iwein forgets his promise to return within the year (I:3051–8), behaving as if he had never entertained more than a passing interest in his wife.

Why, if Lanzelet loves Iblis, does he loll about Pluris for a year? and why, if he admires the obedience of Gilimar, does he not obey his own wife? Why, if Iwein loves Laudine, can he forget her so easily? and why does Hartman praise Iwein's honour in love when he knows what's in store? We are upset by these apparent contradictions, but there is reason to think that the medieval audience was not. Joachim Heinzle speaks of 'a principle of representation that can be observed throughout medieval literature: the emphasis on the individual scene or motif rather than on the coherence of the whole.'[2] Surely it is the concentration with which the authors of *Lanzelet* and *Iwein* devote themselves to the individual scene that leads to the inconsistencies we detected. The author of *Lanzelet* wants to distinguish the Pluris episode by its erotic component; he praises Gilimar by having Lanzelet express admiration; he indicates Lanzelet's eagerness to take on the dragon adventure by having him violate Iblis's wish. Similarly the author of *Iwein* does all he can to dramatize Iwein's love for Laudine; but when Iwein overstays his leave the narrator's mind is no longer on the intensity of new love but on the catastrophe in store for his hero. In every case the author's eagerness to differentiate a particular scene takes precedence over any obligation he might have felt to the overall consistency of his work.

The tendency to concentrate on local effects in ways that offend our twentieth-century notions of coherence can be detected in many areas of medieval art. Wilhelm Messerer discusses a picture of Gregory the Great in which the activity portrayed in the lower half is, from our perspective, logically incompatible with that in the upper half; but the medieval eye could apparently focus on each part with an intensity that we can no longer muster. The whole then has a different meaning.[3] Rhetorical theory too is clearly more interested in local effect than in overall harmony. William Ryding reminds us that the 'theoreticians laid no special stress on unity or simplicity, and seem rather to have been convinced that the secret of elegance lay not in the unification of the matter, but rather in the multiplication of its elements.'[4]

Instances in Arthurian romance in which the multiplication of elements (what I call differentiation) leads to inconsistency are not hard to find; but in almost every case a reason can be advanced to explain why the particular element, contradictory in a larger context, makes sense in the local environment. When Lanzelet leaves for Pluris he tells only Walwein his goal (L:5423–5) – a sign of their special intimacy; but later on Walwein has no idea where Lanzelet is (L:5576–9) – otherwise King Arthur would have no reason to organize the celebration that is the occasion for the 'Mantleprobe.' Twice in *Iwein* we are told that Gawein is responsible for Iwein's neglect of his promise to return (I:3029–30, 3052–8) – this helps to explain Iwein's behaviour; between these two passages Hartman can still maintain, 'her Gawein was der hôfschste man der riters namen ie gewan' (I:3037–8) – this reflects Gawein's traditional role and helps justify *him*.

The narrators are no less contradictory when talking in their own role than when talking of their heroes. Uolrich will not name the one hundred knights whom Lanzelet defeated at Pluris because we would find it tedious, also because no one has told him their names (L:5502–7) – here Uolrich combines two traditional reasons why a narrator might curtail his account. Hartman tells us that Iwein and Ascalon jousted, then destroyed each other's shields in a sword fight (I:1012–28) – he behaves here like a conventional narrator. Then he insists that he won't describe the rest of the fight because no one was there to watch it, Ascalon died, and Iwein is too courteous to talk (I:1029–44) – here Hartman draws our attention to the artificiality of romance conventions.

Over and over in Arthurian romance we find details, each perfectly logical in its local setting, that prove contradictory if we compare them with each other. Yet, given the evidence from the visual arts and from rhetorical treatises as well as the quantity of contradictions themselves, we cannot assume that medieval writers and audiences perceived these discrepancies as contradictions. Perhaps they did not make the comparisons we do. Joachim Heinzle makes just that point: 'The punctuality of representation that results from a particular manner of perception and proceeds from a particular stylistic intent forms the general framework within which inconsistencies are not only tolerable but are simply not perceived and, in this sense, do not even exist.'[5]

Concentration on local effect is not the only cause of what we perceive as contradiction in Arthurian romance. Considering as a group the various structural phenomena that we have investigated, one can isolate two tendencies: on the one hand the tendency of the genre to insist on its own rules, conventions, and traditional meanings; on the other the tendency of each romance to exploit the options that the rules of the genre provide in order to acquire a distinctive profile of its own. The tension between the grammar of the genre and the compositional needs of the individual romance often generates contradiction.

Consider the abduction of Ginover, which plays a role both in *Lanzelet* and in *Iwein* (as well as in *Diu Crone* and *Garel*). A strange knight arrives at Arthur's court (L:Valerin; I:Meljaganz) and makes a claim on the queen; Arthur allows the claim to be decided by combat or else allows the queen to be carried off. This is absurd. One the one hand King Arthur is, according to the conventions of the genre, the unquestioned model for all romance behaviour. In *Lanzelet* we learn, 'der künic selbe ist so wis, daz erz wol erbieten kan eim iegelichen man nach siner werdikheit' (L:1270–3); Hartman tells us, 'er hat bi sinen ziten gelebet also schone daz er der eren krone do truoc und noch sin name treit' (I:8–11). How can this paragon be so foolish as to allow his wife to be carried off? In most cases, by the way, there is no doubt that Arthur has erred: Harpin's victim maintains, 'der künec treit ouch die schande' (I:4526); and the hero of *Garel* says to his king, 'ir wart guoter witze ein kint, daz ir min frowen gabet hin' (G:142–3).[6] On the other hand it seems incredible that none of Arthur's knights could stop the abductor, for the conventions of the genre make Arthur's court the gathering place for the best knights in the world. Uolrich says that those lamenting the abduction were 'die besten von der welte' (L:6865); Meljaganz says to Arthur, 'ir habet der besten ein her' (I:4599). Why is wise King Arthur made to look so foolish? and why are his brave knights suddenly impotent? We find such contradictions strange, but they are merely the reflection of the tension we noted above. Paul Zumthor reminds us that a medieval text possesses 'a double functionality: internal, owing to the fact that it is poetry; and external, owing to the fact that it is traditional. In this sense it is highly predictable, although its predictability is never total.'[7] A text is predictable to the extent that it subscribes to the grammar of the genre, that collection of established meanings, rules, and options that exists outside the individual work; it is not predictable to the extent that, taking advantage of the options allowed by the grammar, it assumes an individual form: it is unique as an individual poetic composition.

In the case of the abduction of Ginover we find that *Lanzelet* and *Iwein* are predictable and unpredictable at the same time. Like all Arthurian romances, they (predictably) proclaim the perfection of Arthur and his knights. Then, however, they take advantage of the opportunities for differentiation that the genre allows and use the abduction of Ginover in the (unpredictable) interests of their own composition. In *Lanzelet* the abduction motivates (multiplication of cause) two separate episodes (the contests with Valerin); the failure of the other knights (multiplication of actor; false heroes) heightens the glory of Lanzelet. In *Iwein* the abduction explains why Lunete and Harpin's victims are left without a champion (multiplication of actor; Gawein as absent hero) and why it is up to Iwein to rescue them (multiplication of cause). In both *Iwein* and *Lanzelet* the appearance of the abduction in two different episodes serves to foster the overall coherence of the romance.

The contradictions that surround the abduction of Ginover could be viewed as the result of the medieval preoccupation with local effect: in one context it suits the author to stress the perfection of Arthur and his knights, in another he finds it more useful to let them fail. Yet, while the tension between grammar and composition may appear as inconsistency of local effect, it reflects a much more general literary phenemenon. Jurij Lotman holds that 'in art two tendencies are simultaneously at work: the tendency to demarcate languages (the language of poetry and prose, the language of various genres, etc.) and to overcome these demarcations ... An artistic text ... functions in a dual structural field consisting of the tendency to establish order and to violate it ... The life of an artistic text depends on their mutual tension.'[8] By praising King Arthur and his knights for their fame and perfection an author establishes unmistakably the language in which he has chosen to write, the genre; by portraying Arthur and his knights as foolish or impotent he violates that order, the grammar of the genre, in the interests of his particular compositional intent. From the logician's point of view this kind of behaviour leads to contradictions; for Lotman this kind of tension produces the semantic richness of art.

The abduction of Ginover is not the only case in which the use of a single element in a non-grammatical way endangers its conventional meaning. Consider the case of Gawein. When he is first mentioned in *Lanzelet*, we are told that 'er zen tiursten was gezalt' (L:2298); at his next appearance we hear of 'Walwein, dem al diu welt wol sprach' (L:2365); Lanzelet considers the publicity value of a fight with such a celebrated hero, 'ichn gehort nie nieman baz geloben' (L:2507). Clearly there is no doubt of Walwein's conventional reputation. Yet the fight that Lanzelet is so eager to begin is suddenly broken off, just when Walwein begins to feel pressed (L:2582–5); and at the tournament at Djofle, where the two heroes briefly come together, their contest is once again mysteriously cut short (L:3372–8) – although Lanzelet does capture Walwein's father.

The author of *Iwein* behaves in a similar fashion. He goes out of his way to establish the conventional perfection of Gawein: 'an dem niht tes enschein ezn waere hövesch unde guot' (I:2698–9); 'der ie in riters eren schein' (I:4718); than whom there was no greater fighter in the world (I:6943–51). As in *Lanzelet* the fight between Gawein and the hero, in which Gawein by his own admission defends the wrong party (I:7621–30), is broken off just as Gawein (and in this case Iwein too) is about to succumb (I:7446–8, 7406–8).

Both works reveal a similar tension. On the one hand their authors are eager to establish the conventional perfection of Gawein and to test their heroes against this standard. On the other, Gawein is perhaps not quite so good as the hero (he allows Lanzelet to capture his father; he defends the wrong sister against Iwein), although neither Lanzelet nor Iwein is allowed to win victory over him. In other words, the authors of both works uphold the conventional role of Gawein, allow their heroes to increase their glory at Gawein's expense, but are careful at the same time not to undermine Gawein's conventional reputation. For without this reputation Gawein would be just another Arthurian knight, like Segramors, and what hero would boast of defeating him?

It is important to emphasize that an author's particular use of Arthur or Gawein does not affect his devotion to the conventional image of

Arthur or Gawein. The extent to which these two potentially contradictory tendencies can exist simultaneously is especially clear in the treatment of Gawein in *Iwein*. At the very same moment that Hartman holds Gawein responsible for Iwein's forgetfulness of Laudine, he calls Gawein 'der höfschste man der riters namen ie gewan' (I:3037–8). In the very same breath, that is, he asserts both Gawein's perfection and his error, both his conventional meaning and his particular function.[9] It is even more important to recognize the simultaneous validity of conventional and particular significance in the case of Arthur. The introduction of Arthur into a romance establishes the genre of the work and proclaims its author's devotion to the conventions of that genre. At the same time it makes available to the author a repertory of stock characters (among them Gawein) and situations (among them the abduction of Ginover) that he can use to give his work the particular differentiation he wants. Although the particular use of Arthur and Gawein in *Lanzelet* and *Iwein* may seem to us to undermine their conventional meaning, the authors of these works clearly feel differently: Arthur presides at both of Lanzelet's coronations, and the beginning of *Iwein* remains the *locus classicus* for 'Artusidealität.'[10]

Discrepancies in Arthurian romance can be attributed to the medieval tendency to focus on local effect; they can be attributed as well to the general tension between a literary work and the tradition in which it is written. The most productive source of apparent inconsistency in Arthurian romance, however, is the interplay between the various systems of which a work is composed.

Consider the treatment of love in *Lanzelet*. For the daughter of Galagandreiz *minne* is clearly nothing but lust (L:854–7, 880–2); for the Künegin von Pluris it is a possessiveness that leads her to keep Lanzelet captive for a year (L:5545–65). Iblis's love of Lanzelet, on the other hand, fits all the courtly forms: she dreams about him before he arrives (L: 4215–33), she addresses Minne in a set speech just before the combat with Iwaret begins (L:4372–406), and she overlooks the death of her father on account of her blind love for the man who killed him (L:4592–601). Elidia is turned into a serpent for some unspecified transgression against a code of love (L:8008–21); returned to human form, she sets up a court of love (L:8033–40). Uolrich regards *minne* as an irresistible force that causes one to behave with foolish excess (L:4054–7, 4330–1, 4597–8, 6644–7), and the inscriptions on the magic tent support his position (L:4849–59).

The evidence from *Iwein* is hardly less diverse. Love overcomes Iwein at the first sight of Laudine (I:1331–9); he regards it as an external power so strong that he is forced to love his mortal enemy – although this same power might also force her to love him (I:1623–59). In fact, however, it is not Vrou Minne who causes Laudine to love Iwein but King Arthur, whose visit to her home she takes as a tribute to her husband's prowess (I:2673–82). According to Gawein it was excess of love that caused Erec to lie about (I:2798). To judge from the reaction of the maid who recognizes the mad Iwein, the effects of love cannot be distinguished from those of poison (I:3404–45). The lion demonstrates *minne* after Iwein kills the serpent (I:3872–6), and the joy of Iwein and Gawein when they recognize each other is also called *minne* (I:7505; cf. I:5107–10). For Hartman *minne* is Vrou Minne: she wounds more dangerously than a sword (I:1537–56); she is nevertheless a great reconciler (I:2054–7); and she can intervene in the narrative itself to expostulate with the narrator (I:2971–3028).

On the basis of such evidence who would dare define the meaning of love in *Lanzelet* or *Iwein*? And what can our authors have in mind by using the term *minne* in so many different ways?[11] Jurij Lotman can help us to an answer. He writes: 'The capacity of a textual element to enter into several contextual structures and to take on different meaning in each context is one of the most profound properties of the artistic text.'[12] The single element, *minne* – a term with a long literary history both within the province of Arthurian romance and in the medieval literary world at large – appears in numerous contexts and has a slightly different meaning in each one. It can serve as multiplication of cause: the lust of Galagandreiz's daughter; the external power that possesses Iwein. It can be rooted in social conventions: the code against which Elidia transgresses; the effect of Arthur's visit on Laudine. It can generate surface effects: the Latin citations on Lanzelet's tent; the personified love who challenges Hartman. In each case *minne* enters into a different set of relations and acquires a different meaning. We are intrigued by the significance of *minne* in *Iwein* not because its author uses the term with unusual precision, but because he uses it with unusual variety. We value precision of meaning in a treatise, richness of meaning in an artistic text.[13]

The semantic richness of the term *minne* results from the different meanings the word has in each of the contexts in which it occurs. At the same time, each particular context is enriched by the relations the single word *minne* sustains with all its other slightly different usages. At the beginning of the Elidia episode Lanzelet is lying in bed with Iblis: 'er do manege rede getet mit siner vriundinne von hübscheit und von minne'

(L:7830–2). What are they talking about? The stylized romance love we associate with Iblis? the uncontrollable sexual needs of Galagandreiz's daughter? the possessiveness of the Künegin von Pluris? the obedience of 'der stumme Gilimar'? Given the fact that Lanzelet is in bed talking to Iblis, with whom he has not exchanged a word since before leaving for Pluris, any of these alternatives is entirely possible. The particular context gains in richness from the resonance of all the meanings of *minne* in the romance.

The word *minne* is not the only element in this passage that sustains relations with other parts of the romance. The more or less obligatory presence of Lanzelet binds this episode into the regular series, the romance, of which he is the hero. That he has just finished celebrating the liberation of Walwein and Erec (end of the last episode) suggests, if the romance is to proceed grammatically, that this is the beginning of a new episode. Markers from the narrator – 'do diu hohgezit ergie' (L: 7817) – imply the same. That we find ourselves at Arthur's establishes a connection between this episode and all the others that begin at the same location. Each particular element – Lanzelet, Arthur, narrator markers, beginning of an episode – belongs to a system that includes all other appearances of the same element. The intersection of these several systems in one context significantly adds to the meaning of that context.

The sentence quoted above, that Lanzelet and Iblis talked of love, continues with Lanzelet's request for news: 'do vragt er si ze leste, waz siu maeres weste aller vremdest nach ir wane' (L:7833–5). The situation is absurd: Lanzelet has been back at court for a thousand lines – long enough for several councils, rescues, and celebrations – but has not yet heard the latest news. Nor, apparently, has he spoken to Iblis until just now (otherwise he would no longer need to congratulate her on her success at the 'Mantelprobe'). Yet, while Lanzelet's request does not satisfy our everyday notions of probability, it does satisfy the needs of the romance, for it elicits from Iblis a reason for Lanzelet to undertake another adventure (multiplication of cause).

That the news which motivates Lanzelet is delivered by Iblis connects this episode with the others in which she appears: the fight with Iwaret and the magic tent, in both of which she is O^+; the conclusion to the first fight with Valerin, where she is little more than Lanzelet's auxiliary; the 'Mantelprobe,' in which she fills the function I. In delivering news of Elidia to Lanzelet Iblis serves as auxiliary to the opponent, for she is the messenger by whom the dragon's challenge reaches the hero. After serving her function she disappears from the episode entirely to make room for Elidia, who becomes O^+. In the course of the romance the name Iblis is attached to a remarkable variety of functions: O^+, I, auxiliary of O^-, auxiliary of I; since each contributes something to the total meaning of the figure Iblis we must account for all of them if we want to understand her. And since they are all attached to the name Iblis they are all present when she delivers the latest news to Lanzelet. She delivers her message as auxiliary of O^-, but she is in bed with Lanzelet as O^+. The tension between these two functions finds expression in her request that Lanzelet forgo the adventure towards which she is leading him (L:7864–7).

We could pursue our investigation of the various systems that intersect in Iblis's speech: her entreaty recalls her attempt to forestall the fight with Iwaret (L:4308–9); Lanzelet's deceptive acquiescence recalls the deceit he practises on the Künegin von Pluris (L:6480–90). We could go on, but by now it must be clear: each element of this or any episode is part of numerous other systems; each appearance of that element recalls its other systemic relations and adds meaning to the particular context in which the element appears.

The examples of apparent contradictions collected above must have shown that for each discrepancy we found in *Lanzelet* we could find a corresponding discrepancy in *Iwein*. It is important to realize that our favourite texts are no less contradictory than those that are not quite so popular. Yet the two works do not have precisely the same attitude towards the contradictions they contain: the author of *Lanzelet* is inclined to ignore contradictions and to rely on us to discover the systemic relations of each element; the author of *Iwein* is more likely to point out contradictions and to exploit the relational systems of each element to further the overall coherence of his work. We can see this tendency in a passage in *Iwein* analogous to Iblis's transmission of news: that in which the imprisoned Lunete explains her plight to Iwein (I:4011–356).

First the situation. Whereas in *Lanzelet* we were left to make the connections ourselves (Arthur's court; Lanzelet and Iblis in bed), here the significance of the setting is fresh in mind: sight of the chapel and the magic well has just caused Iwein to carry on at length about their significance in his life (I:3960–4010). Thus the author himself alerts us to the group of episodes – Kalogrenant's defeat, Iwein's victories over Ascalon and Keie, his final reconciliation with Laudine – to which this episode belongs by virtue of its location.

Like Iblis's message, Lunete's story serves as multiplication of cause, here to motivate Iwein's fight with the malicious steward. But in this case the differentiation is carried further, for the cause, Lunete's imprisonment, is itself given a cause: Lunete's advice to Laudine (I:4127–30, 4196–8; cf. I:2018–24). This advice, in the opinion of the steward (multiplication of perspective), is treasonous. Therefore Lunete stands accused.

Since Lunete devotes her speech primarily to explaining why she is about to be executed, she refers repeatedly to the episode in which she advised Laudine to marry. Yet relations with other episodes are also made explicit. Iwein recognizes that *triuwe*, for the lack of which Lunete denounced him so mercilessly before Arthur (I:3111–96), is at issue here (I:4342), and recognizes as well that his rescue of Lunete from threat of death mirrors her rescue of him when he was trapped in Ascalon's castle (I:4258–60). When Lunete refers to the abduction of Ginover and the absence of Gawein (I:4290–302) a connection is prepared with the Harpin episode, which follows; when she mentions Arthur and when Iwein praises the traditional role of Gawein (I:4276–81) they elicit resonances with the broadest traditions of the genre. To be sure, there are numerous connections that we are left to derive by analogy. Lunete, for instance, as she says herself, is a woman in distress, in need of a champion (I:4072–4); in this she resembles the unmarried Laudine, the Vrouwe von Narison, and the wronged daughter of the Grave von dem Swarzen Dorne. Like this last, Lunete sets the terms of the combat (I:4145–52, 5656–62) and decides later that her cause is not worth the possible death of her champion (I:4315–36, 7304–20). Yet, in spite of the connections that are left for us to derive, it is clear that the author of *Iwein* is more likely than the author of *Lanzelet* to refer directly to the systemic relations of an individual element.

Like Iblis before the Elidia adventure, Lunete in telling her story functions as messenger, bringing the news that causes the hero to accept a particular challenge; but here Lunete functions as messenger in her own behalf: she is the one threatened by O^-, and she, as a result, is O^+. In her first appearance, after the death of Ascalon, Lunete would seem, to judge by conventions of social organization, to be Laudine's auxiliary; yet she functions primarily on Iwein's behalf, that is as his auxiliary. She owes her near execution to the ambiguities of this double functional allegiance. When Lunete denounces Iwein before Arthur's court she clearly functions as messenger for Laudine, now in the position of O^-. When Iwein rescues Lunete from the pyre she is O^+, but by not marrying her Iwein transforms her into his auxiliary – which was her original role and the one in which she functions in the concluding episode. In a further complication of roles and functions Laudine, having witnessed Iwein's rescue of Lunete, willingly turns herself into his – conditional! – auxiliary (I:5471–9, 5521–9).

Hartman does not specify these multiple relationships – although he does predict Lunete's concluding endeavours on Iwein's behalf (I:5555), thus preparing us for the connection that is established later; at the same time his prediction reminds us of the narrator's ability to oversee the entire work and the many systems of which he is a part. Yet if the author of *Iwein* does not specify all the multiple relations of Lunete, still he does not, like the author of *Lanzelet*, merely leave such relations implicit in the individual scene. Iblis disappears from the Elidia episode after she has delivered her message and reappears for the concluding celebrations by virtue of her general position in the romance, not because of anything she said about the dragon. Lunete, however, is still present at the end of the episode that begins with her story, and her function at the end of the romance reflects the position she had at the end of that episode. The rescue episode explains her behaviour at the reconciliation; it functions as multiplication of cause. At the same time, since in the social organization of the romance world Lunete is auxiliary to Laudine, Iwein's winning of the auxiliary brings him materially closer to overcoming the hostility of the principal. Finally, the presence of Lunete in the concluding episode balances her appearance as Laudine's messenger, for the reconciliation resolves the challenge that she then delivered. Objectively the functions filled by Lunete are no less contradictory than those filled by Iblis, yet the author of *Iwein* exploits the systemic relations of these various functions to further the overall coherence of his work, while the author of *Lanzelet* is content to limit his use of these systems to the enrichment of the individual scene.

There are romances that seem to contain fewer contradictions than *Lanzelet* and *Iwein* – *Daniel*, *Garel*, *Tandareis*, for example – but we do not generally count them among our favourites. It seems that we do not regard consistency as such an important quality after all: in Arthurian romance, at least, we seem to value complexity more than logic. As a result our favourite works are not those that remain rigorously logical but those that know how to exploit the many systems of which they are composed in order to generate greater complexity. Wolfram pokes fun at 'vroun Luneten rat' (P:253,10), but the author of *Iwein* is not so naive as Wolfram implies. He recognizes the tension between Laudine's conventional, social obligations to Ascalon and the necessity, forced on her by the structure of the episode and the magic spring, to marry Iwein. In recognition of her apparently contradictory behaviour he has the narrator make a speech (ironically?) praising the flexibility of women, thus attempting to justify her (I:1863–88).[14] The steward's indictment of Lunete is a second recognition of this same tension, and here the victory of Iwein serves to justify Lunete. We have already seen how the multiple meanings of this episode are integrated into the rest of the romance. Hartman's little speech defending Laudine and the careful integration of Iwein's defence of Lunete both derive from the author's awareness of contradictions in his work, and both add to our delight in that work.

One is tempted to appropriate Schiller's categories and divide Arthurian romances into the naive and the sentimental. Naive romances, like *Lanzelet*, tend to exploit the multiple systems of the genre to produce richness of meaning but do not seem to notice the discrepancies they generate at the same time. The sentimental romances, like *Iwein*, do not hesitate to draw our attention to these discrepancies and to capitalize on them. By questioning the conventional exchange of hearts, Hartman exaggerates the tension between the narrator's role as faithful transmitter of the story and his role as a hero in his own right; the relation between story, mediator, and recipient becomes highly charged, and we delight in the tension that is generated. In *Meleranz* there is an exchange of hearts that is accomplished without a hitch (M:4020–9, 4049–53, 4060–6); as a result we hardly notice it. Hartman seizes on the absurdity of this conventional exchange; the verbal surface of the work sparkles, and we prize that sparkle. To whatever extent naive and sentimental make sense in considering Arthurian romance, however, they must be treated as tendencies, not absolute categories: the more naive Ulrich is highly self-conscious in presenting the Iwaret episode; the more sentimental Hartmann seems quite untroubled by the contradictions in Laudine's final acquiescence.

We began with contradictions. First we discovered historical reasons why Arthurian romance appears contradictory; but we realized that the medieval ability to focus on a particular passage – the source of contradiction – would preclude, for the medieval recipient, the perception of such contradictions. Then we considered more general literary reasons why romance appears contradictory; but we realized that romance authors affirm the grammar of genre tradition and the compositional needs of the individual romance simultaneously, apparently unwilling to acknowledge any contradiction in the tension thus produced. Finally we explored structural explanations for the contradictions of romance; but we see now that contradiction is a completely misleading word for the variety of meaning that is generated by the intersection of the various systems of which Arthurian romance is composed. Romance authors are aware of these various systems and, to a greater or lesser extent, delight in the interplay among them. In analysing romance structure we too must try to do justice to the multiplicity of the systems that it comprises.

In general, Arthurian scholarship has attempted to do just the opposite. Its history can be read as a series of attempts to deny the multiple systems of romance and, by isolating one system or level from the rest, to make its subject seem logical and consistent. The first scholars devoted themselves to what we have called the surface of romance and were content if they could produce a reliable text. Later scholars often approached romance with some coherent extra-literary system already in hand – biography, mythology, philosophy, psychoanalysis, theology, courtly love, history, numerology – and as a result only saw in the texts those elements that could be accommodated in the matrix they had selected. More recently scholars have returned to the works themselves, isolated some basic pattern, and interpreted this by structural analogy to an extra-literary system.

What we know about Arthurian romance today is the result of these past efforts. Yet we have paid a price for that knowledge: 'the unequivocal meaning'[15] that Arthurian scholars have discovered and offered to us – one unequivocal meaning after another – has been derived only by isolating one of the many systems of Arthurian romance and analysing it in isolation. Each single interpretation, in order to remain unequivocal, has had to deny the many often contradictory meanings of a romance, has had to deny 'the rich semantics of a text.'[16] We recognize our debt to the scholars, and at the same time we recognize that the many systems they have isolated are but the reflection of the many intersecting and discrepant systems that make up Arthurian romance. The isolated structures that generations of scholars have offered sequentially exist within a romance simultaneously; and the contradictions that distinguish one scholarly approach from another reflect the variety of meaning generated by the interplay of structures within romance. The problems, states William Ryding, 'all stem from the same root: in every case we are faced with a multiplicity where we should like to see unity.'[17]

We ought not to forget, however, that an Arthurian romance, regardless of the multiplicity of its systems and the inconsistencies they sometimes generate, always has a happy end. Iwein, who once forgot his beloved for reasons that were never clear, is finally reconciled with her, for reasons that are equally unclear. In order to enable this reconciliation Laudine is subjected to a transformation so abrupt as to destroy whatever semblance of coherence her character might seem to have had. Hartman, who used to take such delight in unmasking the absurd conventions of romance, reports all this as if it were perfectly reasonable. The narrator's terminal naivety reflects the sudden docility of the author, who, having earlier taken great pains to give his work a distinctive profile and to draw our attention to his sovereign control, is now concerned only to orchestrate a regulation finale. All behave as if the unlikely reconciliation of Iwein and Laudine were perfectly natural. And they are right. The mechanics of the happy ending may strike us as barely credible, even absurd, but the happy ending itself is always natural; indeed, it is obligatory. The special verisimilitude of the genre guarantees that we accept, even welcome, this happy end, even when from any other point of view we would dismiss it as implausible.

One cannot say that the discrepancies of Arthurian romance are reconciled by the happy ending, for they are not; contradictions abound, as the example of *Iwein* shows most clearly, even within the ending itself. One might say, however, that the inconsistencies of Arthurian romance are justified by the happy ending. The bad memory of the devoted Iwein, the sudden submission of the haughty Laudine, the terminal naivety of the perspicacious Hartman, the ultimate docility of the sovereign author: these apparent contradictions are all incorporated, unresolved, in the ending of *Iwein*, and the ending is happy nevertheless. It is the grammar of the genre itself that fosters the generation of these inconsistencies; and it is the grammar of the genre itself that, by incorporating these inconsistencies into the necessarily happy ending, justifies them.

This justification also reflects on our own undertaking. We have investigated at length the various structures that constitute Arthurian romance, and we have repeatedly observed that the imperfect congruence of these structures generates inconsistencies in the system of the genre. We have consistently refused to interpret our texts, because the formulation of a uniform interpretation would require us to ignore the essential noncongruence of romance and thus to misrepresent the structure of the genre. The symptoms of disjuncture, we recognize, are not flaws but simply by-products of the differentiation and elaboration of the many structures of Arthurian romance, an enterprise in which romance authors invested the largest part of their artistic energy and which is responsible for much of the richness and meaning of the works themselves. By incorporating these inconsistencies in the obligatory happy ending of a romance the genre affirms the variety of its constituent, non-congruent systems. Yet if the beneficent teleology of Arthurian romance celebrates

the multiplicity of the structures of which it is composed, then we can
feel justified in our investigation as well, an undertaking that has tried to
recognize and describe the variety of these structures and the system
they form: the structures of Arthurian romance.

Appendix
English Summaries of the
Less Familiar Romances

With few exceptions, the summaries presented here are divided according to the episodic divisions of the romances. The number that precedes each division of the summary refers to the number of the line at which the corresponding episode of the romance begins.

Heinrich von dem Türlin, *Diu Crone*
(Probable date of composition: between 1215 and 1230)

1 Prologue.

256 Brief portrayal of Arthur's youth.

457 Arthur calls a celebration at Christmas. Preparations, arrivals, *vesperie*. A knight arrives with a goblet. Only those can drink out of it without spilling who are true in love ['Becherprobe']. All the knights and ladies try, all except Arthur fail, and Keie mocks them all. Keie fights the knight and is defeated.

3208 A messenger announces a tournament at Jaschune. Most of Arthur's knights set out for it.

3273 Arthur goes hunting, comes back cold, and warms his hand at the fire. Ginover mocks him and claims to know a White Knight who is not afraid of the cold. Arthur is troubled. Keie, Gales, Aumagwin, and Arthur go out at night to find the stranger; they wait for him at different posts. The knight arrives and defeats them one after the other until he gets to Arthur. Arthur and the White Knight trade insults, fight until they are exhausted, and then exchange names. The knight is Gasozein, who claims to be Ginover's first love. Another fight is set in six weeks to decide the claim. Arthur and companions, unsettled, return home. All the knights return except Gawein.

5469 King Flois, much pressed by the giant Assiles, sends to Arthur for help. The messenger stumbles on Gawein, who undertakes to provide that help and sets out for the land of Flois.

5767 Gawein comes to the castle of Riwalin, who tries to get him to turn back (and then lists Gawein's past and future victories). Gawein kills three knights, and a fourth kills himself for shame. Riwalin tends Gawein's wounds.

6747 Gawein passes through a dense forest and comes to Blandukors's castle. A deafening, magical horn betrays Gawein's arrival, and he must defeat two more knights.

7667 A messenger arrives from Amurfina and demands Gawein. En route to Amurfina's we learn of the inheritance controversy between her and her sister Sgoidamur. Gawein is received by Amurfina in bed. His own desire and a threat from a magical sword lead him to promise fidelity. A magical potion robs Gawein of his memory until, after fifteen days, a platter with a picture of a past victory brings him to himself. He sets out.

9129 Gawein rescues a maiden from a monster, is surprised and carried off by a giantess from whom he escapes, then fights Reimambram to free the sister of the lord of the maiden he has just rescued.

9781 Gawein defeats Galaas, a relative of Assiles, and liberates five hundred prisoners. Finally he arrives at Flois's, kills Assiles, and sets out for Arthur's.

10113 Arthur is holding court at Karidol. He seeks advice of his council, who agree that he must fight Gasozein. But as the first joust begins Gasozein turns away. Having discussed their situation at length, Arthur and Gasozein agree that Ginover should choose between them. After a considerable pause she dismisses Gasozein, who departs at once.

11037 Gotegrin, Ginover's brother, feels that her behaviour has disgraced the family and carries her off into the woods. He is about to kill her when Gasozein rescues her. Lament at court.

11608 Gasozein assaults the queen, but Gawein, returning from his giant-killing, arrives in the nick of time. Long fight between Gasozein and Gawein, which ends with their complete exhaustion and their agreement to fight again when healed. Just as this promised battle is to begin Gasozein reveals that his claims on Ginover were fabricated. General pardon and celebration.

12611 Sgoidamur arrives at the celebration seeking a champion against Amurfina [see above, 7667]. Keie takes on the challenge, rides off on her white mule, but turns back at the sword bridge and returns to Arthur's.

12869 Sgoidamur requests Gawein as champion. He accepts, rides off on the mule, crosses the sword bridge, and enters the revolving castle of the magician Gansguoter, uncle of Amurfina and Sgoidamur. A series of contests. Gawein learns that he is fighting for Sgoidamur against Amurfina. He is received by Amurfina and they return to Karidol.

13690 Sgoidamur promises to abide by the will of Gawein, her victorious champion, whereupon he marries her to Gasozein. Gawein seems to marry Amurfina. Celebration. Heinrich on women.

13925 News of a tournament at Orcanie reaches court, and the knights depart.

13940 Gawein goes his own way into the Walt Aventuros, where he encounters a series of grotesque and grisly scenes and adventures, then awakens on a field.

14927 Gawein rides into the land of Fimbeus (from whom Gawein once won a strength-giving stone) and Giramphiel. Deceitful welcome by Giramphiel, who sends Gawein to fight a dragon en route to the castle of Fortuna. Gawein kills the dragon, but his clothes are burnt up.

15220 Gawein arrives at the house of Siamerac, who re-equips him and gives him further directions to Fortuna. He defeats the magician Laamorz and acquires a skein that enables him to reach the palace of Fortuna. He is warmly welcomed there, sees the wheel of fortune, and is given a ring for King Arthur.

15932 Gawein arrives at the home of Aanzim, who gives him directions and tells him to ignore all that he sees and hears in the woods. Another series of grotesque scenes in the woods.

16497 Gawein intervenes in a three-way fight between Gigamec, Zedoech, and Aamanz, Gawein's double. After Gawein leaves, the others murder Aamanz. Gigamec brings the head of Aamanz to Arthur and his court (who are out on the hunt of the white stag) and claims it is the head of Gawein. General lament.

17312 Gawein comes to a floating island, land of maidens, and chooses eternal youth over the love of the queen.

17503 Gawein comes upon Quoikos, who tells him of a tourney called by Leigamar, the prize being the hand of his daughter, Fursensephin. Gawein is taken for a merchant by Fursensephin but admired by her younger sister, Quebeleplus. The sisters fight. Quebeleplus wins Gawein as her champion, and he defeats the knight of Fursensephin.

Since Gawein has outshone all the other knights, he wins the hand of Fursensephin. He marries her off to Quoikos.

18680 Gawein comes upon the goddess Enfeidas, King Arthur's aunt, in a meadow. He is told of the lament over his presumed death at court and warned of danger at Karamphi. At Karamphi Gawein is playing chess with Seimeret when her brother Angaras attacks him. (Gawein had killed his brother in a tournament.) Gawein defends himself with the chessboard, Angaras's father intervenes, and Gawein must promise to reach the grail within a year.

18937 Gawein meets a lamenting woman on whose behalf he kills the black knight, thereby rescuing many.

19346 Gawein comes upon Lohenis, who hates him. Lohenis, pretending to be near death, tricks Gawein out of his horse. Gawein rides off on a nag he takes from a passer-by.

20099 Gawein approaches the castle of Madarp. He defeats Ansgü, a knight sent by Lohenis on Gawein's own horse, which Gawein thereby wins back.

20268 Gawein spends the night with the ferryman Karadas, who tells him about the castle of Salie. It is occupied by Arthur's mother Igern, other relatives, and a magical bed.

20491 En route to Salie Gawein fights a knight sent by Lohenis and accompanied by Mancipicelle.

20562 Gawein enters Salie and sleeps in the magical bed. He remains untouched by the arrows shot at him, is awakened by the women, kills a lion, and thereby wins the hand of Clarisanz – his sister. Gawein postpones the wedding and withholds his name.

21095 Mancipicelle arrives and challenges Gawein to collect a wreath of flowers that will rejuvenate her mistress. Gawein swims to the meadow where the flowers grow, repeatedly stabs his foot to counteract their soporific effect, collects the flowers, and departs.

21413 Returning to Salie, Gawein fights Giremelanz, but the fight is postponed because Gawein is without armour. Giremelanz sends a ring with Gawein as a love token to Clarisanz. Back at Salie Mancipicelle admits that she had acted at the behest of Lohenis and Ansgü when she challenged Gawein to collect the flowers.

21792 Gawein invites Arthur's court to the contest with Giremelanz. The court, overjoyed to learn that Gawein is still alive, travels with a huge host to Salie. Reunion of Arthur and his family. Clarisanz reconciles Gawein and Giremelanz; she will marry Giremelanz. All return to Karidol for the wedding.

22571 Gawein tells of his obligation to seek the grail. He gives Arthur the ring from Fortuna.

22990 A messenger (from Giramphiel: more on the history of her conflict with Gawein) arrives with a magical glove that renders one half of the wearer invisible – except for those parts that are guilty of indiscretion ['Handschuhprobe']. Only Gawein and Arthur pass the test. Keie mocks all the others in turn.

24720 The 'Ritter mit dem boc' arrives with the matching glove. Under the pretext of helping Gawein in the search for the grail, the knight gets possession of the ring of Fortuna and the stone of Fimbeus. A maiden borne in by the wind prophesies danger – in vain. The 'Ritter mit dem boc' puts on both gloves and thus becomes invisible, declares himself an agent of Giramphiel, and flies away on his ram, taking the magical props with him. Lament.

25571 In spite of this Gawein remains steadfast. The maiden borne by the wind suggests help be sought from Gansguoter. Arthur wants to accompany Gawein but is dissuaded. Keie, Lanzelet, and Calocreant leave with Gawein after Keie has made a speech entreating the ladies not to give way to sorrow at his departure.

26099 En route to Gansguoter they fight with four knights. Keie is wounded but recovers.

26191 They ride through treacherous terrain and are captured in the mountains by Baingranz, brother of the giant Assiles [see above, 9781]. They sleep three days. Gawein awakens. By eavesdropping on a conversation between two lovers passing by in a swan-drawn boat he discovers how to escape. Gawein gets the key that opens the trap, rides forth, and kills a dragon. He can just barely get to a magical spring that renews his strength, water from which he then brings to his companions. Gawein is praised by those whom the dragon has dispossessed. Gawein and his fellows defeat Baingranz and three other giants.

27183 They reach Gansguoter, who gives Gawein armour that protects from magic. Gansguoter's magical powers lead them safely through several dangers into the land of Fimbeus and Giramphiel. Gansguoter gives Gawein a magical box and departs.

27701 At the castle of Fimbeus and Giramphiel, Gawein puts most of the company to sleep with Gansguoter's magical box. Fimbeus and three knights fight Gawein and his companions, and the latter (Gawein protected from Fimbeus's magical stone by Gansguoter's neutralizing armour) win. Gawein gets the magical props back from Fimbeus.

28262 Arthur's knights set out, swim all day and night across a lake, and split up to seek the grail.

28375 Gawein is led (in a ring of flames) to Gansguoter's sister, who gives detailed instructions on how to seek the grail. She has him send the magical properties back to Arthur (who thinks Gawein is dead).

28608 Gawein rides past another series of surreal sights and after more than a month finds Lanzelet and Calocreant. (Keie is in prison.) A page invites the three knights to the castle of his lord. There they are welcomed and served. Lanzelet and Calocreant fall asleep, but Gawein (by not drinking, according to instructions) does not. Grail ceremony. At the right moment Gawein asks, what is the meaning of all this? Great rejoicing: he has saved many living and dead. Gawein is told how Parzival had disappointed them. Most of the company disappear.

29670 Gawein and his comrades depart. Angaras [see above, 18680] joins the party. They reach Keie and Gawein leaves his magic armour to aid Keie in freeing himself.

29756 Gawein, Lanzelet, Calocreant, and Angaras arrive at Arthur's. Angaras joins the Round Table. Keie, having defeated his nine opponents, soon arrives too. Great celebration.

29910 Epilogue.

[Konrad von Stoffeln], *Gauriel von Muntabel*
(Probable date of composition: between 1240 and 1270)

1 Prologue.

52 Gauriel rides off into a land of women and declares that they are the most beautiful women he has ever seen save one. This one, his lady, has forbidden him to mention her and, since he did so, she withdraws her favour and transforms him into an ugly man. He will regain his former good looks only when he has regained her favour. After a sickness of six months, Gauriel sets out on adventures in the company of a ram. He is known as the knight of the ram. After one year a messenger from his lady arrives: he will regain her favour if he can bring the three greatest knights of Arthur's court to Fluratrone, the land where his lady wears the crown.

401 Gauriel sets off and encamps not far from Arthur's court. A damsel is sent to invite him to court but he takes her captive, resolving to hold her honourably until Arthur's knights can win her back. In three days Gauriel fights and defeats a series of knights from Arthur's court including Keie, Segramors, Walban, and Dodines.

1288 Gawan, Iwein, and Erec are away from court. They encounter a maiden who had sought help at Arthur's court for her lady, a duchess who is under attack by a rejected suitor in league with her own cupbearer. The maiden reports that, on account of Gauriel's challenge, she could get no help at Arthur's. Gawan and Iwein return to court to help there. Erec sets out to help the duchess, to whom he is related.

1444 Gawan and Iwein return to court. Gawan fights Gauriel and, since his sword breaks, must give surety. Iwein and his lion fight Gauriel and his ram, and the latter team wins.

1904 King Arthur sets out to fight Gauriel, but Gauriel refuses the challenge. He then explains to Arthur why he was compelled to challenge the court, and Arthur pardons him. The queen forgives him for holding her maiden captive, on the condition that Gauriel remain one year as member of Arthur's court. He promises to do so after he has regained his lady's favour. To do so Gawan, Iwein, and Walban, who have all given surety, must accompany Gauriel to Fluratrone.

2130 Erec arrives at the seat of his threatened relative, kills her traitorous cupbearer, and her troublesome suitor concedes defeat. Erec returns to Arthur's.

2300 Erec joins Gawan, Iwein, Walban, and Gauriel, and all depart for Fluratrone. They come upon a page who sets them off in the right direction.

2400 In order to enter the country they kill two dragons who guard the way.

2464 They ride through a wood. A hunter gives them directions to a bridge, where Gauriel defeats two giants. The Arthurian knights are attacked by a crowd, but news of their arrival has reached the queen, who orders her subjects to lay down their arms.

2788 Gauriel and his companions arrive at their goal. After a bath and a salve, Gauriel regains his original good looks and marries the queen.

2870 Erec preaches his moral – one must not lie about – and Gauriel remembers his obligation to Ginover. Therefore they all set out for Arthur's, Gauriel having obtained a one-year's leave from his lady.

2986 En route they defeat a heathen army that was ravaging the land of Pronaias.

3010 The heroes return to Arthur's court, which then departs on a hunting expedition. Gauriel, Erec, and Pliamin leave the party to seek adventure. A hunter tells them of the abduction of the daughter of Asterian, and they undertake her rescue.

3240 After a round of harmless jousts they are welcomed into a dwelling at the edge of a wood. Their host tells them about this enchanted wood and its lord, the abductor of Asterian's daughter.

3452 They make their way through the wood fighting dragons and other fierce animals. Gauriel defeats the abductor, the son of Pallas, who receives them graciously. They ride off with the daughter of Asterian and are welcomed extravagantly by their earlier host at the edge of the wood.

3755 En route back to Arthur's the heroes defeat Geldipant who, with his army, is trying to force the goddess Juno into marriage.

3784 They arrive at Arthur's. Asterian is notified and comes to fetch his daughter. Gauriel, recalling the term set by his lady, is about to depart when a messenger arrives and instructs him to wait. Gauriel's lady arrives with a marvellous retinue. Celebration. Asterian returns home. Gauriel's lady returns home, where she lives admirably.

4168 Epilogue.

der Pleier, *Garel von dem Blüenden Tal*
(Probable date of composition: between 1260 and 1280)

1 Garel arrives at Arthur's Pentecostal festival and finds the king nearly alone. The rest of the court has ridden off in pursuit of Meliakanz, who had ridden off with the queen. A well-mannered giant, Karabin, arrives and delivers the challenge of Ekunaver: Arthur is responsible for the death of Ekunaver's father; Ekunaver will attack in a year's time. Garel, mocked by Keie for his resolve, sets off after Karabin to collect information.

743 Garel arrives at Merkanie. After according Garel a most courteous welcome his host tells his predicament: Gerhart von Riviers, having been refused the hand of the host's daughter Sabie, has attacked Merkanie for ten years and will do so again tomorrow. Garel defeats Gerhart and his kinsman Rialt, makes peace, and receives promises of support for Arthur from Gerhart and the lord of Merkanie.

2148 Garel comes upon Gilan, whom he defeats after a long fight. Gilan promises thousands of soldiers for Arthur's cause, then tells his Tristan adventure (Petitcreiu) and his present purpose: he is en route to fight Eskilabon, who holds captive two of Gilan's nephews, Floris and Alexander. Garel resolves to fight Eskilabon. Garel and Gilan stay at Pergalt with the parents of the captive nephews.

3162 Garel and Gilan arrive at Belamunt, the seat of Eskilabon. Garel makes wreaths from the flowers in Eskilabon's garden and dispatches a falcon: these constitute the challenge. Gilan defeats three underlings. Garel defeats Eskilabon, who promises to release his four hundred captives. Eskilabon tells the history of his garden and the adventure that has left so many captive. Garel tells his ancestry (his mother's brother is Gahmuret) and his present purpose. Eskilabon pledges thousands of soldiers to Arthur's cause. Large celebration. The captives (among them Floris and Alexander) are freed. They promise to help Arthur. Garel declines the hand of Flordiane, Eskilabon's sister.

5472 Garel, still following after Karabin, comes upon the giant couple Purdan and Fidegart, whom he kills. He thereby liberates Klaris, a knight whom Purdan had carried off from a neighbouring land, Albewin, a dwarf king who along with his subjects had been forced to serve the giants, and Duzabel, who along with twelve maidens had been abducted by Fidegart. Albewin provides food, riches, and armour. Klaris promises help for Arthur.

7183 Garel arrives at Anferre, a land decimated by Vulganus, a centaur who bears a Gorgon head in his shield. Garel is admitted to the castle of Laudamie, the queen of the country, and falls in love with her. With the aid of Albewin, who steals off with the fatal shield and hides it, Garel is able to kill Vulganus. He marries Laudamie (lots of ceremony), has the Gorgon head covered with lead and sunk in the sea, and remains at Anferre until the following spring.

9343 At Pentecost all who promised help arrive at Anferre and join with the local forces. Lengthy celebration. Knighting of Klaris. Lavish gifts for all. Departure.

10999 At a fortified pass that guards the entrance to Kanadic, the land of Ekunaver, Garel defeats the giant Malseron, who informs him of Ekunaver's forces. Malseron and his fellow giants (among them Karabin [see above, 1]) pledge to remain neutral in the battle. They withdraw their allegiance from Ekunaver. Ekunaver holds a war council and decides to await Garel rather than march forth to meet him. Tjofrit arrives at the council to deliver Garel's formal challenge. Garel occupies the pass.

12782 Galvan arrives, intending to occupy the pass for Ekunaver. Galvan and most of his force are killed.

13224 Garel's forces advance. Eskilabon rides ahead and destroys a brass lion whose cry could have undone them. Skirmishes at a ford. Garel's forces rout the enemy. The army camps for the night.

14219 A truce is called so that Ekunaver's army can cross to Garel's side of the ford. The armies are divided into battalions. They attack each other and reach a stalemate. Then the various battalions of Garel begin to defeat those of Ekunaver. Garel captures Ekunaver, whose forces, after more heavy fighting, are forced to flee. Lament for the casualties. Garel requires Ekunaver and two other royal captives to deliver themselves to Arthur, but Ekunaver is allowed to return first to his queen, Kloudite, and order his affairs. He does so and then returns. The giants heal many with salves. The victors and captives march off towards Arthur. Garel sends a messenger to Laudamie.

17635 Arthur, knowing nothing of all this, has assembled a huge army and has begun to march towards Ekunaver. His forces approach those of Garel, and Keie, after berating the absent Garel, rides out to reconnoitre. Garel, riding in advance of his army, comes upon Keie, defeats him, and sends him back to Arthur on foot.

18297 Malseron [see above, 10999] is sent to Arthur with Keie's horse and helmet and with the news of Garel's victory and approach. The captive kings are sent to Arthur, who treats them graciously. The army camps. Elaborate greetings all round. All move, at Arthur's invitation, to Dinazarun for a huge celebration. At the intercession of many, Arthur pardons the captives, and they join the Round Table. Departure.

20429 On his way home Garel stops at Merkanie [see above, 743], where he marries Sabie to Floris [see above, 2148], at Pergalt [see above, 2148], where he marries Flordiane [see above, 3162] to Alexander [see above, 2148], and at Turtus, where he marries Klaris to Duzabel [see above, 5472]. Garel greets Albewin [see above, 5472] and at last reaches Anferre and Laudamie.

21064 Epilogue, in which a monastery is founded at the site of the battle.

der Pleier, *Meleranz*
(Probable date of composition: between 1260 and 1280)

1 Prologue.

127 King Arthur has three sisters, one of whom is married to the king of France. Meleranz is their son. Inspired by his uncle's reputation, young Meleranz sneaks away from home and sets out for Arthur's court. He gets lost in the mountains and stumbles upon Queen Tydomie at her bath in a forest clearing. They talk, fall in love, eat, spend the night in tents, and the next morning Meleranz is guided out of the woods and shown the road to Arthur's. Tydomie confesses her love to her mistress who, having consulted the stars, prophesies a happy outcome.

1910 Meleranz comes upon Arthur's master of the hunt. They find a stag, which Meleranz leads by the horns into Arthur's camp. Meleranz is received into the retinue. More than a year later a messenger dispatched by the king of France in search of his son arrives at court and recognizes Meleranz. Gawein notices Meleranz's love-struck behaviour and correctly diagnoses its cause. Meleranz pretends he is merely distressed at not yet being a knight. Arthur plans a festival in May for the knighting. Tydomie sends a page with trinkets and a love letter. Just after the knighting, Lybials arrives to seek, at the request of his lady, the first joust with the new knight. Neither is unhorsed. Lybials tells the story of his lady and departs. Arthur's festival ends. Tydomie's page is sent home with a love letter from Meleranz, which has a powerful effect on her.

4208 Meleranz sneaks away in search of adventure and of Tydomie. He comes to the house of the giant Pulaz, who treats him hospitably and informs him that a band of giants is compelled to capture whomever they can and deliver the captives to Godonas, king of Terrandes. The giants appear with a group of captives. Among them is a messenger on her way to Arthur to seek help for her mistress, Dulceflor, who is beleaguered by Verangoz. Meleranz promises to aid Dulceflor if he is successful against Godonas.

4943 En route to Terrandes Meleranz first defeats Godonas's steward, Cursun, who tries in vain to convince Meleranz to turn back. At Godonas's castle Meleranz blows three times on a horn, thus summoning Godonas, whom he fights and kills. After some initial resistance from Godonas's vassals, Meleranz is crowned lord of Terrandes, the captives are freed, and Cursun is installed as viceroy.

7033 Meleranz sets out to help Dulceflor, who turns out to be the cousin of Tydomie. After welcoming Meleranz, Dulceflor reports that Tydomie's uncle wants her to marry Libers, that Libers has camped with twenty-three knights in the forest clearing, but that Tydomie has set her heart on another. By his reaction to this news Dulceflor recognizes that Meleranz is the one. The next day Meleranz kills Verangoz in battle, and Verangoz's army is defeated by Dulceflor's forces. Meleranz sets out for Tydomie's country, stops at Terrandes, and continues, led by Cursun.

9192 They camp in a meadow, challenge the knights in Tydomie's forest clearing, and defeat them all, ending on the fourth day with Libers. Libers is sent to Arthur. Meleranz and Tydomie are reunited and send messengers inviting Arthur and the king of France to their wedding. Tydomie's uncle, thwarted in his plans for her, invades the country.

Dulceflor, King Arthur, and the king of France arrive. When the uncle learns Meleranz's ancestry he is placated. Meleranz marries Tydomie and Dulceflor marries Libers. Celebration and departures. As he leaves, the king of France gives his son advice on good government. 12766 Epilogue.

der Pleier, *Tandareis und Flordibel*
(Probable date of composition: between 1260 and 1280)

1 Prologue.
197 Tandareis, Ginover's cousin, grows up at Arthur's court. Flordibel arrives at Arthur's Pentecostal festival and desires to become a member of the court on the condition that anyone who desires her as his wife will lose his life. The condition is accepted, Tandareis is assigned to serve her, and the two fall in love. They do not confess this love until Tandareis, distracted by love, cuts his hand while slicing bread for Flordibel. When the court departs for another Pentecostal festival, the lovers sneak off and arrive at Tandernas, the castle of Tandareis's father.
1597 Angry that Tandareis has disgraced him, Arthur assembles an army and beseiges Tandernas. Tandareis in single combat captures Keie, Dodineis, Kalogriant, and Iwanet but refuses to fight his relative Gawein. Peace negotiations are introduced by Flordibel, who proposes to claim that Tandareis had never sought her love. Tandareis returns his prisoners, who intercede with Arthur on his behalf. Tandareis and his court come to Arthur for a trial at which Gawein acts as the lovers' advocate. The court acquits them of all but having left court without leave.
3789 Tandareis is sentenced by Arthur to ride off in search of adventure; Flordibel must return to court. Departures.
4057 Second prologue.
4092 Tandareis, riding through the woods, is lost in thoughts of Flordibel. Robbers attack his retinue. Tandareis, without his armour, beats off the robbers but is wounded. He enters a town and is nursed back to health by the merchant Todila.
4891 Tandareis re-enters the woods and rescues Liodarz and his lady from an attack by twenty-five robbers. The few surviving captive robbers tell Tandareis that they are one of several bands compelled by the giant Karedos to pillage those who travel through the woods. Tandareis sends Liodarz with the captured horses as a present to Todila.

5540 Tandareis sets out for Malmontan, the castle of Karedos. To reach Malmontan he must travel a causeway blocked at three places by guardhouses. At each he kills the giant guard, liberates captives, and burns the guardhouse.

6390 Tandareis reaches Malmontan and kills Karedos, then defeats one of his guards. The captives are freed; Liodarz and Todila are summoned. The freed captives are dispatched to Arthur to intercede for Tandareis.

7969 The envoys arrive at Arthur's. Everyone entreats Arthur to pardon Tandareis, which he does. Dodineis is dispatched to fetch Tandareis.

8301 Leaving Malmontan in the charge of Liodarz, Tandareis rides out to seek adventure and arrives at the castle of Albiun. She has been under attack by Kurion, who wants her land. Tandareis defeats Kurion and the leopards that fight with him, and sends Kurion to King Arthur and Flordibel. Tandareis learns that Albiun is served by vassal dwarfs, rejects her offer of marriage, and rides off.

10201 He rides into a wood where he comes upon Kalubin beating Claudin. Tandareis fights Kalubin, who, defeated, explains that he had served Claudin but that she had treated him with scorn. Kalubin is sent to King Arthur and Flordibel. Tandareis sets off to return Claudin to her home.

10815 They come upon Kandalion and his party. Tandareis unhorses Kandalion but is attacked by fifty of his followers. After Tandareis has killed thirteen and wounded twenty, he himself is wounded. Kandalion threatens to rape Claudin then and there if Tandareis does not surrender; he does and is thrown into Kandalion's dungeon. Antonie, the sister of Kandalion, learns the story, rescues Tandareis, and cares for him secretly.

11662 Claudin returns home and laments Tandareis's fate.

11746 Dodineis returns to Arthur with the news that Tandareis is out searching for adventure. In order to lure him to court Arthur resolves to hold a tournament once a month for one year.

11931 Tandareis has spent more than a year with Antonie, who has fallen in love with him, when he hears of Arthur's tournaments. He gets Antonie's permission to attend as her knight, provided that he return to her. At the tournament Tandareis (anonymous, in black armour) unhorses Kandalion, is recognized as the best, but sneaks off before anyone discovers who he is. Return to Antonie. Kandalion is angry about his lack of success at the tournament.

13496 Tandareis attends a second tourney under the same conditions.

Before it begins, he and Flordibel see each other and are transfixed by love. At the tournament Tandareis (in red armour) once again un-horses Kandalion and hastens off before being discovered. Return to Antonie. Kandalion is angry about his lack of success.

14084 At the third tourney Arthur suspects that Tandareis (in white armour) is fighting as the knight of a woman who keeps him captive. Arthur determines to capture him, but Tandareis thwarts the plan and returns to Antonie.

14443 Arthur, having correctly deduced Tandareis's condition, pro-mises a duchy to whoever brings him to court. Kandalion realizes from the description that the knight Arthur seeks is the one he aban-doned in his dungeon. Kandalion laments his murder of Tandareis to his vassals, and Antonie, after various assurances have been negoti-ated for her protection and that of Tandareis, reveals all. They head off for King Arthur in time for the fourth tournament. Kandalion expects the duchy in reward, but Arthur gives it to Antonie.

15412 Claudin hears of Tandareis's liberation and comes to court with her father. Since she, Antonie, and Flordibel all claim Tandareis's hand, Arthur convenes a council. Gawein defends Flordibel's claim. Since the council is split, Arthur leaves the choice up to Tandareis, who, guided by his heart, chooses Flordibel. Antonie is married to Beacurs (Gawein's brother), and Claudin to Kalubin [see above, 10201]! Celebrations and lengthy departures.

17515 Flordibel, Tandareis, and his parents return to Tandernas [see above, 197], then proceed to Karmil, the chief city in the land that had been subject to Karedos [see above, 5540, 6390]. They go to Malmon-tan, where Tandareis dispenses great riches and sends Liodarz home [see above, 8301]. Finally they return to Karmil for coronation, enfeoff-ment, and celebration. Tandareis's father returns to Tandernas.

18241 Epilogue.

der Stricker, *Daniel von dem Blühenden Tal*
(Probable date of composition: between 1220 and 1230)

1 Prologue.

33 Information about Arthur, customs of his court, Keie.

143 Daniel approaches Arthur's court. Keie rides out to fight and is un-horsed. Many others ride out to joust with Daniel, but he remains undefeated. Gawein, Iwein, and Parzival invite him to court where he is welcomed into the company by Arthur.

408 A giant arrives at court with the demand that Arthur offer himself as vassal of Matur, the king of Cluse. To gain time to assemble an army Arthur pretends to be willing. The giant will wait one week.

987 Daniel, who cannot wait, rides out until he reaches the brother of the messenger giant, who guards the entry to Cluse. While Daniel is debating whether to fight the giant, the Frouwe von dem Trüeben Berge throws herself at his feet and beseeches his aid against Juran, a dwarf with an invincible sword who wants her as his wife. After weighing his obligations, Daniel follows the lady, tricks Juran out of his sword, and kills him.

1782 As he leaves, Daniel is met by the Frouwe von dem Liehten Brunnen, who entreats his aid against 'der buchlose valant,' a monster from the sea that has decimated her land with the help of a Gorgon head. Daniel follows her, kills the monster with the help of a mirror, and throws the deadly head into the sea. The Grave von dem Liehten Brunnen, who has been hiding in a tower, resolves out of gratitude to accompany Daniel.

2361 They come to a tent filled with food in the middle of a field. A knight (Knight X) passes by and does not return Daniel's greeting. They pursue him. Knight X gallops through a pass and a stone gate falls, leaving Daniel alone on the outside. He returns to the tent.

2670 After pondering his predicament Daniel sets off and, with Juran's sword, kills the giant who guards the pass (brother of the messenger giant).

2845 Just then Arthur arrives with his forces. Daniel and several others ride ahead and, by pulling a banner out of its mouth, cause a statue of a beast to roar. This, as the messenger giant told them at the outset, is the way to summon Matur. Matur appears; Arthur fights and kills him.

3072 Matur's army battles Arthur's. The messenger giant is a particular problem (Keie gets thrown into the air) until Daniel kills him. Matur's forces are routed.

3914 Daniel sneaks off at midnight to see if he can't rescue the Grave von dem Liehten Brunnen. He cuts his way through one stone barrier, fights Knight X, whom he cannot get to say a thing, and enters the land where the Grave von dem Liehten Brunnen is trapped.

4127 Daniel gets caught in an invisible net from which he is released only after he promises obedience to the maiden who had set the trap. She, the Frouwe von der Grüenen Ouwe, explains that the country has been destroyed by a monster whose voice renders all obedient to his will and who thereby procures the victims in whose blood he bathes once a week. Daniel stops his ears with wax, kills the monster, and liberates the last group of (near) victims – including the Grave von dem Liehten Brunnen. They set off for the battleground at Cluse along with Knight X, who turns out to be the father of the Frouwe von der Grüenen Ouwe.

5000 Daniel and his comrades arrive early the next day in time for the battle with a second army from Cluse. After the victory of Arthur's forces all praise Daniel.

5379 On the next day Arthur's army defeats a third army from Cluse.

5444 The following day the remaining forces of Cluse arrive. Early on the second day of this battle Arthur's soldiers, acting on a suggestion of Daniel's, stop their ears and then cause the statue of the beast to roar [see above, 2845]. This paralyses Matur's forces, and they surrender.

5808 Arthur sets about placating Cluse. He is reconciled with Matur's widow, Danise, whom on the advice of his council he marries to Daniel. Festival at which hundreds of widows of Cluse are married to Arthurian knights.

6900 The father of the two slain giants arrives at the celebration, carries off King Arthur, and holds him on a dangerous precipice. Parzival tries to rescue the king but is also captured. Daniel fetches the Frouwe von der Grüenen Ouwe with her net. The giants' father is caught in the net; Daniel talks him into reconciliation; Arthur and Parzival are released. Festival resumes.

7914 Ginover is fetched for the final celebration. Arthur marries the Frouwe von der Grüenen Ouwe to Beladigant and rewards the giants' father.

8444 Epilogue.

Ulrich von Zatzikhoven, *Lanzelet*
(Probable date of composition: between 1194 and 1205)

1 Prologue.

41 Pant, the tyrannical king of Genewis, is killed by his barons. Pant's son, X, is snatched away from his mother by a water fay. He is raised in the magic kingdom of which she is queen, educated in virtue and arts by various of her subjects (all women) and in fighting (not knightly combat) by mermen. X leaves because he wants to find out about knightly things and also because he wants to learn his name,

which will be revealed to him only after he has killed Iwaret. X rides off, the horse leading him. A dwarf (at Pluris) slaps him in the face. X meets Johfrit, who instructs him in knightly behaviour. Celebration at Johfrit's.

676 X meets two knights, Kuraus and Orphilet, fighting in the woods. They stop at his request. All three seek shelter at the castle of Galagandreiz. During the night Galagandreiz's daughter offers her love to Kuraus and Orphilet, who refuse out of loyalty to their host. X accepts, even before she offers. Galagandreiz challenges X to a knife fight. X attacks and wins, killing Galagandreiz. The daughter offers X her hand and kingdom; X accepts. Orphilet leaves for Arthur's court, where he praises X. X sneaks off from his new kingdom, having recalled why he had left the water fay.

1357 X fights hundreds of opponents in trying to reach the castle of the absent Linier. When the fighting gets too much he gives surety to Linier's niece, Ade, who gives him safe passage. When Linier returns, X is unable to give his name and is thrown into prison. Ade tells X of the *aventiure* that Linier has established, and X agrees to undertake it. By defeating one giant, two lions, and finally killing Linier, X breaks the *aventiure* and wins Ade. She tends his wounds. He gains her hand and her kingdom.

2239 X's fame reaches Arthur's court. Walwein, sent out to find X, comes across X and Ade out riding. Walwein invites X to court, but X insists on a fight. Walwein is in difficulty, but before the fight is decided a page arrives, separates them, and announces a tournament at Djofle. Walwein accepts the invitation; X declines. Walwein leaves. X changes his mind and sets off for Djofle with Ade and her brother Diepalt. X distinguishes himself on the first day of the tournament as a green knight, on the second day as a white knight, and on the third day as a red knight. Arthur and Walwein seek out X and praise him. X leaves for Pluris.

3526 X, Ade, and Diepalt arrive at Schatel le Mort. The magic of the castle renders X weak and cowardly. Ade and Diepalt desert him in disgust. X is imprisoned by Mabuz (the weakling son of the water fay, who gave him this magic castle for his protection). Mabuz sends X out against a band of pillagers that Iwaret has sent into Mabuz's land. (This is why the water fay wants Iwaret killed.) As soon as X is out of the castle he regains his prowess and defeats the robber band.

3826 X meets an abbot in the woods who tells him about Iwaret. X suddenly remembers that he must fight Iwaret. The abbot promises to pray for X's soul. X goes off into Iwaret's magic forest, where he finds a spring and a tree with a gong. Iblis (Iwaret's daughter) dreams of X and comes to the woods. She declares her love. X hits the gong three times, Iwaret appears, they fight, and X kills Iwaret. X and Iblis leave the woods, passing the abbot, who is dragging an empty bier on which he had expected to place the body of X.

4661 X and Iblis dismount in a meadow and make love under a linden. A messenger from the water fay appears and tells X his name – Lanzelet – and his parentage. She gives him a precious magic tent (bejewelled, with Latin inscriptions; when folded a damsel can carry it) and tells him he is Arthur's nephew.

4960 Lanzelet and Iblis set off for Arthur's. They meet a page who reports that Valerin claims Ginover (he asserts a prior claim). The date for judicial combat has been set. Lanzelet rushes on to Kardigan (Iblis stays with relatives), replaces Walwein as Ginover's champion, and defeats Valerin (whom he does not kill). Iblis is fetched, and Lanzelet becomes one of the Round Table. Big celebration.

5429 Lanzelet sneaks off to Pluris (he tells only Walwein) to avenge his earlier insult [see above, 41]. He breaks the *aventiure* of the Künegin von Pluris (fighting one hundred knights in succession) and she holds him her 'prisoner' – out of love. He can't help himself. Arthur organizes a fete for his own glory and to see if anybody knows where Lanzelet is. (Walwein seems to have forgotten.) A messenger from the water fay appears with a magic cloak: it fits only women of flawless virtue ['Mantelprobe']. After not fitting properly over two hundred ladies of court (including Ginover), it fits Iblis perfectly. Then the messenger tells Lanzelet's whereabouts. Erec, Walwein, Tristant, and Karjet ride off to Pluris and take on the one hundred knights. Finally Lanzelet persuades the Künegin von Pluris to let him fight a single joust. Tristant turns back when charging and appears to flee. Lanzelet pursues him and escapes.

6563 While returning to Arthur's the five knights spend a night with 'der wise stumme Gilimar,' who in obedience to the command of his lady will not utter a word, and learn from a page that Ginover has been abducted by Valerin and is being held in his magically protected castle. Council at Arthur's (including his son, Lout). They seek help from the magician Malduc, who requires in exchange that Erec and Walwein be given over to him as prisoners (they had injured him earlier). Malduc paralyses Valerin's defences with a spell. Ginover is freed. Malduc throws Erec and Walwein in a dungeon; sadness at court. Lanzelet attacks Malduc's castle with one hundred knights and a giant, Esealt. The castle is taken and all are killed except Malduc's daughter, who had aided the Arthurian knights. All return to court for a festival.

7830 Lanzelet asks Iblis for news. She mentions a dragon in the forest that wants a knight to kiss it. Lanzelet leaves to seek it out, even though Iblis requests he not do so. The dragon says the knight who kisses it is the best knight in the world. Lanzelet does so, and the dragon turns into a beautiful woman. They return to court.

8050 Lanzelet, Arthur, and an army set off for Genewis [see above, 41]. Peace is made with the rebellious barons, and Lanzelet is crowned king of his father's land.

8469 Messengers from Iwaret's land, Dodone [see above, 3826], seek out Lanzelet, bringing rich gifts. A great celebration is planned for Dodone. Lanzelet, Arthur, and a huge company prepare and travel there. Glorious coronation. Arthur stays three months, then returns home.

9309 Epilogue, including information on the source.

Wigamur
(Probable date of composition: around 1250)

1 In books we read of Paldriot, king of Lendrie. While he and his wife are attending a celebration at Arthur's court their young son Wigamur is abducted by Lesbia, who keeps him in a cave at the sea. Shortly thereafter he is carried off by a partly human sea creature who raises Wigamur, teaches him various courtly skills and values, and sends him off when he is old enough to bear a sword.

419 Wigamur comes upon a castle as it is being pillaged and burned. He finds and takes a horse and armour. Wigamur meets Glakotelesfloyer; they fight. Wigamur wins and asks childish questions. Wigamur's horse leads him back to the burned castle, where he finds a maiden, Pioles. She tells her story: the Kunig von Nordein had left her at the castle while he went off to a tourney at Pelrapeire; she was the only survivor of the attack.

988 Wigamur rides out the next day and again on the following day, when he comes upon the castle at Dalmflamür. [Missing page in the manuscript: Wigamur fetches Pioles and returns?] He is instructed there and knighted by Yttra, Arthur's uncle.

1444 Wigamur leaves, comes upon a vulture and an eagle fighting, and kills the former. The eagle becomes his devoted companion.

1526 Wigamur encounters Eydes, who is looking for a champion to fight at King Arthur's in defence of her claim to a magic spring. Wigamur volunteers. They arrive at Arthur's. Wigamur wins the combat but, citing his unworthy poverty, will not accept Eydes's offer of her hand and her country.

1974 Arthur proclaims a tourney, the victor of which will win Eydes. Wigamur outshines all the others but again refuses the prize. Eydes gives Arthur a beautiful tent and leaves.

2476 Arthur has a festival. A messenger from Ysope, queen of Holdrafluos, arrives. The court sets out to meet the approaching queen, and she tells her story: she is threatened by a heathen suitor. Arthur raises an army.

2852 Wigamur and a few companions are sent out to reconnoitre. They defeat a party of heathen scouts, who deliver themselves to Ysope the next morning.

3103 Ysope welcomes Arthur, and Arthur sends a letter of challenge to Morroch, the heathen king. Battle, in which Wigamur captures Marroch. Ysope is advised to marry Wigamur but she knows he will refuse. She gives Arthur a crown of gold. Wigamur leaves.

3457 Wigamur rides into Deleferant, a land laid waste by Atroclas and Paldriot, two kings who claim it. Wigamur joins Atroclas. After a day of battle it is agreed that the contest should be decided the next day in single combat: Wigamur will represent Atrocles against Paldriot. Paldriot insists that he will only fight against a king, whereupon Wigamur tells his own story. Paldriot recognizes Wigamur as his son, the enemies are reconciled, and it is agreed that Wigamur shall marry Dulceflur, the daughter of Atroclas. Paldriot and Wigamur return to Lendrie, where Paldriot installs Wigamur as king and gives him advice on how to govern. They set out for Rerat, the kingdom of Atroclas, and the marriage of Wigamur and Dulceflur is celebrated.

4656 At the wedding celebration a page arrives with news of a tourney to be held at Musygrallt in two days. Dinifogar, the queen, will give herself and her crown to the victor. Atroclas and Wigamur set out. At the tourney Wigamur fights and defeats Lypondrigan.

5311 The next morning Lypondrigan leaves, comes upon Dulceflur, who is en route to the tournament, and abducts her. Wigamur and Atroclas set out for the land of Lypondrigan.

5576 On their way they come upon the Kunig von Nordein lamenting the presumed death of Pioles [see above, 419]. Wigamur realizes that they are near the castle where he left her. He rides there, fetches her, and reunites Pioles and the Kunig von Nordein.

5827 Wigamur and his companions approach the country of Lypondrigan and learn that he has set out with Dulceflur for a tournament at
Gemorigal. They arrive. Wigamur defeats Lypondrigan, rescues Dulceflur, and they return to Rerat. [Four leaves missing in the manuscript:
celebration at Rerat and return to Lendrie?]
6095 Epilogue.

Wirnt von Gravenberc, *Wigalois*
(Probable date of composition: between 1210 and 1215)

1 Prologue.
145 An unknown knight (Joram) appears at Arthur's court and defeats
many knights, last of all Gawein, whom he leads back to his own
magical kingdom. Gawein must marry Florie, Joram's niece. He then
receives permission to visit Arthur's, but he cannot find his way back
to Florie. Gwigalois, the son of Florie and Gawein, inspired by his
father's fame, wants to make a name for himself. He leaves home and
comes upon an errant page who directs him to Arthur's. He dismounts
on a stone that will not tolerate those ever guilty of the slightest false-
hood (only Arthur and Gawein's hand). Gwigalois is welcomed,
entrusted to Gawein (Gwigalois seems to have forgotten that this is
his father), and knighted.
1717 A messenger appears at Arthur's court seeking help for her mistress. She needs a knight willing to attempt an adventure 'like death.'
Gwigalois gets Arthur's permission, the messenger leaves in a huff
(she had wanted Gawein), and Gwigalois hurries off after her.
1927 They need a place to spend the night. The messenger knows of a
knight who grants hospitality only to those who defeat him. Gwigalois kills him, and the travellers sleep out of doors.
2038 They hear cries of help. Gwigalois rescues a maiden from two
giants who had stolen her from Arthur's.
2184 The messenger, still sorry to have Gwigalois's company, spots a
spaniel she fancies. Gwigalois catches it for her, then kills its master.
2349 They come across Elamie, who has been robbed of her horse and
talking parrot, prizes awarded because of her beauty, by Hojir, the red
(-haired) knight. Gwigalois returns to the site of the courtly assembly
where the prizes had been awarded, fights Hojir, and regains horse
and parrot.
3297 They arrive at the camp of Schaffilun, who also wants to attempt
the adventure for the messenger's mistress. They fight; Schaffilun
dies.

3607 The messenger, finally satisfied of Gwigalois's valour, tells him the history of Korntin. It was taken from the father of her mistress by the heathen Roaz; the hand of the mistress is the reward for the liberator. This is the adventure Gwigalois undertook back at Arthur's court.

3885 They arrive at their goal, Roimunt. On entering Gwigalois unhorses the steward. We learn that the messenger's name is Nereja and that her mistress is Larie. Gwigalois and Larie fall in love. Gwigalois promises to attempt the adventure.

4370 Gwigalois sets off, following a marvellous beast into the land of Korntin. He follows the beast past a demonic tourney to its home, whereupon it turns into Lar, Larie's father. Lar explains about Korntin, predicts Gwigalois's success, tells him his father is Gawein, and equips him with a special lance and flower.

4863 Gwigalois comes upon Beleare, who is lamenting the abduction of her husband, Moral, by a dragon. Gwigalois kills the dragon with the special lance but is crushed unconscious by the dragon. He is robbed of his armour and therefore, on awakening, supposes he cannot possibly be the knight Gwigalois. Beleare discovers him, cares for him, and gives him lordly armour.

6251 The giantess Ruel captures Gwigalois and nearly kills him; but God, answering Gwigalois's prayer, frees him from his bonds, and he escapes.

6539 Gwigalois fights Karrioz, a heathen dwarf who, wounded, flees into a smog, where he dies.

6775 Caught on a bridge between the smog and a wheel of swords, Gwigalois prays again to God, who stops the wheel; Gwigalois enters the city of Glois.

6910 Gwigalois hears mysterious voices foretelling his doom; he defeats the fire-throwing centaur, Marrien; voices warn Roaz. Gwigalois kills one porter and defeats another.

7246 Gwigalois enters the castle, fights and kills Roaz, who is lamented by his wife Japhite. She dies of grief. Adan saves the unconscious Gwigalois from angry women and, by saying the name of Larie, gives Gwigalois new strength. Roaz's body is carried away by the Devil, which prompts Adan to convert to Christianity. Japhite is buried, and Adan is installed as viceroy at Glois.

8533 Gwigalois returns to Joraphas, home of Moral [see above, 4863], and prepares a celebration. The vassals are summoned; an embassy is sent for Larie; coronation and marriage. Gawein, Erec, Lanzelet, and Iwein arrive late. Reunion of Gawein and Gwigalois.

9799 A page brings the news that Lion has killed Amire. Elaborate preparations are made for a campaign against Lion, under the direction of Gawein. Namur is beseiged, and Lion is killed by Gawein.

11295 Gwigalois and the others set off for King Arthur's and learn en route of Florie's death [see above, 145]. Brief visit with Arthur.

11518 Gwigalois sets out for Korntin. Gawein tells Gwigalois how to govern well, then leaves. Gwigalois and Larie arrive at Korntin.

11610 Epilogue, including advertisement for the story to be told of Gwigalois's son and information on Wirnt's source.

Notes

INTRODUCTION

1 Kuhn, 'Erec'; Köhler, *Ideal und Wirklichkeit.*
2 Ruh, *Höfische Epik*, pp. 16–23, 92; Cormeau, *'Wigalois' und 'Diu Crone,'* pp. 12–13, 18; Haug, 'Symbolstruktur,' pp. 668–75.
3 Ruh, 'Der "Lanzelet" Ulrichs von Zatzikhofen,' p. 50. For a more detailed argument against the thematic importance of Lanzelet's namelessness see Schultz, 'Lanzelet,' pp. 166–7. Note as well that Kuhn, after venturing his own tentative analysis of Ulrich's work, remains uncertain about the accuracy of his own observations (Kuhn, 'Die Klassik des Rittertums,' p. 136).
4 Mitgau, 'Bauformen,' pp. 18, 23.
5 Moelleken, 'Minne und Ehe,' p. 50.
6 'Dem Danielroman fehlt das wichtige Movens der Minne' (de Boor, 'Der Daniel,' p. 77). See also Brall, 'Strickers *Daniel*,' pp. 242–3.
7 Frye, *The Secular Scripture*, pp. 180–1.
8 As Jurij Lotman writes: 'the study of the unique in a work of art can be carried out only after we have discovered what features regularly occur' (*Structure*, p. 77).
9 For text and discussion of the surviving fragments (all from a single manuscript) see Viskelety, 'Neue Fragmente.' For the knowledge of *Cligés* in Germany see Brogsitter, *Artusepik*, pp. 55–6.
10 On the relation between *Wigalois* and French romance see Cormeau, *'Wigalois' und 'Diu Crone,'* pp. 68–105. Cormeau concludes that *Wigalois's* relation to its possible sources is determined by its position in German literary history (pp. 103–5).
11 On the distinctions between Arthurian and Tristan traditions see Kuhn, *Tristan, Nibelungenlied, Artusstruktur*, pp. 16–38, and Ferrante, *The Conflict of Love and Honor*, pp. 14–18.

12 'Die Erforschung isolierter Genres ohne Berücksichtigung der Zeichen des Genresystems, mit dem sie in Korrelation stehen, ist unmöglich. Der historische Roman Tolstojs steht in Korrelation nicht zum historischen Roman Zagoskins, sondern zur zeitgenössischen Prosa' (Tynjanov, 'Über die literarische Evolution,' p. 447).

13 A number of German works that do contain Arthurian material have for various reasons been excluded from the investigation. The prose *Lancelot*, the *Jüngerer Titurel*, and *Lohengrin* do not belong formally to the tradition of Hartmann: they are composed in prose or in strophes, whereas the traditional Arthurian romance requires rhymed couplets. Further, the prose *Lancelot* and the *Jüngerer Titurel* belong, along with the Tristan romances, to a different world, in which the happy ending of Arthurian romance is not possible (See Cormeau, *'Wigalois' und 'Diu Crone,'* p. 13). The works of Ulrich Fuetrer, written nearly three centuries after those of Hartmann (after the end of the Middle High German period), are the product of an altogether different spirit.

14 Kuhn begins by expressing the hope 'aus einer neuen Anschauung der Komposition ... zu einer neuen Deutung des Gedichts zu gelangen' ('Erec,' p. 133).

15 'Die Form besiegelt die Erfahrung einer doppelten Wahrheit, die für das höfische Rittertum wieder zu einer einzigen zu machen der höfische Roman bestimmt ist. Diese neue literarische Gattung wird aus dem geistigen Zwang der ritterlichen Welt zur Überbrückung der aufgerissenen Kluft geboren und lebt vom Bewusstsein dieser Möglichkeit' (Köhler, *Ideal und Wirklichkeit*, pp. 242–3).

16 Todorov, *Introduction*, p. 149; trans., p. 141.

17 To draw attention to this distinction between author and narrator I will, in referring to the author of a work, give his name in its modern form: Hartmann, Chrétien. In referring to the narrator, however, that character within the work who usually goes by the same name, I will give the name as it appears in the text: Hartman, Crestïens.

18 'It is not "things" themselves, but the relations of things, which are the material substance in sign systems. This is likewise manifested in the artistic text, which is constructed as a form of organization, as a system of relations between constituent material units' (Lotman, *Structure*, p. 53).

19 Barthes, 'Style,' p. 10.

CHAPTER ONE

1 Todorov, 'The Place of Style,' p. 31. Note that Kuhn's description of the 'Gattungstendenzen' of courtly romance consists of two points, one functional ('wie kann er [der adlige Laie] diesen seinen Ort, jetzt und hier, aus

"Heilsgeschichte" begründen und rechtfertigen?') and one structural ('Gerüstepik') (Gattungsprobleme,' p. 59).

2 I have called my categories functions because each category fills a particular, essential function in Arthurian romance. Thus I use the term differently from Propp, for whom 'function is understood as an act of a character, defined from the point of view of its significance for the course of the action' (*Morphology*, p. 21). My functions are categories that generate characters and the actions of characters, while Propp's are limited strictly to the actions themselves.

3 Köhler, *Ideal und Wirklichkeit*, p. 77.

4 On the role of religion in *Wigalois* see Cormeau, *'Wigalois' und 'Diu Crone,'* pp. 44–8, 122.

5 After listing a series of parallels between the ordinary natural order (water becomes grapes, grapes become wine) and miracles (Christ turns water to wine), Augustine states: 'But when these things happen, as it were, in a river where things move and flow in a neverending succession, and pass from the hidden to the visible and from the visible to the hidden along the usual course for such transitory things, they are called natural; but when the same effects are brought about through an unusual change, in order to teach men some lesson, then they are called miracles' (*De Trinitate*, p. 138; trans., pp. 106–7).

6 Among the parallels in the list mentioned in note 5, Augustine includes the following: 'Who ordinarily clothes the trees with leaves and flowers except God? But when the rod of Aaron the priest flowered, then it was the divinity that conversed in a certain manner with doubting humanity.' Later he says: 'But even though all these things that I have just mentioned [the regular course of nature] are excluded, there are still other things; although they are formed from the same corporeal matter, yet they appear before our senses for the sole purpose of announcing a divine message. These are properly called miracles and signs' (*De Trinitate*, pp. 137–8, 146; trans., p. 106, 114–15).

7 Todorov, *Introduction*, p. 116; trans., p. 110.

8 In his essay 'Roman und Legende im deutschen Hochmittelalter' (p. 163) Max Wehrli remarks the transformation of 'das Wunder' of legend into 'das Wunderbare' of romance. 'Es [das Wunder] verliert vielleicht seine religiöse Verbindlichkeit, es wird zum bloss Wunderbaren, wenn nicht zum Phantastischen oder zum blossen Reiz.' In romance the divine has become simply strange, and God is the equivalent of a water fay. For a discussion of miracles in the strict sense and their role in romance (*Gregorius, Parzival, Tristan*) along with a consideration of the theological tradition see Lofmark, 'The Miraculous.'

9 Arthurian romance stands, then, with Dante, for whom 'fortuna' is one with the will of God; the wheel of fortune is simply a tool of divine providence (*Inferno*, 7:67–96). Therefore it is no surprise that in *Wigalois* the wheel of fortune is in the work of a priest (W:1036–52). On the treatment of chance as a function of genre see Köhler, *Der literarische Zufall*, pp. 122–37.

10 See Zumthor, *Essai*, pp. 137–40.

11 See Kuhn, 'Parzival,' pp. 159–61, 176.

12 Köhler, *Ideal und Wirklichkeit*, pp. 36, 66–78, 242–3; Kaiser, *Textauslegung*, pp. 124–6; Kaiser, '*Der Wigalois*,' p. 443; Brall, 'Strickers *Daniel*,' pp. 251–6.

13 Kaiser, '*Der Wigalois*,' p. 431.

14 On the general attitude of our genre to cities see Kaiser, '*Der Wigalois*,' pp. 431–3. One might point out here that, Köhler notwithstanding (*Ideal und Wirklichkeit*, pp. 16–18), the French *Erec* and *Yvain* are considerably more interested in city life than are their German counterparts. When Iwein enters 'diu burc' ravaged by Harpin (I:4372–85), he passes through the gate and is at once greeted by 'sehs knappen' and 'der wirt'; only after he has entered his host's dwelling does he meet 'ritter unde vrouwen.' When Yvain enters the equivalent 'chastel' (CY:3797–811), however, he is met by 'chevaliers, dames et sergenz, et dameiseles' who greet him and escort him 'a l'ostel.' In Chrétien the space between *la porte del chastel* (CY:900–1) and *la porte del palés* (CY:906) is invariably filled with 'dames, chevalier et borjois' (CE:4705). If the situation is not right for a welcome (Erec is borne into Limors), they may simply follow along (CE:4704–5); if they are not out on the streets (Yvain pursues Esclados into his fortress), this is cause for a remark (CY:903–6). Except in the case of Erec's arrival at Brandigan (CE:5445–93; E:8056–172), where the ominous remarks of the townspeople prepare the stage for the 'joie de la curt,' Hartmann ignores completely the bourgeois life within the French castles. He will say merely, 'uf Limors vuorten si in dan' (E:6315) or, 'sus vuoren si ... unz an daz palas' (I:1077–9).

At times of celebration – the inhabitants of Laluth prepare for the fight over the falcon; King Lac welcomes Erec and Enide at Carnant; King Arthur arrives at Laudine's – the difference between the French and German castles is even more obvious. In Chrétien the *borjois* are engaged decorating *ses meisons* (CY:2321) and bedecking *les rües* (CE:351) with tapestries and silken awnings (CE:2310–12; CY:2342–4); they ring the bells (CE:2279, 2307; CY:2350), play all sorts of musical instruments (CY: 2350–5), and fill the place with *joie* (CE:348–50, 2282, 2313, 2316; CY:

2341, 2359–60). All Hartman has to say is, 'nu reit der künec Artus durch sine bete mit im [Iwein] ze hus' (I:2653–4) or, 'er [Lac] vuorte si [Erec und Enite] heim ze Karnant' (E:2918). Once there the guests may enjoy *guotiu handelunge* and *kurzwile* (I:2656, 2658), but the welcome by the townspeople is missing.

One finds the same contrasting treatment of towns when comparing French and German Tristan romances. In Beroul, when Yseut returns to Marc after the years in the woods, more than four thousand townspeople come out to greet her and lead her into the 'cité'; there the bells are ringing and the streets are hung with silk and tapestries (Beroul, *Tristran*, vv. 2957–69). In Eilhart, at the analogous moment, we learn only, 'do reit der koning Marke dar und nam die koninginne wedir und hate sie abir sedir manich jar mit libe' (ETr:4978–81). Otherwise our attention is devoted entirely to Tristrant's parting words and departure.

15 See Emmel, *Formprobleme*, for an extended discussion, limited primarily to the works of Chrétien, Hartmann, and Wolfram, of the composition of Arthur's court.

16 Compare Heinrich's lament when Gawein fails at the 'Becherprobe' (C:2031–69).

17 See Haupt, *Der Truchsess Keie*, pp. 107–8. Unfortunately Haupt hardly considers the non-classical works, because they do not treat Keie as Hartmann and Wolfram do.

18 Haupt, *Der Truchsess Keie*, pp. 94–102; Emmel, *Formprobleme*, pp. 20–34, 60–2.

19 For an extensive discussion of the appearance of earlier heroes in *Diu Crone* see Cormeau, *'Wigalois' und 'Diu Crone,'* pp. 165–208.

20 Note the inclusiveness of the list of famous heroes that the author of *Gauriel* assembles at Arthur's for the terminal *hochzit*: Iwein, Erec, Gawan, Wigalois, Tristrant, Garel, Kalokreant, Lanzelot, der wilde Dodones, Parzival, Daniel von Plüental (GM:3857–67).

21 The fate of Parzival is ambiguous. Even those authors who mention him by name (Wirnt, W:6329; Konrad, GM:3866; der Pleier, T:2540, G:4187) tend not to assign him an active role in their works (as do der Stricker and, to a very slight extent, Heinrich). And this is not because they hesitate to remove Parzival from the lofty world of the grail: our authors think nothing of recalling Erec from Karnant, of separating Iwein once more from Laudine, or of raising Tristan from the dead. See as well note 72.

22 Ruh, *Höfische Epik*, p. 18.

23 Haug, *Das Land*, p. 27.

24 This same function is served also by the requirement, invented by the author of *Daniel* and mentioned a bit later, that Arthur's knights could not return to court until their shields had been battered to pieces (D: 125–42). Ingeborg Henderson is certainly right in criticizing Peter Kobbe's assertion that the custom undermines Arthur's ideality (Henderson, *Strickers Daniel*, p. 134; Kobbe, 'Funktion und Gestalt,' pp. 430–1).

25 Note how, at the very end of *Diu Crone*, when at long last the author can find no need to generate more episodes, he allows Keie to joke with the well-known convention of the postponed meal (C:29855–65).

26 See Köhler, *Ideal und Wirklichkeit*, p. 83.

27 Even in those works in which the hero does not reach Arthur's court until quite far along the author will take pains to introduce him earlier. In *Lanzelet* Arthur is praised by an errant member of his own court after Lanzelet's first victory (L:1258–86); in *Parzival* Arthur and Gawan are mentioned even before the hero himself is born (P:66,1–22); and in *Gauriel* and *Meleranz* Arthur is worked into the prologue along with Hartman and Wolfram (GM:19–31; M:101–69).

28 Ruh, *Höfische Epik*, p. 13.

29 Karin Gürttler distinguishes two tendencies in the post-classical treatment of Arthur: one, conservative, in which he remains passive, the symbol of the good old times; the other in which he plays an active role (*Künec Artus*, pp. 279–81).

30 Note that this single *hochzit*, at which 'manc edele herze ... vröude unde hohen muot gewan' (GTr:585–6), occurs at the outset of the romance, where Marke's reputation – he is called 'höfsch und ... erbaere' (GTr: 421) – is able to lure Riwalin to Cornwall. The author of *Tristan* recognizes the relation of courtly ideality, *hochzit*, and *vreude*; but once the ideality of Marke is undermined the rest disappear as well.

31 The situation seems to have been different in France, at least according to Beroul. When Yseut returns to court after the years in the woods, the townspeople come to greet her ('mervellose joie menoient' [*Tristran*, v. 2961]), a mass is celebrated, and then she is led to the palace: 'grant joie i ont le jor menee' (v. 2999). All are welcome to the feast; Yseut is greatly honoured; there is great joy; Marc knights twenty squires: it is a regulation festival. Such a celebration accords with those elements of Beroul's narrative that serve to justify the court at the expense of the lovers, elements that conflict with the strong partisan sympathies of the narrator (See Le Gentil, 'La Légende de Tristan,' pp. 111–18).

32 Wolfram does the same when he says of the home of Plippalinot, 'daz stuont also daz Artus ze Nantes, da er dicke saz, niht möhte han gebuwet baz' (P:548,24–6).

33 Arthurian *vreude* is of course completely foreign to the world of the *Nibelungenlied* as well. At the festivities that accompany the arrival of Prünhilt at Worms, *vreude* appears as a personal expectation (Nbl:600,3) and a cause of noise (Nbl:603,4), but the main activity of the court is jousting (Nbl:596–8). When Kriemhilt marries Etzel the celebrations begin 'vroelichen' (Nbl:1362,4), but they consist exclusively of 'milte' (Nbl:1372,1) and 'ritterschefte' (Nbl:1375,1). We see in both cases courtly behaviour and various joyful activities but never that collective emotion, the *vreude* of an Arthurian *hochzit*.

34 See Jameson, 'Magical Narratives,' p. 161.

35 As Barthes says, 'the epic is a narrative broken at the functional level [by function he means smallest narrative unit] but unitary at the actantial level' ('Introduction,' p. 15; trans., p. 104).

36 Greimas, 'Éléments,' p. 180.

37 See Schultz, 'Lanzelet,' pp. 183–4.

38 See Moelleken/Henderson, 'Die Bedeutung der *liste*,' pp. 188–99.

39 'Damit ihm auch wirklich zu-fällt, was ihm zu-kommt, begibt der Protagonist des Artusromans sich auf die Suche nach der *aventure* – *adventura*. Aventure wird zum auszeichnenden, "zukommenden," vorherbestimmten ... Ereignis ...' (Köhler, *Der literarische Zufall*, p. 29).

40 See Todorov, 'Les Hommes-récits,' pp. 78–82; trans., pp. 66–70.

41 Ruh, 'Der "Lanzelet" Ulrichs von Zatzikhofen,' p. 50.

42 Ehrismann, *Geschichte*, 2,2,1:229.

43 Köhler, *Ideal und Wirklichkeit*, p. 77.

44 Warning, 'Formen narrativer Identitätskonstitution,' pp. 561–2.

45 Huby, 'L'Approfondissement psychologique,' p. 23.

46 Hahn, 'Parzivals Schönheit,' p. 232.

47 Wehrli, 'Strukturen,' p. 49. Eberhard Lämmert, after considering the nature of time in medieval epic, expresses a general reservation about the study of 'development' in literature: 'Diese Erscheinung ... macht aber gleichzeitig darauf aufmerksam, dass das Problem der Lebensdarstellung durch die erzählte Geschichte nicht grundsätzlich unter dem Aspekt der Entwicklung gesehen werden darf' (*Bauformen*, p. 31).

48 See Cormeau, *'Wigalois' und 'Diu Crone,'* p. 50.

49 Benveniste, *Problèmes*, pp. 238–43.

50 See Rosenhagen's note to D:169 (der Stricker, *Daniel*, p. 180). For an extensive discussion of the 'episches Präteritum' see Hamburger, *Logik*, pp. 59–72.

51 The examples given by Ingeborg Schröbler (Paul, *Mittelhochdeutsche Grammatik*, §§ 301–5) show that the functional distinction between preterite and perfect that we have derived from Benveniste and observed in the

passage from *Lanzelet* is in general true of all Middle High German texts – although exceptions are not uncommon (§ 302,b). Schröbler mentions as well the occasional use of the present within a narration primarily in the preterite (§ 297, notes 1–2) as a technique by which the narrator reduces the 'Erzähldistance.'

52 The narrators of *Wigalois*, *Gauriel*, and *Garel* do not claim a French source for their tales. Wirnt says he has his story from 'ein knappe' (W:596, 11687). Although scholars have seen in this 'knappe' the transmitter of various French works (for a consideration of the literature see Cormeau, *'Wigalois' und 'Diu Crone,'* pp. 68–105), Wirnt himself says nothing about the language spoken by his informant. In a passage not accepted as genuine by the editor of *Gauriel*, Maister Cuonrat von Stoffel says of himself: 'zuo Hispania er daz puoch gewan' (see note to GM:4064). Der Pleiaere does not reveal the origin of the 'fremdez maere' (G:31) he offers us as *Garel*, although he may well have had something to say on the subject in the missing prologue. In each of these works, however, we find hints that the language of the original actors must have been French: clearest is the case of Gwigalois, who himself apparently speaks 'franzois' (W:8340); the hero of *Gauriel* comes from 'Muntabel' (GM:167, 1013) and Erec is called 'fil de roi Lac' (GM:1398, 3160); Garel adopts Arthur's battle cry of 'Nantes' (G:14506, 14519, 14876).

53 On Wolfram's exploitation of his bilingual role in *Willehalm* but with regard as well to *Parzival* and other Arthurian romances see Curschmann, 'The French,' especially pp. 553–8 and note 12.

54 Gotfrit's audience, on the other hand, seems to understand French quite well. We see this first of all in the much greater amount of French that is incorporated into the narrative: characters often greet one another in French (GTr:743–4, 2681, 2685–6, 3353–5) and the reaction of courtly society is often given in the original: the lament at the kidnapping of Tristan (GTr:2397–8); their impression of the newly arrived Tristan (GTr:3363–4) or Isolt (GTr:12559–60). The cowardly Irish steward attacks the dragon (GTr:9165–6) and Tristan begs mercy (GTr:10229) – both in French. Although some of the lines mentioned above are translated immediately into German (GTr:2682–3, 2687–8, 2399–400, 12561–2), the rest are not; it seems that Gotfrit's audience is assumed to understand French while the Arthurian audience only knows German. Thus Gotfrit can build the scene in which Tristan and Isolt reveal their love for one another around a triple pun in French (GTr:11985–12015); he can leave untranslated the three-line exchange of greetings when Marke and Tristan first meet (GTr: 3353–5); even the narrator is allowed half of a line in French: '"merci!"'

dit la buzele' (GTr:744). This last example shows quite clearly that the internal audience in *Tristan* is assumed to be bilingual, just like Gotfrit himself.

55 Ong, 'The Writer's Audience,' p. 16.
56 Curschmann, 'The French,' p. 554.
57 Todorov, *Introduction*, p. 19; trans., pp. 14–15.
58 This principle is violated in *Daniel*, where the father of the two slain giants snatches Arthur away from his victory festival after the taking of Cluse (D:6948–53). In *Lanzelet*, however, when Valerin carries Ginover away the deatils of the abduction are kept unclear (L:6725–51). The page who relates the event mentions only that the court was off on the hunt of the white stag. Apparently they had left the realm of S for that of W, where an encounter with O⁻ is to be expected.
59 My system of romance space has its roots in Genette's analysis of narrative aspects and levels and in Lotman's discussion of artistic space, plot event, and persona (Genette, 'Discours du récit,' pp. 71–2, 239, note 1; trans., pp. 25–6, 228, note 41; Lotman, *Structure*, pp. 217–44). I have taken elements from both theorists and arranged them with regard to the particular characteristics of Arthurian romance.
60 The critical distinction between story and plot – plot adds relations of cause or meaning to the simple time sequence of the story – has provided this technical definition of story (see Lämmert, *Bauformen*, pp. 24–6); yet the distinction between story and plot is not of importance in my system. Plot relations – cause and meaning – may be part of the narrator's source; they may be implied in the action; they may figure as speech acts by the personae of the story; or they may be added by the narrator as he fashions his account. Although we can often isolate explanatory interruptions by the narrator and thereby establish that they are features of the narration, we cannot tell whether the causal explanations that appear in our text originate with the narrator or his source. The critical distinction between plot and story is of no consequence in distinguishing levels of romance space.
61 Tzvetan Todorov, writing of the *Odyssey*, makes a similar point. 'Within speech-as-narrative, we now see two distinct poles ... At one pole, there is the bard's song ... At the other pole, we read the many brief narratives the characters utter throughout the poem, without thereby becoming bards. This category of discourse marks a stage in the movement toward speech-as-action: here speech remains constative [like that of the principal narrator], but it also assumes another dimension which is that of action' (Todorov, 'Le Récit primitif,' pp. 72–3; trans., p. 60).

218 Notes to pages 58–73

62 See Barthes, *S/Z*, pp. 74–5; trans., 67–8.
63 Todorov, *Grammaire*, p. 28.
64 See Propp, *Morphology*, p. 20.
65 See Todorov, *Grammaire*, p. 29.
66 'Tragedy is an imitation, not of men but of action and life ... The purpose of action on the stage is not to imitate character, but character is a by-product of the action' (Aristotle, *Poetics*, § 1450a, pp. 13–14).
67 Almost one hundred years ago Max Jellinek and Carl Kraus cautioned against drawing psychological conclusions from the inconsistent behaviour of characters: 'Als Widerspruch kann es auch bezeichnet werden, wenn dieselbe Person in ganz gleichen Situationen sich verschieden benimmt, ohne dass der Dichter sie dadurch als launenhaft oder unbeständig charakterisieren will' ('Widersprüche,' p. 690).
68 Curschmann, 'Das Abenteuer des Erzählens,' pp. 631–62.
69 Bezzola, *Le Sens de l'aventure*, p. 86. See Fromm, 'Doppelweg,' p. 71.
70 See Kermode, *Genesis*, pp. 75–99, especially p. 98.
71 What Franz Stanzel writes about the 'auktorialer Roman' can be said of many Arthurian romances as well: 'Das Spannungsfeld, das sich zwischen beiden [Erzähler/dargestellter Welt] bedeutungsvoll aufbaut, ist ein entscheidendes Spezifikum seines Sinngefüges' (*Typische Formen*, p. 21).
72 See Zumthor, *Essai*, p. 81.
73 Might not the anomalous reception of Parzival (see note 21) indicate that later authors (and not only modern scholars) questioned Parzival's allegiance to the world of Arthur?

CHAPTER TWO

1 Haug, 'Symbolstruktur,' p. 696. Jurij Lotman makes the same point from a more general perspective: 'Thus the initial point of plot movement is the establishment of a relation of distinction and mutual freedom between the hero-agent and the semantic field surrounding him: if the hero's essence coincides with his environment, if he is not invested with the capacity to distinguish himself from that environment, the development of plot is impossible' (*Structure*, p. 240).
2 Karl Uitti makes the same point in discussing the immodest damsel in the *Charrete*: 'In other words, Lancelot accepts her hard conditions (despite their ridiculous overtones) because, precisely, the romance must go on' (*Story, Myth, and Celebration*, p. 180).
3 For a brief but perceptive discussion of sea voyages in the German Tristan romances but with reference as well to Arthurian adventure see Schindele, *Tristan*, pp. 25–6.

4 Nolting-Hauff, 'Märchen und Märchenroman,' pp. 155–6. Nolting-Hauff
goes on to say: 'Es spricht für das Niveau des Autors [Chrestiens], dass
er im Gegensatz zu den meisten späteren Autoren von Ritterromanen
aus der strukturellen Notwendigkeit zahlreicher verfehlter happy ends
eine thematische Tugend macht' (p. 156). But this is unfair, at least for
German romance. Lanzelet is the only profligate in the group. Gwigalois,
Daniel, Gauriel, Meleranz, and Tandareis are all just as chaste as Erec or
Parzival.

5 Thus Kurt Ruh: 'Das Mit- und Ineinander von Aventiure und Minne
gehört in der Tat zu den konstitutiven Elementen des Artusromans'
(*Höfische Epik*, p. 21). Similarly, Karl Otto Brogsitter: 'Nach aussen sind es
nur zwei Dinge, die im Mittelpunkt dieser Erzählungen zu stehen schei-
nen: Waffentaten und Liebe' (*Artusepik*, p. 50).

6 Todorov, *Introduction*, p. 172; trans., pp. 163–4.

7 In a few cases S is absent from the episodes of equilibrium. After Lanzelet
wins Iblis they choose to adjourn to a beautiful meadow rather than face
the political problems in Dodone; one is not surprised, for both have
strong connections to W. When Iwein and Laudine are reconciled the only
one present is Lunete; why is there no recognition by society? Kurt Ruh,
trying to connect the scene at Arthur's court with the reconciliation with
Laudine that follows, says: 'Was im epischen Bericht sich notwendigerweise als ein Nacheinander darstellen musste, das ist dem Sinne nach ein
Miteinander: Aventiure u n d Minne' (*Höfische Epik*, p. 157). But why
'notwendigerweise'? Chrétien did after all compose a conclusion to *Erec*
that united the hero, the heroine, and Arthur's court. Why did he not do
the same in *Yvain*?

8 See above, chapter one, pp. 24–5.

9 See Ruh, *Höfische Epik*, pp. 92–3; Cormeau, '*Wigalois' und 'Diu Crone*,' pp.
14–15; Zumthor, *Essai*, pp. 356–7.

10 Propp, *Morphology*, p. 100.

11 Nolting-Hauff, 'Märchen und Märchenroman.'

12 Propp, *Morphology*, p. 101–4.

13 For a more general critique of Nolting-Hauff's proposals see Cormeau,
'Artusroman und Märchen,' pp. 64–74. I agree with him that the
'Verhaltenserwartung' that motivates much of Arthurian romance is an
essential component of the genre; in my system it derives from the ideology of S and plays the most important role in the multiplication of cause.
But I do not agree with Cormeau when he says of this 'Verhaltenserwartung': 'Sie ist eine Konstituente, ohne die genaugenommen die Handlung
auseinanderfällt ...' (p. 72). There are many cases in which an Arthurian
plot is motivated in ways directly contrary to the 'Verhaltenserwartung' of

the genre: Gawein induces Iwein to forget his promise to Laudine; Lanzelet kills his host, Galagandreiz, after having slept with Galagandreiz's daughter; Arthur functions as hero for a long stretch near the beginning of *Diu Crone*. In each of these cases – and there are many others – the hero behaves contrary to expectation, yet the plot does not fall to pieces. As a result I am convinced that the conventional kinds of Arthurian motivation do not define romance plot at its basic level. They provide, instead, a repertory of motivational patterns on which an author can draw to make the predetermined movement of his plot seem plausible and which we, familiar with the conventions of Arthurian verisimilitude, accept as credible; but the integrity of the skeletal plot does not depend on these motivations.

14 Dorfman, *The Narreme*.
15 For a more extensive presentation and critique of Todorov's *Grammaire* see Culler, *Structuralist Poetics*, pp. 215–17.
16 See Stierle, *Text als Handlung*, pp. 208–11.
17 For a more extensive presentation and critique of Greimas's 'Éléments' see Stierle, *Text als Handlung*, pp. 202–11. For a discussion of the problems involved in transferring Greimas's system to Arthurian romance see Warning, 'Formen narrativer Identitätskonstitution,' pp. 558–73.
18 My distinction between skeleton and substance is similar to Barthes's distinction between sets of 'nuclei,' which provide a framework that is both necessary and sufficient, and 'the other units' (catalysers, indices, informants), which fill out the framework 'according to a mode of proliferation in principle infinite' (Barthes, 'Introduction,' p. 11; trans., p. 97).
19 I realize that by beginning with the episodic skeleton and treating the techniques of differentiation as additions to that skeleton ('an episode *acquires* special characteristics') I may seem to offer a model of the actual generation of an Arthurian episode. This is not my intention at all. The various levels I propose are merely ways of isolating various kinds of romance organization, arranged here from most abstract (functions, skeleton) to least (surface). Perhaps Wolfram began the composition of *Parzival* with the 'Bogengleichnis,' the 'Selbstverteidigung,' and a handful of puns, then added the rest of the work 'underneath' – precisely the reverse, that is, of the order in which I develop my structural model. This should not affect the usefulness of my categories and levels for analysing the different kinds of organizational patterns of which the finished work is actually composed. The order in which these categories and levels have been introduced has been determined by the hope of achieving some measure of expository clarity, not by any theory of how a romance was actually written.

20 The system of differentiation that we are investigating here parallels in many ways the system of attributes that Wilhelm Messerer has detected in medieval visual art. He speaks of '"Attribuierung" im Sinne von "erläuternder Zuordnung"' ('Einige Darstellungsprinzipien,' p. 160), terms that could very well describe the function, in this passage, of Enite and of Erec's armour in relation to Erec himself.

21 See Köhler, *Ideal und Wirklichkeit*, p. 74. On the more complex relation between Parzival's appearance and his essential worth see Hahn, 'Parzivals Schönheit.'

22 Wilhelm Messerer speaks of the 'Attribut eines Attributs eines Attributs' and of 'das Astwerk der Zuordnung' ('Einige Darstellungsprinzipien,' pp. 169, 162).

23 Faral, *Les Arts poétiques*, p. 76.

24 Zumthor, *Essai*, p. 354.

25 See Barthes on 'sequences' ('Introduction,' pp. 13–15; trans., pp. 101–4); see also Jameson, 'Magical Narratives,' p. 139.

26 On the way in which additional characters (multiplication of actor) generate more narrative see Kermode, *Genesis*, pp. 78–94.

27 This is not, however, true of *Cligés*. There, in the fights against Count Angrés and the Duke of Saxony, the love of the hero for his lady is very carefully interwoven with the progress of the battle.

28 One can observe this distinction between tournament and battle quite clearly in the thirty-first *aventiure* of the *Nibelungenlied*. There, what begins as a regulation *buhurdieren* ('Swes iemen da pflaege, so was ez niwan schal' [Nbl:1881,1]) threatens to turn into a battle when Volker kills a rich Hun (Nbl:1889,3). The battle is averted, but only by the active intercession of Etzel, who asserts that Volker is *ane schulde* and that he killed his opponent by accident (Nbl:1896,3–4). Had Volker *intended* to kill the Hun, this would violate the rules of tournament and justify a counterattack – which in this case would certainly mean battle.

29 Taking all these together one sees that the fighting in book seven of *Parzival* follows the pattern of a tournament much more closely than that of a battle – even though the fighting is intense and, as we are told in passing, lives are lost (P:386,15–18).

30 *Dietrichs Flucht* (= *Das Buch von Bern*), lines 8502–673; *Rabenschlacht*, strophe 536. In the second part of Eilhart's *Tristrant*, which is in fact very much like a series of Arthurian adventures, Tristrant leads an army in a large battle on behalf of his future father-in-law, Havelin. In the middle of the fray we are told:
    da vacht so [gar] vreisliche
    Kehenis und Tristrant,

daz Dieterich noch Hildebrant
ni so vele mochte getun.   (ETr:5974–7)
Eilhart compares Tristrant and Kehenis to Dietrich and his master, not to
Erec or Eneas; he indicates thereby that the model for large battles – even
when they appear in 'courtly' works – is heroic poetry.

31 Brall, 'Strickers Daniel,' p. 227; see also Henderson, Strickers Daniel, p.
169.

32 Like Helmut de Boor: 'Die Massenschlacht ist dem klassischen Artusroman überhaupt fremd. Der Pleier hat sie beibehalten, um zu zeigen, wie
sie etwa einzustilisieren wäre' ('Daniel,' p. 79). The large-scale battle
may be foreign to the classical Arthurian romance, but it is not at all
strange if we regard the whole corpus; fully one-third of the romances
contain battles. And why, if the author of Garel retained Daniel's battle
only to make a stylistic point, did he expand it to more than three times
its original length?

33 In Jurij Lotman's system the capacity of Arthurian romance to present one
event from several perspectives would be classed as a kind of 'internal
recoding'; 'reality comes to be viewed as the mutual intersection of various points of view' with the result that the amount of (artistic) information carried by such a text is increased (Lotman, Structure, pp. 41–6).

34 Robert Hanning devotes a chapter of The Individual in Twelfth-Century
Romance to 'Multiple Perspectives on Reality' (pp. 171–93). It includes
many perceptive observations on the mechanics and significance of multiple perspective; and yet, as his is an interpretive study, his conclusions
are very different from my own. Hanning finds 'that multiple perspective
is a technique rendering, and expressing the importance of, the individual's subjective experience of reality' (p. 180); he is concerned with multiple perspective as 'an educational force,' with what characters and
readers 'learn' from it (p. 187), and the way it contributes 'to the complexity and attractiveness of the romances as statements about the problematic limitations of individuality' (p. 193). Hanning's analysis of
multiplication of perspective in the French Erec can doubtless increase our
understanding of its German adaptation and perhaps of the other canonical works as well. Yet I do not think we can turn his observations into a
definition of the function of multiplication of perspective for the entire
Arthurian genre. The author of Garel, for instance, is quite at home with
the technique of multiplication of perspective; yet in his case this common
technique is not made to bear any of the epistemological or developmental
meaning that it seems to bear in some of the French romances.

35 Gérard Genette, writing in a more general context, makes a similar point
with regard to the relation of the apparent and real motivation in works

of fiction: 'La motivation est donc l'apparence et l'alibi causaliste que se donne la détermination finaliste qui est la règle de la fiction: le *parce que* chargé de faire oublier le *pour quoi?* – et donc de naturaliser, ou de *réaliser* (au sens de: faire passer pour réelle) la fiction en dissimulant ce qu'elle a de *concerté*, comme dit Valincour, c'est-à-dire d'artificiel: bref, de fictif' ('Vraisemblance,' p. 97).

36 Culler, *Structuralist Poetics*, p. 145.

37 Culler, *Structuralist Poetics*, p. 147.

38 Propp, *Morphology*, p. 78.

39 Albert Leitzmann calls this 'eins der häufigsten mhd. sprichwörter' and gives a number of other citations ('Lanzelet,' p. 301).

40 Eugène Vinaver considers the introduction of causal explanations to be Chrétien's great contribution to the Arthurian matter: 'The purpose of poetic composition as he [Chrétien] saw it was to give meaning and shape to amorphous matter. His most subtle and most effective method of achieving this was an analysis – sometimes simply an explanation – of the characters' motives and feelings. The narrative proper might remain simple and even base; what mattered was its systematic and careful elucidation' (*Form and Meaning*, p. 7).

41 The confusion that results from not distinguishing between the needs of the romance structure and the motives ascribed to the characters can be observed in a remark of Luise Lerner. She states: 'Lanzelet besteht sämtliche Kämpfe nur gezwungen, nicht aus freiem Willen wie Iwein und Parzival' (*Studien*, p. 18); but she is wrong on two counts. On the level of the story Lanzelet is often said to act of his own free will: he chooses to leave the water fay; he rides deliberately to Galagandreiz's and Linier's castles even though he knows there will be trouble; he elects to take on the defence of Ginover and to attempt the *aventiure* at Pluris. On the other hand, none of Lanzelet's decisions really allows room for free will: the decisions are taken for him by the requirements of the episodic skeleton – but it is the same for Iwein and Parzival.

42 Geoffrey of Vinsauf, *Poetria nova*, vv. 115–17; trans., p. 37.

43 By giving away the end of the romance first from the perspective of Anfortas and then from that of Condwiramurs, the narrator demonstrates his sympathy for the diad (*gral, minne*) that inspires Parzival without having to claim that sympathy explicitly (cf. P:737,27–30). *Gral* and *minne* are not only Parzival's goal but, as Wolfram makes clear here, that of the work itself.

44 Geoffrey of Vinsauf, *Poetria nova*, vv. 55–61; trans., pp. 34–5.

45 In the following I have, wherever possible, given the medieval rhetorical term (from Geoffrey of Vinsauf) for each of Wolfram's ornaments. I have

done so to show that Wolfram's narrative bravura can be analysed in contemporary terms, not to make any point about the author's possible rhetorical schooling or lack of it. With regard to this latter issue, Eberhard
Nellmann is surely right in concluding that there is no need to assume
any direct influence of classical or medieval Latin rhetoric on the author
of *Parzival* (*Wolframs Erzähltechnik*, pp. 179–80).

46 Curtius's 'inexpressibility' topos (*European Literature*, pp. 159–60).

47 Or perhaps one should say 'that only modern punctuation can create': the
punctuation of Leitzmann/Deinert assumes a considerably more elaborate
hyperbaton than that of Lachmann et al.

48 The meaning of the line is not entirely clear. For the various readings that
have been suggested see Nellmann, *Wolframs Erzähltechnik*, p. 101 and
p. 101, note 99.

49 For a comprehensive catalogue of the types and functions of narrative
intervention as practised by Wolfram, both within the single episode and
with regard to the whole romance, see Nellmann, *Wolframs Erzähltechnik*,
pp. 34–164.

50 Curschmann, 'Das Abenteuer des Erzählens.'

51 Curschmann, 'Das Abenteuer des Erzählens,' pp. 662, 666–7.

52 Rainer Warning holds that the contradictions of the Arthurian tale are
harmonized 'auf der Ebene ironischer Vermittlung,' by the consistent
irony of the narrator ('Formen narrativer Identitätskonstitution,' pp.
578–83, here p. 579). But the ironical stance is only one of the postures
that the narrator assumes, and these various postures can be reconciled
(another point of Warning's, see below pp. 166–7) only from the perspective
of the author. From the narrator himself we can expect, and indeed we
get, no more consistency than from any other Arthurian character.

CHAPTER THREE

1 *Wigamur* differs from the other Arthurian romances in many respects.
Among them is that the hero has not won his wife before he marries her.
The marriage is arranged between the bride's father, on whose side Wigamur is fighting, and Wigamur's own father, whom unwittingly he nearly
fights. As if knowing that an arranged marriage is inadequate, Wigamur
runs off for the tournament at Musygrallt as soon as he hears of it, without even pausing to consummate the marriage. While he is at the tournament his bride is abducted, and he must win her back. Only then, at the
very end of the romance, is the marriage finally consummated.

2 Frye, *Anatomy*, p. 186.

3 Murphy, *Rhetoric*, pp. 288–9.
4 Faral, *Les Arts poétiques*, pp. 59–60.
5 See Cormeau (*'Wigalois' und 'Diu Crone,'* pp. 205–8), who talks of 'Weitererzählen im abgesteckten Genreraum' (p. 208).
6 Cervantes, *Don Quixote*, 2:241.
7 The beginning of *Diu Crone* is problematic. The first episode, the 'Becherprobe,' belongs to Keie, who comments on the proceedings and loses the single combat (type-two episode). After harmony has been restored, news of the tournament at Jaschune reaches court and Gawein departs (type-one episode). Then Arthur hears of Gasozein, sets out, and eventually fights him (type-two episode). Since Arthur never actually defeats Gasozein while Gawein ultimately does, one might consider Arthur a false hero (!). This is harder to do in the case of Keie, even though he is defeated outright, because the 'Becherprobe' messenger disappears after his victory and Keie is never avenged by anyone who could be called the 'true' hero. In the following I will ignore the 'Becherprobe' and consider both the first Arthur episode and the first Gawein episode. On the function of the 'Becherprobe' see Cormeau, *'Wigalois' und 'Diu Crone,'* pp. 223–4.
8 Although the basic pattern of Tristan's childhood shows similarities with that of an Arthurian hero, the two traditions differ in important respects with regard to child-rearing. Whether one follows Eilhart or Gottfried, the portrayal of Tristan's childhood requires only four stages; first, some information about his parents; second, a description of his early childhood and education; third, his departure by sea and arrival at Cornwall; finally, his life at Marke's court leading to his knighting. Although the Tristan pattern lacks the flexible fourth position of Arthurian romance, its skeleton is otherwise the same. Both traditions also agree on the obligatory anonymity of their young heroes: in the case of Tristan he *chooses* to hide his true identity (ETr:269–85; GTr:2696–721, 3097–123).

Tristan's childhood, however, differs from that of an Arthurian hero in several respects, all of which affect his education as a knight. First, Tristan is not raised by his mother, for his mother dies when he is born: in Eilhart, he is educated at his father's court by Kurneval (ETr:120–89); in Gottfried, by 'einem wisen man' (GTr:2061) at the castle of Rual. Although Tristan's true identity is not publicly known in Gottfried, in neither version can he be said to spend his early years hidden from the world, like an Arthurian hero. Second, Tristan *does* learn knightly skills at home (ETr: 148–52; GTr:2103–16). Therefore, third, he does not leave out of a desire to learn more about knighthood but simply because he wants to see something of the world (ETr:198–9, 211–19), or because he is kidnapped (GTr:

2279–339). Fourth, although Tristrant is entrusted to a guardian, Tinas (ETr:303–45), in neither version does the hero learn any more about knightly skills or courtly behaviour once he reaches Marke's court. At this point Eilhart's narrative introduces the challenge of Morolt, while Gottfried, after following Tristan as his various proficiencies gradually win him the confidence of Marke, turns his attention to Rual's search for his foster child and the revelation of Tristan's identity. Both versions include the ceremony in which their hero is knighted: Eilhart, after brief negotiations, accomplishes the knighting in two lines (ETr:499–522); Gottfried, in spite of all the tangential commotion, is hardly more detailed (GTr:5012–52). The knighting is not, as in Arthurian romance, followed by a tournament at which the hero distinguishes himself; Eilhart does not mention a tourney at all; Gotfrit reports the occurrence of such an event but refuses outright to describe it (GTr:5054–68).

Thus, although the portrayals of childhood in the Tristan romances and in Arthurian romance share a similar skeletal pattern, we see by the comparison of the two traditions that Arthurian romance has given the pattern a particular focus and a clear purpose: to demonstrate the hero's knightly vocation. To this end the early childhood of an Arthurian hero is isolated from the world, his father is dead or absent, and his education is limited to books, games, music, and courteous behaviour: he is systematically deprived of contact with the world of knighthood. Therefore we are all the more impressed when he wants to go off and learn more about knightly skills: somehow he senses that he must become a knight. The fourth section demonstrates the hero's great need of further instruction. Once he reaches an appropriate tutor, however, he makes up for his earlier deficient training in no time at all – another sign of his calling – and demonstrates his knightly perfection by excelling at a tournament. In Arthurian romance, then, the childhood sequence is a carefully staged demonstration of the hero's knightly calling.

9 Northrop Frye, speaking of romance in general, writes: 'Identity means a good many things, but all its meanings in romance have some connection with a state of existence in which there is nothing to write about. It is existence before "once upon a time," and subsequent to "and they lived happily ever after." What happens in between are adventures, or collisions with external circumstances, and the return to identity is the release from these circumstances' (The Secular Scripture, p. 54).

10 One might be tempted to attribute the unorthodox ending of Iwein to its French source if it were not for two facts: first, Hartmann felt free to write a new beginning to the work; second, Hartmann felt no hesitation in reworking the conclusion of Chrétien's Erec.

11 One must resist the temptation to overinterpret this generic happy ending or to write the qualities peculiar to the happy endings of the most famous works into our definition of the genre. Rainer Warning, who deals so admirably with disjuncture in the course of a romance plot ('Formen narrativer Identitätskonstitution,' pp. 558–73), is less willing to accept it at the end. He regards the ending of a romance as the conclusion of the hero's 'Identitätssuche' (p. 562), as the successful conclusion of his internalization of courtly norms (p. 568), and as the second, this time proper, winning of the hero's lady (pp. 569, 571). Yet Lanzelet discovers his identity (i.e. his name) the first and only time he wins his wife – midway through the romance; and the Arthurian court admires his understanding of courtly norms from the outset (see Schultz, 'Lanzelet,' pp. 167–71). Daniel, Gwigalois, and the Gawein of *Diu Crone* all need to win wives only once – Gawein only to forget his entirely for the rest of the romance; and all of these heroes are paragons of knighthood from the outset of their romances. They all *display* their understanding of courtly norms throughout the work, but we have no reason to assume that they have *grown* internally in the understanding of these norms. One may want to interpret the ending of *Erec*, *Iwein*, or *Parzival* as the happy conclusion of a process of growth for which the reunion with court and wife are visible signs; one cannot describe the required happy ending of Arthurian romance, however, in any but the most concrete terms without doing violence to the nature of the genre. The hero gets what is destined for him – a kingdom, a wife, the festival reunion with Arthur's court; that is the happy ending. Once again we can observe the consequences of deriving the rules of the genre by interpreting the particular qualities of the most celebrated romances.

12 For *Iwein* see Selbmann, 'Strukturschema,' pp. 82–3; for *Parzival* see Ehrismann, *Geschichte*, 2,2,1, p. 261, also Bumke, *Wolfram von Eschenbach*, pp. 43–4; for *Wigalois* see Mitgau, 'Nachahmung,' pp. 334–7.

13 See the 'Conclusion,' pp. 172–5.

14 See Ruh, *Höfische Epik*, pp. 11–15.

15 In the *Charrete* the initial challenge is not conclusively resolved until the final episode, but this is the fight between Lancelot and Meleaganz rather than the courtly fete that typically concludes a German romance.

16 William Ryding distinguishes three types of medieval episodic narrative. In the first type 'none of the episodes may be considered as more legitimately a beginning, middle, or end than any other. Each is a separate unit' (*Structure*, p. 47). In the second type, 'the writer points early in the story to a terminal objective, then artfully delays its coming'; the beginning and end are fixed, but any number of episodes can come between

them (p. 48). The third type begins with 'an initial impulse that calls into play the series of episodes of which the story is composed, but which leads nowhere, or, it may be, only to an arbitrarily designated conclusion' (p. 50). The German romances seem to be modified versions of types two or three. *Garel* would be type two. So would *Wigalois, Daniel,* and *Gauriel* – except that in *Gauriel* the bracket is followed by an unrelated episode, and in *Wigalois* and *Daniel* it is preceded by unrelated material as well. Lunete's accusation in *Iwein* and Cundrie's in *Parzival,* as well as Tandareis's banishment, imply, at least, a terminal objective, but these 'beginnings' occur about a third of the way into the romance. *Erec, Lanzelet, Diu Crone,* and *Meleranz* would be type three; the 'initial impulse,' even when it comes rather late in the work (*Erec, Meleranz*), has little effect on the way it ends.

17 See Kuhn, 'Erec,' pp. 133–50.
18 Köhler, *Ideal und Wirklichkeit,* p. 240.
19 Ryding, *Structure,* p. 43.
20 See de Boor, 'Daniel,' p. 72; also Moelleken/Henderson, 'Die Bedeutung der liste.'
21 Structural interpretations of Arthurian romance often depend on analogies of this kind. Hugo Kuhn says of *Erec*: 'Programm der A-Reihe ist: *ungemach* durch *arbeit* für Erec und Enite. Da ist zuerst die *arbeit* der Reise selbst, die Abenteuer, die Verwundung Erecs; dann aber verstärkte *arbeit* durch alles, was Erec darüber hinaus sich und Enite auferlegt: Verzicht auf Begleitung, Verzicht auf höfische Bequemlichkeit und Repräsentation' ('Erec,' p. 142). Kurt Ruh's analysis of *Iwein* depends on the same sort of interpretative analogies: 'Er [Iwein] bewährt sich nicht nur in der *triuwe* gegenüber Laudine (durch zweimalige Zurückweisung eines Minneangebots) und in der Dankbarkeit (gegenüber der Frau von Narison und Lunete), sondern auch in der Pünktlichkeit (durch zweimalige Terminnot)' (*Höfische Epik,* p. 155). Rainer Warning, in explaining his category of intensified reprise ('Formen narrativer Identitätskonstitution,' pp. 561–8), also relies on analogous interpretation to establish connections between several episodes. That Lunete's aid of Yvain just after he kills Esclados, the damsel's enthusiasm in healing the mad Yvain, and Yvain's active intercession for the imprisoned Lunete constitute a series of related episodes (p. 564) is clear only if we link them by a common interpretation: they all share the element of rescue from death. In other respects, however, these episodes do not represent the kind of reprise Warning claims: in what regard, for example, is the imprisoned Lunete an intensification of the mad Yvain, or the damsel with the salve an intensification

of the much more active Lunete with her ring? Warning speaks of 'der sinngebenden Kontrastierung analoger Stationen' (p. 565). The 'analoge Stationen' are generated by the coincident realization of the Arthurian functions in disjunct episodes, and the existence of the analogy cannot be disputed: Lunete aids Yvain when he first arrives at Laudine's, and she is the one who aids him when he returns at the end. The 'sinngebende Kontrastierung,' however, is not the work of the author but of the critic and carries no greater authority than any other interpretation: what is gained by linking the damsel with the salve to the Yvain who rescues Lunete? While on the subject of Warning's intensified reprise we should note that although there are many episodes in Arthurian romance joined by the coincident realization of functions, only a small number of these are intensified reprises: Lanzelet wins Iblis and Elidia by accomplishing a fixed adventure, but the reprise is surely less 'intense' than the first version; Erec's return to Arthur's near the end of the romance is clearly less 'intense' than his earlier appearances. To speak of such episode pairs as *figura* and *implementum* is to transform familiar exegetical categories into the tools of structural analysis, a transformation in which the familiarity of the categories may well blind us to the violence they do in their new application. The last combat of the *Charrete* is in some senses the fulfilment of earlier episodes; yet few would call it an intensification of them except in the very narrow sense that it is terminal. I do not mean to deny the usefulness of Warning's category in understanding Arthurian romance, where the intensified reprise can often serve an important function in structuring the sense of the work; I do want to stress, however, that the intensified reprise is merely a special category derived in the process of interpretation (the exegetical terminology should alert us to this fact) from the much larger category of episodes linked by the coincident realization of functions.

22 Frye, *The Secular Scripture*, p. 130.
23 Henderson speaks of 'Daniels grundsätzliche Bereitschaft, in jeder Situation der Überlegung die Handlung folgen zu lassen' (*Daniel*, p. 154).
24 'Als episches Erlebnis ist der Auftritt Parzivals auf Munsalvaesche in feiner Psychologisierung ganz aus der Perspektive des Helden gesehen' (Curschmann, 'Abenteuer,' p. 636).
25 'Usually the hero is a covert (potential) narrator' (Tomashevsky, 'Thematics,' p. 77).
26 Genette, 'Discours du récit,' pp. 211, 223–4; trans., pp. 195, 210.
27 I would be tempted to call Enite the hero of the episode with Oringles: by her resistance she transforms the hostile Oringles (O^-) into a friendly

Erec (O^+). Yet we dare not ignore the fact, mentioned in passing (E: 6621–2), that Erec does kill Oringles, thus in the accepted manner defeating the opponent and winning the woman. Indeed, two transformations take place at once, forming a sort of narrative chiasmus:

I(Enite)/O^-(Oringles) → I(Enite)/O^+(Erec)

I(Erec)/O^-(Oringles) → I(Erec)/O^+(Enite)

Such an episode, with a double hero, makes one prefer the French title *Erec et Enide* to the German *Erec*.

28 As William Ryding says: 'The main thing, however, is that Chrétien apparently found it convenient, in the absence of logical sequence, to construct this story in a fairly geometrical way' (*Structure*, p. 91). For the classic interpretation of the geometry see Kuhn, 'Erec.'

29 Propp, *Morphology*, p. 75.

30 Haug, *Das Land*, p. 74.

31 As Roland Barthes says: 'Language, as sentence, period, and paragraph, superimposes on these discontinuous categories [of content] ... an appearance of continuity' ('Style,' p. 6).

32 On the importance of such 'specific signals' see Lotman, *Structure*, pp. 155–6.

33 The prologues to *Erec*, *Garel*, and *Wigamur* are lost and thus cannot be included in the discussion.

34 Hennig Brinkmann ('Der Prolog') and Peter Kobbe ('Funktion und Gestalt') have traced the two-part pattern of the Middle High German prologue from antique rhetoric into medieval poetics and thence into the works themselves. Although I have borrowed from Kobbe (p. 414) in formulating my characterization of the two parts, I hesitate to follow him or Brinkmann further. After considerable searching I have been unable to discover a two-part prescription in any of the authorities they cite, nor do the terms they borrow to name the parts have in the sources anything like the precision that Brinkmann and Kobbe attribute to them.

35 Kobbe, 'Funktion und Gestalt,' p. 421.

36 Kobbe calls this the 'Typus *einliniger Verschränkung*,' which exhibits the 'Bestreben ... die Grenze zwischen Prolog und Erzählung zu verundeutlichen ... der Erzählinhalt wird vorgestellt, das Publikum wird über ihn "unterrichtet," und aus dem einleitenden Bericht, der "Information," geht der Erzählanfang ohne weiteren Kommentar hervor' ('Funktion und Gestalt,' p. 417). Note, however, that, while works like *Lanzelet* and *Parzival* do introduce the public – in the most general way – to the 'Erzählinhalt' (L:25–40; P:4,14–26), the three Arthurian prologues that fit into Kobbe's category either keep their particular story a complete mystery

(*Wigalois, Daniel*) or else deliberately lead us astray (*Diu Crone* implies that its hero will be Arthur himself [C:217–19]).

37 On the importance of the frame in literature see Lotman, *Structure*, pp. 209–17.

38 Mitgau, 'Bauformen,' p. 91.

39 The very clear way in which the narrator of *Tandareis* marks changes of focus reminds one of similar markers in the prose *Lancelot*. The wording in both texts is similar as well: 'nu lazen daz beliben hie unt hoeret wie ez dort ergie Tandareis, dem werden man' (T:8301–3); 'Nu lassen wir die rede von im und sprechen furbas von mym herren Ywan wie das er gefûre' (*Lancelot*, 1:549,14–15).

40 Eberhard Nellmann attempts to divide *Parzival* into 'Erzählphasen,' taking as boundary markers those passages where Wolfram interrupts the story with introductory or concluding remarks (*Wolframs Erzähltechnik*, p. 85). Although Nellmann eliminates from consideration those interruptions that do not themselves explicitly introduce or conclude a narrative segment (P:291,1–293,18 or P:583,1–587,14, for instance), he is still not able to perform his division without contradictions. He cannot decide whether to put the end of his first phase at P:112,8, which conforms to his rules, or at P:116,4, the much bolder break at the end of the 'Selbstverteidigung,' which, however, does not refer to the sections of the narrative at all (pp. 86–7, 104). Nellmann begins his fifth phase at P:399,11 but notes that 'disiu burc' at P:399,11 is meaningless unless the audience recalls information provided before the beginning of the phase (P:398,28–30). He devotes an excursus to the question 'ob die hier erwartete Leistung des Hörers mit dem Anzatz eines Phasenbeginns vereinbar ist' (p. 97), but avoids the problem entirely with a series of evasionary manoeuvres (phases have nothing to do with performance; the books of the *Aeneid*!). (For a better idea of what the narrator is doing in book eight see Curschmann, 'Das Abenteuer des Erzählens,' pp. 627–31, 662–6.) Finally, Nellmann's determination to match his sixth phase with Lachmann's book nine forces him to disregard P:452,9–10, just the kind of remark that, according to Nellmann, ought to indicate the start of a new phase (pp. 98–9). It turns out that Nellmann, in establishing his 'Erzählphasen,' treats the remarks of the narrator just as Lachmann, in establishing his books, used the initials of ms D: each takes a limited number of markers from a series of potentially equal markers, assigns those selected basic structural importance, and ignores the rest. From my own perspective I would say as well that Nellmann's procedure, besides being inconsistent, is based on a false premise. Nellmann assumes that the behaviour of the

narrator must necessarily reflect the divisions of the story, but this, as we have just seen and as the inconsistencies of Nellmann's own attempt clearly show, is not the case. Wolfram, for instance, says nothing in his own right to mark Parzival's approach to Pelrapeire.

41 On the various functions of *Vorausdeutung* in Arthurian romance but especially in *Wigalois* see Cormeau, *'Wigalois' und 'Diu Crone,'* pp. 59–64. For a general discussion of the significance of *Vorausdeutungen* in literature see Lämmert, *Bauformen*, pp. 139–94.

42 When Yvain leaves Laudine only he forfeits his heart; Crestïens considers it a 'mervoille' that Yvain should live without a heart, but is able to think up an explanation (CY:2641–62). Cligés and Fenice are said to exchange hearts; again Crestïens stops short, but here too he is able to reason his way past his doubts (CCl:2777–814). Hartman denies the convention; Crestïens finds a way to explain it. The exchange of hearts plays a large role elsewhere in *Cligés* (CCl:5118–95) and, in its one-sided variant, in the *Charrete* (CCh:3970–80, 4692–7, 6827–53); but in these cases the narrator does not raise any objections.

43 Northrop Frye wonders if there is not a 'character in romance corresponding to the *agroikos* type in comedy, the refuser of festivity or rustic clown. Such a character would call attention to realistic aspects of life, like fear in the presence of danger, which threaten the unity of the romantic mood' (*Anatomy*, p. 197). When the Arthurian narrator introduces his (momentarily) ordinary reactions into the special atmosphere of romance, he seems to fill the function that Frye envisions.

44 Tomashevsky, 'Thematics,' p. 84; see also pp. 94–5.

45 Warning, 'Formen narrativer Identitätskonstitution,' p. 578.

CONCLUSION

1 Jellinek/Kraus, 'Widersprüche.'

2 Heinzle, *Dietrichepik*, p. 170.

3 Messerer, 'Einige Darstellungsprinzipien,' p. 162.

4 Ryding, *Structure*, pp. 115–16.

5 Heinzle, *Dietrichepik*, p. 173.

6 We might note that the criticism of Arthur is not so strong in *Erec* and *Iwein* as it is in their French sources. In reporting the abduction of the queen, Chrétien's Lunete remarks: 'don li rois fist que fors del san' (CY:3702); Harpin's victim says of the king and queen, 'cil fu fos et cele musarde qui an son conduit se fïa' (CY:3920–1). At the beginning of the romance, as well, the characters in *Yvain* are more critical than those in

Iwein. When Arthur and the queen retire in the midst of the opening feast there are many, amazed and aggrieved, 'qui molt grant parole an firent' (CY:45); but this criticism is suppressed in German. The much greater extent to which the author of the French romance is willing to subvert the traditional ideality of Arthur's court is evident not only in the critical words of his characters but also in the actual presentation of the queen's abduction. According to Crestïens, Meleaganz is successful only because Arthur is tricked by his own seneschal, as Harpin's victim clearly states (CY:3915–19). According to Hartman, however, Arthur is led astray by the generous courtesy of his court (I:4566–78). In the *Charrete*, after Keu leads the queen away all are distraught; 'mes a nelui n'an pesa tant que del sivre s'antremeïst' (CCh:222–3) until Gauvain ventures the suggestion that they might perhaps set out to see what has happened. In *Iwein* the court is also distraught, 'doch warens unervaeret' (I:4622); all call for their arms at once and go dashing off. Finally, in the *Charrete*, Arthur's courtiers dissipate in the woods without attracting any notice and we are led off into the main plot on the heels of Lancelot. In *Iwein*, however, we learn the names of seven knights who, in addition to Keie, actually fight with the abductor in their effort to rescue the queen, and many more remain unnamed (I:4685–715). While the abduction of Arthur's queen is a major crisis in any romance, in Hartmann's version the court at least retains its coherence and its ability to act. In Chrétien, on the other hand, it is betrayed from within and is unable to organize a respectable defence. At the beginning of the *Charrete* we see Arthur's court dissolve in front of our eyes, something that never happens in the German romances (See Haug, *Das Land*, pp. 26–8).

7 Zumthor, *Essai*, p. 81.
8 Lotman, *Structure*, pp. 298–9.
9 See Ruh, *Höfische Epik*, pp. 150, 157.
10 See Ruh, *Höfische Epik*, pp. 11–15.
11 Note, however, that every instance in which *minne* is portrayed (including the lion and Gawein) conforms to our *functional* definition: *minne* is the theme that exists in the field of tension between O^+ and I.
12 Lotman, *Structure*, pp. 59–60.
13 Eberhard Nellmann, in analysing Wolfram's behaviour as narrator, is troubled by various contradictions: some he dismisses by calling them 'unbeabsichtigt' (*Wolframs Erzähltechnik*, p. 25), others by limiting their impact to the actual performance situation (p. 29) or short-term narrative strategy (p. 22), still others by distinguishing traces of the real author from the hopefully coherent figure of the narrator (pp. 21, 29). By deacti-

234 Notes to pages 181–2

vating these contradictions Nellmann is able to isolate a relatively consistent Wolfram; in doing so, however, he robs the work of much of its sparkle and, I am quite sure, much of its meaning.

14 See Warning, 'Formen narrativer Identitätskonstitution,' pp. 570–3, 578–83. Warning deals at length with the contradictions of romance and explains them as the consequence of the non-congruence of two fundamental systems: the actantial scheme (borrowed from Greimas, related to the basic patterns of folklore, and close to our skeletal pattern) and the figural scheme (borrowed from typological exegesis and based on the intensified reprise); the former is cyclical, the latter teleological. Where I prefer to derive the contradictions of Arthurian romance from the conflicts among many systems, Warning limits himself to two; that one of these, the figural scheme, is a peculiarly medieval pattern makes his explanation especially attractive. Yet the explanation is inadequate for two reasons. First, the number of systems in Arthurian romance is, as I have tried to show, much greater than two. Second, the figural scheme is of major importance only in a few (of the most celebrated) romances; it may, as Warning claims, generate contradictions in *Yvain*, but it will only lead us astray if we look for it in *Lanzelet* or *Garel*. See note 21, chapter three.

15 Kuhn, 'Struktur,' p. 19.

16 Lotman, *Structure*, p. 300.

17 Ryding, *Structure*, p. 61.

Bibliography

For obvious reasons this bibliography does not attempt a systematic presentation of the literature on Middle High German Arthurian romance; it is simply a listing of the works to which reference is made in the text. For a more complete introduction to the critical literature see Brogsitter, *Artusepik* and de Boor, *Die höfische Literatur*; for individual topics see the second edition, as far as it has appeared, of Stammler/Langosch, *Verfasserlexikon*.

PRIMARY WORKS

Beroul *The Romance of Tristran: A Poem of the Twelfth Century*. Edited by Alfred Ewert. New York: Barnes and Noble, 1971
Chrétien de Troyes *Le Chevalier au lion (Yvain)*. Edited by Mario Roques. Les Romans de Chrétien de Troyes, 4. Paris: Champion, 1970
– *Le Chevalier de la charrete*. Edited by Mario Roques. Les Romans de Chrétien de Troyes, 3. Paris: Champion, 1975
– *Cligés*. Edited by Alexandre Micha. Les Romans de Chrétien de Troyes, 2. Paris: Champion, 1975.
– *Le Conte du graal (Perceval)*. Edited by Félix Lecoy. Les Romans de Chrétien de Troyes, 5. Paris: Champion, 1975
– *Erec et Enide*. Edited by Mario Roques. Les Romans de Chrétien de Troyes, 1. Paris: Champion, 1973
Dietrichs Flucht. In *Deutsches Heldenbuch*, part 2, edited by Ernst Martin, pp. 55–215. Berlin: Weidmann, 1866. Reprint Dublin/Zürich: Weidmann, 1967
Eilhart von Oberge *Tristrant*. Edited by Franz Lichtenstein. Quellen und Forschungen, 19. Strassburg: Trübner, 1877
Gottfried von Strassburg *Tristan und Isold*. Edited by Friedrich Ranke. 15th ed. Dublin/Zürich: Weidmann, 1970

Hartmann von Aue *Erec*. Edited by Albert Leitzmann; 5th ed., edited by
Ludwig Wolff. Altdeutsche Textbibliothek, 39. Tübingen: Niemeyer, 1972
– *Iwein*. Edited by Georg Friedrich Benecke and Karl Lachmann; 7th ed.,
edited by Ludwig Wolff. Berlin: de Gruyter, 1968
Heinrich von dem Türlin *Diu Crône*. Edited by Gottlob Heinrich Friedrich
Scholl. Bibliothek des Litterarischen Vereins in Stuttgart, 27. Stuttgart:
Litterarischer Verein, 1852. Reprint. Amsterdam: Rodopi, 1966
[Konrad von Stoffeln] *Gauriel von Muntabel: Eine höfische Erzählung aus dem 13.
Jahrhunderte*. Edited by Ferdinand Khull. Graz: Leuschner und Lubensky, 1885
Lancelot: Nach der Heidelberger Pergamenthandschrift pal. germ. 147. Vol 1.
Edited by Reinhold Kluge. Deutsche Texte des Mittelalters, 42. Berlin:
Akademie-Verlag, 1948
Das Nibelungenlied. Edited by Karl Bartsch; 19th ed., edited by Helmut de
Boor. Wiesbaden: Brockhaus, 1967
der Pleier *Garel von dem Blüenden Tal: Ein höfischer Roman aus dem Artus-
sagenkreise*. Edited by Michael Walz. Freiburg i.B.: Wagner, 1892
– *Meleranz*. Edited by Karl Bartsch. Bibliothek des Litterarischen Vereins in
Stuttgart, 60. Stuttgart: Litterarischer Verein, 1861
– *Tandareis und Flordibel*. Edited by Ferdinand Khull. Graz: Styria, 1885
Rabenschlacht. In *Deutsches Heldenbuch*, part 2, edited by Ernst Martin, pp.
217–326. Berlin: Weidmann, 1866. Reprint. Dublin/Zürich: Weidmann, 1967
Rosengarten A. In *Die Gedichte vom Rosengarten zu Worms*, edited by Georg
Holz, pp. 1–67. Halle: Niemeyer, 1893
der Stricker *Daniel von dem Blühenden Tal: Ein Artusroman*. Edited by Gustav
Rosenhagen. Germanistische Abhandlungen, 9. Breslau: Koebner, 1894
Ulrich von Zatzikhoven *Lanzelet: Eine Erzählung*. Edited by K.A. Hahn. Frank-
furt/Main: Brönner, 1845. Reprint. Berlin: de Gruyter, 1965
Wigamur. Edited by Johann Gustav Büsching. In *Deutsche Gedichte des Mittel-
alters*, edited by Friedrich von der Hagen, vol. 1, no. 4. Berlin: Realschul-
buchhandlung, 1808
Wirnt von Gravenberc *Wigalois: Der Ritter mit dem Rade*. Edited by J.M.N.
Kapteyn. Rheinische Beiträge und Hülfsbücher zur germanischen
Philologie und Volkskunde, 9. Bonn: Klopp, 1926
Wolfram von Eschenbach *Parzival*. Edited by Albert Leitzmann; 7th ed.,
edited by Wilhelm Deinert. Altdeutsche Textbibliothek, 12–14. Tübingen:
Niemeyer, 1961–5

PRIMARY WORKS IN ENGLISH TRANSLATION

Beroul *The Romance of Tristan by Beroul and the Tale of Tristan's Madness*.
Translated by Alan S. Fedrick. Harmondsworth: Penguin, 1970

Chrétien de Troyes *Arthurian Romances* [*Erec et Enide, Cligés, Yvain, Lance-lot*]. Translated by W.W. Comfort. Everyman's Library, 698. New York: Dutton, 1970
Chrétien de Troyes *The Story of the Grail* [*Perceval*]. Translated by Robert White Linker. Chapel Hill, N.C.: University of North Carolina Press, 1960
Eilhart von Oberge *Eilhart von Oberge's Tristrant*. Translated by J.W. Thomas. Lincoln, Nebraska: University of Nebraska Press, 1978
Gottfried von Strassburg *Tristan*. Translated by A.T. Hatto. Harmondsworth: Penguin, 1960
Hartmann von Aue *Iwein: The Knight with the Lion*. Translated by J.W. Thomas. Lincoln, Nebraska: University of Nebraska Press, 1979
The Nibelungenlied. Translated by A.T. Hatto. Harmondsworth: Penguin, 1965
Ulrich von Zatzikhoven *Lanzelet: A Romance of Lancelot*. Translated by Kenneth G.T. Webster. Records of Civilization, Sources and Studies, 47. New York: Columbia University Press, 1951
Wirnt von Grafenberg *Wigalois: The Knight of Fortune's Wheel*. Translated by J.W. Thomas. Lincoln, Nebraska: University of Nebraska Press, 1977
Wolfram von Eschenbach *Parzival*. Translated by A.T. Hatto. Harmondsworth: Penguin, 1980

SECONDARY WORKS

Aristotle *The Poetics*. In Aristotle, *On Poetry and Style*, translated by G.M.A. Grube, pp. 1–62. Indianapolis: Bobbs-Merrill, 1958
Augustine *Sancti Aurelii Augustini de Trinitate Libri XV*. Edited by W.J. Mountain. Corpus Christianorum, Series Latina, 50. Turnhout: Brepols, 1968. English translation: *The Trinity*. Translated by Stephen McKenna. *The Fathers of the Church*, 45. Washington, D.C.: The Catholic University of America Press, 1963
Barthes, Roland 'Introduction à l'analyse structurale des récits.' *Communications* 8 (1966): 1–27. English translation: 'Introduction to the Structural Analysis of Narratives.' In Roland Barthes, *Image Music Text*, translated by Stephen Heath, pp. 79–124. New York: Hill and Wang, 1977
– 'Style and its Image.' In *Literary Style: A Symposium*, edited by Seymour Chatman, pp. 3–15. London: Oxford University Press, 1971
– *S/Z*. Paris: Seuil, 1970. English translation: *S/Z*. Translated by Richard Miller. New York: Hill and Wang, 1974
Benveniste, Émile *Problèmes de linguistique général*. Bibliothèque des sciences humaines. Paris: Gallimard, 1966
Bezzola, Reto R. *Le Sens de l'aventure et de l'amour (Chrétien de Troyes)*. Paris: La Jeune Parque, 1947

Brall, Helmut 'Strickers *Daniel von dem Blühenden Tal*: Zur politischen Funktion späthöfischer Artusepik im Territorialisierungsprozess.' *Euphorion* 70 (1976): 222–57

Brinkmann, Hennig 'Der Prolog im Mittelalter als literarische Erscheinung: Bau und Aussage.' *Wirkendes Wort* 14 (1964): 1–21

Brogsitter, Karl Otto *Artusepik*. 2nd ed. Sammlung Metzler, 38. Stuttgart: Metzler, 1971

Bumke, Joachim *Wolfram von Eschenbach*. 3rd ed. Sammlung Metzler, 36. Stuttgart: Metzler, 1970

Cervantes, Miguel de *The History of Don Quixote of the Mancha*. Translated by Thomas Shelton. London: David Nutt, 1896

Cormeau, Christoph 'Artusroman und Märchen: Zur Beschreibung und Genese der Struktur des höfischen Romans.' In *Wolfram-Studien V*, edited by Werner Schröder, pp. 63–78. Berlin: Schmidt, 1979

– *'Wigalois' und 'Diu Crône': Zwei Kapitel zur Gattungsgeschichte des nachklassischen Aventiureromans*. Münchener Texte und Untersuchungen zur deutschen Literatur des Mittelalters, 57. Munich: Artemis, 1977

Culler, Jonathan *Structuralist Poetics: Structuralism, Linguistics and the Study of Literature*. Ithaca: Cornell University Press, 1976

Curschmann, Michael 'Das Abenteuer des Erzählens: Über den Erzähler in Wolframs "Parzival."' *Deutsche Vierteljahrsschrift für Literaturwissenschaft und Geistesgeschichte* 45 (1971): 627–67

– 'The French, the Audience, and the Narrator in Wolfram's "Willehalm."' *Neophilologus* 59 (1975): 548–62

– *Der Münchener Oswald und die deutsche spielmännische Epik: Mit einem Exkurs zur Kultgeschichte und Dichtungstradition*. Münchener Texte und Untersuchungen zur deutschen Literatur des Mittelalters, 6. Munich: Beck, 1964

Curtius, Ernst Robert *European Literature and the Latin Middle Ages*. Translated by Willard R. Trask. Bollingen Series, 36. Princeton: Princeton University Press, 1967

Dante Alighieri *The Divine Comedy: Inferno*. Translated by Charles S. Singleton. Bollingen Series, 80. Princeton: Princeton University Press, 1970

de Boor, Helmut 'Der Daniel des Stricker und der Garel des Pleier.' *Beiträge zur Geschichte der deutschen Sprache und Literatur* (Tübingen) 79 (1957): 67–84

– *Die höfische Literatur: Vorbereitung, Blüte, Ausklang, 1170–1250*. 7th ed. *Geschichte der deutschen Literatur von den Anfängen bis zur Gegenwart*, vol. 2. Edited by Helmut de Boor and Richard Newald. Munich: Beck, 1966

Dembowski, Peter F. 'Monologue, Author's Monologue and Related Problems in the Romances of Chrétien de Troyes.' In *Approaches to Medieval Romance*, edited by Peter Haidu. *Yale French Studies* 51 (1974): 102–14

Dorfman, Eugene *The Narreme in the Medieval Romance Epic: An Introduction to Narrative Structures*. University of Toronto Romance Series, 13. Toronto: University of Toronto Press, 1969

Eggers, Hans 'Strukturprobleme mittelalterlicher Epik, dargestellt am Parzival Wolframs von Eschenbach.' *Euphorion* 47 (1953): 260–70.

Ehrismann, Gustav *Geschichte der deutschen Literatur bis zum Ausgang des Mittelalters*, part 2, vol. 2, 1st half. Handbuch des deutschen Unterrichts an höheren Schulen, 6,2,2,1. Munich: Beck, 1927

Emmel, Hildegard *Formprobleme des Artusromans und der Graldichtung: Die Bedeutung des Artuskreises für das Gefüge des Romans im 12. und 13. Jahrhundert in Frankreich, Deutschland und den Niederlanden*. Bern: Francke, 1951

Faral, Edmond *Les Arts poétiques du XIIᵉ et du XIIIᵉ siècle: Recherches et documents sur la technique littéraire du moyen âge*. Paris: Champion, 1962

Ferrante, Joan M. *The Conflict of Love and Honor: The Medieval Tristan Legend in France, Germany and Italy*. De proprietatibus litterarum, Series practica, 78. The Hague: Mouton, 1973

Fischer, Hanns *Studien zur deutschen Märendichtung*. Tübingen: Niemeyer, 1968

Fromm, Hans 'Doppelweg.' In *Werk-Typ-Situation: Studien zu poetologischen Bedingungen in der älteren deutschen Literatur: Hugo Kuhn zum 60. Geburtstag*, edited by Ingeborg Glier, Gerhard Hahn, Walter Haug, Burghart Wachinger, pp. 64–79. Stuttgart: Metzler, 1969

Frye, Northrop *Anatomy of Criticism*. Princeton: Princeton University Press, 1971

– *The Secular Scripture: A Study of the Structure of Romance*. Cambridge, Mass.: Harvard University Press, 1976

Genette, Gérard 'Discours du récit.' In *Figures III*, pp. 65–282. Paris: Seuil, 1972. English translation: *Narrative Discourse: An Essay in Method*. Translated by Jane E. Lewin. Ithaca: Cornell University Press, 1980

– Vraisemblance et motivation.' In Gérard Genette, *Figures II*, pp. 71–99. Paris: Seuil, 1969

Geoffrey of Vinsauf *Poetria nova*. In *Les Arts poétiques du XIIᵉ et du XIIIᵉ siècle: Recherches et documents sur la technique littéraire du moyen âge*, edited by Edmond Faral, pp. 194–262. Paris: Champion, 1962. English translation: *The New Poetics*. Translated by Jane Baltzell Kopp. In *Three Medieval Rhetorical Arts*, edited by James J. Murphy, pp. 27–108. Berkeley: University of California Press, 1971

Greimas, Algirdas Julien 'Éléments d'une grammaire narrative.' In Algirdas Julien Greimas, *Du sens: Essais sémiotiques*, pp. 157–83. Paris: Seuil, 1970

Gürttler, Karin R. *'Künec Artûs der guote': Das Artusbild der höfischen Epik des 12. und 13. Jahrhunderts*. Studien zur Germanistik, Anglistik und Komparatistik, 52. Bonn: Bouvier, 1976

Hahn, Ingrid 'Parzivals Schönheit: Zum Problem des Erkennens und Verkennens im "Parzival."' In *Verbum et Signum*, edited by Hans Fromm, Wolfgang Harms, Uwe Ruberg, 2: 203–32. Munich: Fink, 1975

Hamburger, Käte *Die Logik der Dichtung*. 2nd ed. Stuttgart: Klett, 1968

Hanning, Robert W. *The Individual in Twelfth-Century Romance*. New Haven: Yale University Press, 1977

Haug, Walter *'Das Land, von welchem niemand wiederkehrt': Mythos, Fiktion und Wahrheit in Chrétiens 'Chevalier de la Charrete', im 'Lanzelet' Ulrichs von Zatzikhoven und im 'Lancelot'-Prosaroman*. Untersuchungen zur deutschen Literaturgeschichte, 21. Tübingen: Niemeyer, 1978

– 'Die Symbolstruktur des höfischen Epos und ihre Auflösung bei Wolfram von Eschenbach.' *Deutsche Vierteljahrsschrift für Literaturwissenschaft und Geistesgeschichte* 45 (1971): 668–705

Haupt, Jürgen *Der Truchsess Keie im Artusroman: Untersuchungen zur Gesellschaftsstruktur im höfischen Roman*. Philologische Studien und Quellen, 57. Berlin: Schmidt, 1971

Heinzle, Joachim *Mittelhochdeutsche Dietrichepik: Untersuchungen zur Tradierungsweise, Überlieferungskritik und Gattungsgeschichte später Heldendichtung*. Münchener Texte und Untersuchungen zur deutschen Literatur des Mittelalters, 62. Munich: Artemis, 1978

Henderson, Ingeborg *Strickers Daniel von dem Blühenden Tal: Werkstruktur und Interpretation unter Berücksichtigung der handschriftlichen Überlieferung*. German Language and Literature Monographs, 1. Amsterdam: Benjamins, 1976

Huby, Michel 'L'Approfondissement psychologique dans *Erec* de Hartmann.' In *Études germaniques* 22 (1967): 13–26

– 'Remarques sur la structure du "Lanzelet."' In *Mélanges pour Jean Fourquet*, edited by P. Valentin and G. Zink, pp. 147–56. Munich: Hueber/Paris: Klincksieck, 1969

Jameson, Frederic 'Magical Narratives: Romance as Genre.' In *New Literary History* 7 (1975–6): 135–63

Jauss, Hans Robert 'Theorie der Gattungen und Literatur des Mittelalters.' In *Grundriss der romanischen Literatur des Mittelalters*, edited by Hans Robert Jauss and Erich Köhler, 1: 107–38. Heidelberg: Winter, 1972

Jellinek, Max H. and Kraus, Carl 'Widersprüche in Kunstdichtungen.' *Zeitschrift für die österreichischen Gymnasien* 44 (1893): 673–716

Kaiser, Gert *Textauslegung und gesellschaftliche Selbstdeutung: Die Artusromane Hartmanns von Aue*. 2nd ed. Wiesbaden: Athenaion, 1978

– 'Der *Wigalois* des Wirnt von Grâvenberc: Zur Bedeutung des Territorialisierungsprozesses für die "höfisch-ritterliche" Literatur des 13. Jahrhunderts.' *Euphorion* 69 (1975): 410–43.

Kermode, Frank *The Genesis of Secrecy: On the Interpretation of Narrative.*
    Cambridge, Mass.: Harvard University Press, 1979
Kobbe, Peter 'Funktion und Gestalt des Prologs in der mittelhochdeutschen
    nachklassischen Epik des 13. Jahrhunderts.' *Deutsche Vierteljahrsschrift für
    Literaturwissenschaft und Geistesgeschichte* 43 (1969): 405–57
Köhler, Erich *Ideal und Wirklichkeit in der höfischen Epik: Studien zur Form der
    frühen Artus- und Graldichtung.* 2nd ed. Beihefte zur *Zeitschrift für romanische
    Philologie*, 97. Tübingen: Niemeyer, 1970
– *Der literarische Zufall, das Mögliche und die Notwendigkeit.* Munich: Fink,
    1973
Kuhn, Hugo 'Erec.' In Hugo Kuhn, *Dichtung und Welt im Mittelalter,* pp.
    133–50. Stuttgart: Metzler, 1959
– 'Gattungsprobleme der mittelhochdeutschen Literatur.' In Hugo Kuhn,
    Dichtung und Welt im Mittelalter, pp. 41–61. Stuttgart: Metzler, 1959
– 'Die Klassik des Rittertums in der Stauferzeit.' In *Annalen der deutschen
    Literatur,* edited by Heinz Otto Burger, pp. 99–177. 2nd ed. Stuttgart:
    Metzler, 1971
– 'Parzival: Ein Versuch über Mythos, Glaube und Dichtung.' In Hugo
    Kuhn, *Dichtung und Welt im Mittelalter,* pp. 151–80. Stuttgart: Metzler, 1959
– 'Struktur und Formensprache.' In Hugo Kuhn, *Dichtung und Welt im Mittel-
    alter,* pp. 15–21. Stuttgart: Metzler, 1959
– *Tristan, Nibelungenlied, Artusstruktur.* Bayerische Akademie der Wissen-
    schaften, Philosophisch-historische Klasse, Sitzungsberichte, 1973, 5.
    Munich: Akademie der Wissenschaften, 1973
Lämmert, Eberhard *Bauformen des Erzählens.* 6th ed. Stuttgart: Metzler, 1975
Le Gentil, Pierre 'La Légende de Tristan vue par Béroul et Thomas: Essai
    d'interprétation.' *Romance Philology* 7 (1953–4): 111–29
Leitzmann, Albert 'Zu Ulrichs Lanzelet.' *Beiträge zur Geschichte der deutschen
    Sprache und Literatur* 55 (1931): 293–305
Lerner, Luise *Studien zur Komposition des höfischen Romans im 13. Jahrhundert.*
    Forschungen zur deutschen Sprache und Dichtung, 7. Münster in Westf.:
    Aschendorff, 1936
Lofmark, Carl 'The Miraculous in Romance.' *German Life and Letters* n.s. 30
    (1976–7): 110–26
Loomis, Roger Sherman *Arthurian Tradition and Chrétien de Troyes.* New York:
    Columbia University Press, 1949
Lotman, Jurij *The Structure of the Artistic Text.* Translated by Ronald Vroon.
    Michigan Slavic Contributions, 7. Ann Arbor: Dept. of Slavic Languages
    and Literatures, 1977
Maddox, Donald 'Greimas in the Realm of Arthur: Toward an Analytical
    Model for Medieval Romance.' *L'Esprit Créateur* 17 (1977): 179–94

Messerer, Wilhelm 'Einige Darstellungsprinzipien der Kunst im Mittelalter.' *Deutsche Vierteljahrsschrift für Literaturwissenschaft und Geistesgeschichte* 36 (1962): 157–78

Mitgau, Wolfgang 'Bauformen des Erzählens im "Wigalois" des Wirnt von Gravenberc.' Dissertation, Göttingen, 1959

– 'Nachahmung und Selbständigkeit Wirnts von Gravenberc in seinem "Wigalois."' *Zeitschrift für deutsche Philologie* 82 (1963): 321–37

Moelleken, Wolfgang W. 'Minne une Ehe in Strickers "Daniel von dem Blühenden Tal": Strukturanalytische Ergebnisse.' *Zeitschrift für deutsche Philologie* 93 (1974), Sonderheft, pp. 42–50

– and Henderson, Ingeborg 'Die Bedeutung der *liste* im "Daniel" des Strikkers.' *Amsterdamer Beiträge zur älteren Germanistik* 4 (1973): 187–201

Murphy, James J. *Rhetoric in the Middle Ages: A History of Rhetorical Theory from Saint Augustine to the Renaissance.* Berkeley: University of California Press, 1974

Nellmann, Eberhard 'Die Komposition des *Parzival*: Versuch einer neuen Gliederung.' *Wirkendes Wort* 21 (1971): 389–402

– *Wolframs Erzähltechnik: Untersuchungen zur Funktion des Erzählers.* Wiesbaden: Steiner, 1973

Nolting-Hauff, Ilse 'Märchen und Märchenroman: Zur Beziehung zwischen einfacher Form und narrativer Grossform in der Literatur.' *Poetica* 6 (1974): 129–78

Ong, Walter J. 'The Writer's Audience Is Always a Fiction.' *PMLA* 90 (1975): 9–21

Paul, Hermann *Mittelhochdeutsche Grammatik.* 20th ed., by Hugo Moser and Ingeborg Schröbler. Tübingen: Niemeyer, 1969

Pörksen, Uwe *Der Erzähler im mittelhochdeutschen Epos: Formen seines Hervortretens bei Lamprecht, Konrad, Hartmann, in Wolframs Willehalm und in den 'Spielmannsepen.'* Philologische Studien und Quellen, 58. Berlin: Schmidt, 1971

Propp, Vladimir *The Morphology of the Folktale.* Translated by Laurence Scott. 2nd ed., revised by Louis A. Wagner. Austin: University of Texas Press, 1971

Ruh, Kurt *Höfische Epik des deutschen Mittelalters I: Von den Anfängen bis zu Hartmann von Aue.* Grundlagen der Germanistik, 7. Berlin: Schmidt, 1967

– 'Der "Lanzelet" Ulrichs von Zatzikhofen: Modell oder Kompilation?' In *Deutsche Literatur des späten Mittelalters: Hamburger Colloquium 1973*, edited by Wolfgang Harms and L. Peter Johnson, pp. 47–55. Berlin: Schmidt, 1975

Ryding, William W. *Structure in Medieval Narrative.* De proprietatibus litterarum, Series maior, 12. The Hague: Mouton, 1971

Scheunemann, Ernst *Artushof und Abenteuer: Zeichnung höfischen Daseins in Hartmanns Erec.* Breslau: Maruschke & Berendt, 1937

Schindele, Gerhard *Tristan: Metamorphose und Tradition.* Studien zur Poetik und Geschichte der Literatur, 12. Kohlhammer: Stuttgart, 1971

Schultz, James A. '"Lanzelet": A Flawless Hero in a Symmetrical World.' *Beiträge zur Geschichte der deutschen Sprache und Literatur* (Tübingen) 102 (1980): 160–88

Selbmann, Rolf 'Strukturschema und Operatoren in Hartmanns *Iwein.*' *Deutsche Vierteljahrsschrift für Literaturwissenschaft und Geistesgeschichte* 50 (1976): 60–83

Stammler, Wolfgang, and Langosch, Karl, eds. *Die deutsche Literatur des Mittelalters: Verfasserlexikon.* Berlin: de Gruyter, 1953. 2nd ed., edited by Kurt Ruh. Berlin: de Gruyter, 1978–

Stanzel, Franz K. *Typische Formen des Romans.* 8th ed. Kleine Vandenhoeck-Reihe, 1187. Göttingen: Vandenhoeck und Ruprecht, 1976

Stevens, John *Medieval Romance: Themes and Approaches.* London: Hutchinson University Library, 1973

Stierle, Karlheinz *Text als Handlung: Perspektiven einer systematischen Literaturwissenschaft.* UTB, 423. Munich: Fink, 1975

Todorov, Tzvetan *Grammaire du Décaméron.* Approaches to Semiotics, edited by Thomas Sebeok, 3. The Hague: Mouton, 1969

– 'La Grammaire du récit.' In *Poétique de la prose,* pp. 118–28. Paris: Seuil, 1971. English translation: 'The Grammar of Narrative.' In *The Poetics of Prose,* translated by Richard Howard, pp. 108–19. Ithaca: Cornell University Press, 1977

– 'Les Hommes-récits.' In *Poétique de la prose,* pp. 78–91. Paris: Seuil, 1971. English translation: 'Narrative-Men.' In *The Poetics of Prose,* translated by Richard Howard, pp. 66–79. Ithaca: Cornell University Press, 1977

– *Introduction à la littérature fantastique.* Paris: Seuil, 1970. English translation: *The Fantastic: A Structural Approach to a Literary Genre.* Translated by Richard Howard. Ithaca: Cornell University Press, 1975

– 'The Place of Style in the Structure of the Text.' In *Literary Style: A Symposium,* edited by Seymour Chatman, pp. 29–44. London: Oxford University Press, 1971

– 'La Quête du récit.' In *Poétique de la prose,* pp. 129–50. Paris: Seuil, 1971. English translation: 'The Quest of Narrative.' In *The Poetics of Prose,* translated by Richard Howard, pp. 120–42. Ithaca: Cornell University Press, 1977

– 'Le Récit primitif.' In *Poétique de la prose,* pp. 66–77. Paris: Seuil, 1971. English translation: 'Primitive Narrative.' In *The Poetics of Prose,* translated by Richard Howard, pp. 53–65. Ithaca: Cornell University Press, 1977

Tomashevsky, Boris 'Thematics.' In *Russian Formalist Criticism: Four Essays*, translated by Lee T. Lemon and Marion J. Reis, pp. 61–95. Lincoln, Nebraska: University of Nebraska Press, 1965

Tynjanov, Jurij 'Über die literarische Evolution.' In *Russischer Formalismus*, edited by Jurij Striedter, UTB 40, pp. 434–61. Munich: Fink, 1971

Uitti, Karl D. *Story, Myth, and Celebration in Old French Narrative Poetry: 1050–1200.* Princeton: Princeton University Press, 1973

Vinaver, Eugène *Form and Meaning in Medieval Romance.* Modern Humanities Research Association, 1966

Vizkelety, András 'Neue Fragmente des mhd. Cligès-Epos aus Kalocsa (Ungarn).' *Zeitschrift für deutsche Philologie* 88 (1969): 409–32

Warning, Rainer 'Formen narrativer Identitätskonstitution im höfischen Roman.' In *Identität*, edited by Odo Marquard and Karlheinz Stierle, pp. 553–89. Poetik und Hermeneutik, 8. Munich: Fink, 1979. This essay has appeared also in a shorter form: 'Heterogenität des Erzählten – Homogenität des Erzählens: Zur Konstitution des höfischen Romans bei Chrétien de Troyes.' In *Wolfram-Studien V*, edited by Werner Schröder, pp. 79–95. Berlin: Schmidt, 1979. English translation: 'Heterogeneity of Plot – Homogeneity of Narration: On the Constitution of Chrétien de Troyes' Romances.' *L'Esprit Créateur* 18, no. 3 (1978): 41–54

Wehrli, Max 'Roman und Legende im deutschen Hochmittelalter.' In Max Wehrli, *Formen mittelalterlicher Erzählung: Aufsätze*, pp. 155–76. Zürich: Atlantis, 1969

– 'Strukturen des mittelalterlichen Romans – Interpretationsprobleme.' In Max Wehrli, *Formen mittelalterlicher Erzählung: Aufsätze*, pp. 25–50. Zürich: Atlantis, 1969

Zumthor, Paul *Essai de poétique médiévale.* Paris: Seuil, 1972

Index

This index includes references to medieval romance and contemporary scholarship only where the romances and the scholars are themselves objects of analysis. Where literary and scholarly passages serve merely as illustrative examples they have been ignored.